# Modernity and politics in the work of Max Weber

'This is an exciting book with a strong thesis about the way in which Max Weber conceived the modern personality and its relation to politics. Turner provides us with an analysis of Weber that is both scholarly and original.'

J.R.R. Thomas, *Head of the School of Sociology, Bristol Polytechnic*

In the last decade an increasing amount of Anglo-American scholarship has been devoted to the importance of politics within Max Weber's work. While broadly sympathetic to this approach, the author argues that none of its representatives have dealt adequately with Weber's concept of the political. In particular, some have attempted to demonstrate the centrality of politics by reading Weber as a neo-Aristotelian, and playing down the role of neo-Kantian value philosophy. This book argues that while Weber's work should indeed be seen in the light of the neo-Aristotelian critique of modernity, the analytical and ethical centrality of politics is quite consistent with the manner in which he drew upon the neo-Kantian philosophy of his contemporaries. The key to this, believes Turner, is an understanding of what Weber means by 'personality' and by the tragedy of culture.

One of the most distinctive features of the book is that it encourages Weber specialists to situate their work within a wider range of debates about modernity and post-modernity, and suggests that contributors to those debates reconsider Weber's significance for them.

**Charles Turner** studied at the Universities of Durham and London. He teaches in the faculty of Social and Political Sciences at the University of Cambridge.

# Modernity and politics in the work of Max Weber

Charles Turner

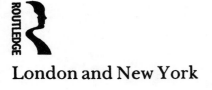

London and New York

First published 1992
by Routledge
11 New Fetter Lane, London EC4P 4EE

Simultaneously published in the USA and Canada
by Routledge
29 West 35th Street, New York, NY 10001

Reprinted 1994

© 1992 Charles Turner

Typeset in Baskerville by
NWL Editorial Services, Langport, Somerset
Printed and bound in Great Britain by
Antony Rowe Ltd, Chippenham, Wiltshire

*British Library Cataloguing in Publication Data*
A catalogue record for this book is available from the British Library

*Library of Congress Cataloging in Publication Data*
A catalog record for this book is available from the Library of Congress

ISBN 0-415-06490-2

For my parents

# Contents

# Preface

It is regarded as the mark of a cultivated intellectual sensibility to care whether Gadamer or Habermas, Popper or Adorno, Freud or Jung, phenomenology or Marxism, or Foucault or Derrida got it right, to get hot under the collar when reading Bloom or Rorty. Perhaps the reason is that, beyond their substantive differences, these thinkers, even the ones who worry about 'the role of intellectuals', share a belief in the enduring relevance of what they do, so that by devoting oneself to the study of any one of them one can find oneself on the cutting edge of social and political debate.

As a graduate student my initial interest in these people was based on the same belief. Yet it was precisely because of this that that interest waned. My reading kept being disrupted by the thought that these types of questions had all been raised before, by Max Weber. In itself this was no argument for going back to him, especially if his problems are merely identical to theirs. What made me go back was the thought that while many contributors to contemporary debates seemed to be engaged in an indefinable, interdisciplinary exercise known as 'theory', Weber had forced himself constantly to ask himself about the status of what he called his science, about the limits of that science and what lay beyond them. So much so that Leo Strauss accused him of reducing science to the same dignity as stamp collecting, of giving us no reason to listen to its results. That he could produce the work he did and lay himself open to such a charge seemed like the best reason to listen to him.

For comments on earlier versions of parts of the manuscript, I would like to thank: Paul Filmer, Phil Manning, Irving Velody and members of the BSA Max Weber Study Group. I have benefited from conversations with Chris Clark, Patrick Dassen,

Felicitas Dörr, Sven Eliassen, Tapani Hietanieni, Andreas Hirseland, Yolanda Ruano and Rüdiger Suchsland. I am also grateful to Dr Karl-Ludwig Ay of the *Arbeitstelle und Archiv der Max Weber Gesamtausgabe*, Munich, for his assistance, and to the German Academic Exchange Service, who provided a grant for the time I spent there.

# Abbreviations

| | |
|---|---|
| *AJ* | *Ancient Judaism*, New York, Free Press, 1952. |
| *ASAC* | *The Agrarian Sociology of Ancient Civilizations*, London, New Left Books, 1977. |
| *ES* | *Economy and Society*, Berkeley, University of California Press, 1978. |
| *FMW* | *From Max Weber*, London, Routledge & Kegan Paul, 1948. |
| *GARS* | *Gesammelte Aufsätze zur Religionssoziologie*, Tübingen, J.C.B. Mohr (Paul Siebeck), 1920. |
| *GPS* | *Gesammelte Politische Schriften 4. Auflage*, Tübingen, J.C.B. Mohr (Paul Siebeck), 1980. |
| *MSS* | *The Methodology of The Social Sciences*, New York, Free Press, 1949. |
| *MWGA* | *Gesamtausgabe II: Briefe 1906–8*, Tübingen, J.C.B. Mohr (Paul Siebeck), 1990. |
| *NS* | ' The National State and Economic Policy', *Economy and Society*, vol. 9, no. 4, 1980. |
| *PE* | *The Protestant Ethic and the Spirit of Capitalism 2nd edn*, London, Allen & Unwin, 1976. |
| *PV* | 'Politics as a Vocation', *in FMW*. |
| *RC* | *The Religion of China*, New York, Free Press, 1951. |
| *RI* | *The Religion of India*, New York, Free Press, 1958. |
| *RK* | *Roscher and Knies*, New York, Free Press, 1975. |
| *ST* | *Selections in Translation*, Cambridge, Cambridge University Press, 1978. |
| *WL* | *Gesammelte Aufsätze zur Wissenschaftslehre 3. Auflage*, Tübingen, J.C.B. Mohr (Paul Siebeck), 1968. |
| *WuG* | *Wirtschaft und Gesellschaft 5. Auflage*, Tübingen, J.C.B. Mohr (Paul Siebeck), 1972. |
| *Zg* | 'Zwischenbetrachtung', in GARS, vol. 4. |

# Introduction

Is that the same Weber who has written on Roman agrarian history?

(Benedetto Croce)

When those who take thinking to be a form of cultural therapy and their duty to be the construction of diagnoses of our time are asked to justify themselves, they will probably do so by an appeal to the Hegelian idea that philosophy is its time grasped in thoughts. If their Hegelianism is anything more than journalistic, they will go beyond this bald claim and argue that the aim of all responsible thought or reflection is to underwrite the culture in whose soil it grows, to formulate that culture's presuppositions, to give an account of those principles without which no modern human being could live his or her life. And in the majority of cases, reference will be made at some point to the theory of modernity of Max Weber.

The seminal status of Weber's work for a theoretical under-standing of the modern self, modern capitalism, the modern state, modern science, modern law, modern culture, modern society or the modern age, is undeniable. But did he have a theory of modernity in a diagnostic sense? Did he take seriously the idea of the birth of the modern world out of the womb of the old or the crossing of a threshold into the modern epoch? He certainly uses the term 'threshold' more than once, and there is an unmistakably diagnostic tone to several passages in his driest works. But do they make sense in terms of what he took to be the meaning of his science? I want to give the perhaps obvious answer that they do not, but then employ the analysis which leads to this conclusion in an interpretation of 'Politics as a Vocation' (PV). My concern will be less Max Weber and the theory of modern politics[1] than what, in the light of the manner in which he sets up the object domain of his science, Weber believes the concept of the political can mean for modern human beings.

The phrase 'modernity and politics' can imply a disjunction as well as a conjunction. For a whole strand of twentieth-century conservatism, modernity is synonymous with the usurpation of a properly political account of human conduct by one which grounds human identity in an apolitical, anti-political, or at best pre-political realm – the social, the ethical, the economic, the intellectual. Whether modernity entails the impossibility of reasonable talk about the good[2] or a pluralism which threatens to render the idea of state sovereignty incoherent,[3] or the replacement of a classical opposition between public and private by a modern one between social and individual,[4] reasonable talk about modernity is talk about the reduction of politics to a means for the achievement of an extra-political purpose. One implication of this is that liberalism and Marxism are two sides of the same modern, non-political coin.

Yet in the last twenty years, neo-Marxism in particular has been notable for the extent to which it has begun to talk less of capitalism and more of 'modernity'. And hand in hand with this has gone the attempt to establish neo-Marxism's political credentials by placing less emphasis on the capitalist state and more on 'civil society'. This in turn has entailed the identification of 'the political' with Foucault's local struggles, Laclau and Mouffe's alliance politics, Guattari's 'molecular revolution' or 'new social movements'.[5] Here, a concern with modernity appears to imply the repoliticisation of an increasing number of areas of social and cultural life. Reasonable talk about modernity is talk about the rediscovery of politics.

From the conservative point of view, to expand the political in this way is to stretch it to the point at which it is unable to bear much of a theoretical load. The combination of an identification of ever more domains in terms of their 'modern' characteristics, and their repoliticisation turns into a romantic exercise. As Carl Schmitt said of romanticism's treatment of the romantic: 'this type of literature always turns the romantic into nothing more than a predicate, never into the subject of a definitional proposition.'[6] At the same time, this exercise in (political) predication satisfies the neo-Marxist need for a contemporary version of ideology critique which avoids simply opposing ideology to science. The task of the critique of ideology is no longer to find the magico-scientific needle which will play the same tune no matter what record is placed on the turntable,[7] but to set free 'ideologically-frozen relations of dependence'[8] in the name of human possibility. In the words of one of the sharpest feminist theorists: 'innovative and revolutionary thinkers are those who declare politics to exist where politics was thought not to exist before'.[9] The declaration that a particular mode of human connection is not natural is no longer made in order to contrast it with the truly natural mode, nor out of a conviction that the achievement of the truly natural mode is the task of politics. Now, politics is that declaration, that predicative activity, the assertion that a state of affairs could have been and can be otherwise.

At the time of writing the rediscovery of civil society by western neo-Marxists, the extension of 'the political' into ever more previously non-political domains, coincides with the rejection by the peoples of Eastern Europe of regimes based precisely upon this extension. If this book has any relevance to the immense theoretical problems this throws up, problems unlikely to be solved by the eastward projection of a concept rooted in the concrete historical experience of a western industrial bourgeoisie, it will be to recall Durkheim's remark that if the state is everywhere it is nowhere,[10] and to suggest that the potentially political character of everything is politics' potential trivialisation.

The deeper reasons for writing the book are twofold. Firstly, the undeniably political nature of Weber's thought leads neither to the classicist conclusion that to be a political animal is to lead the truly human life, or that the only adequate account of a common human life is a political account, nor to what that classicism might view as the contemporary degeneration of the political into a predicate. There is an argument for the increasingly popular view that Weber took the political to be the most important dimension of cultural life, but it is not the neo-Aristotelian one its proponents think it ought to be.[11] Secondly, the contemporary romanticisation of modernity and of politics is often tied to a 'politics of culture'. I will argue that it is precisely the fact that Weber took 'culture' to be the object of his intellectual curiosity that accounts both for the lack of a systematic or diagnostic Weberian account of modernity, and for his understanding of the limits of political action.

Chapter 1 argues that a fully fledged theory of modernity must satisfy one of two theoretical criteria. It must be a synthesis of all conceivable elements which together constitute an epoch's identity, or at least treat one of those elements as foundational for all others. In addition, and by implication, many theories of modernity which meet these requirements will adopt a normative perspective which is either pre-or post-modern. There are few genuine theories of modernity which are not critiques of modernity, which neither yearn for a lost, but analytically recoverable golden age, nor anticipate a utopian future. Max Weber never steps outside what he takes to be the modern world in any systematic sense, but nor does he commit himself to a 'modern project'. His frequently nostalgic references to pre-modern cultural forms are, at most, dramatic asides.

Since Weber takes his science to be a cultural science, Chapter 2 discusses the possible sense in which he might have used the term 'culture', and suggests that Weber had wholly detached culture from the polemical context of German self-cultivation, in which it referred to some realms of human endeavour while 'civilisation' referred to others, a distinction with which critical theory operates even today. Weber understood culture less in terms of the need to defend a sense of inwardness and depth against the encroachments of modern bureaucracy, than as a means of conceptualising the relationship between the unity and differentiation of the personality, the ordeal of determinate human conduct as such.

Weber was sceptical towards claims that the task of a cultural science was to define an epoch's underlying principles because he was sceptical towards the concept of an epoch itself. Chapter 3 argues that the foundation for this scepticism was neo-Kantian value philosophy. In contrast to speculative philosophies of history, and the theoretical vitalism of Nietzsche and Dilthey, both of which generated undifferentiated accounts of history, selfhood and historical epoch, Weber formulated his theory of culture in neo-Kantian terms.[12] To be a cultural being is to be thrown into different spheres of cultural activity grounded in values which are mutually irreducible. Even were a synthesis of these values possible, even if it made sense to talk of the one value which was the ground of all, this move is closed to an empirical cultural science. Since cultural science belongs to one value sphere, it is implicated in the conflict it investigates, and it can neither legislate for those others nor achieve the level of abstraction required for cultural diagnosis.

If the object of a cultural science is the ordeal of determinate conduct, that ordeal takes the form of a struggle to actualise ultimate values, a struggle which for Weber was tragic because eternal, a struggle not just between different modes of making one's way in the world, but between rival principles upon which the unity of any culture could be held to be based. His studies in the sociology of religion examine tensions between those principles and the reality of cultural practices, a reality which includes rival universalist principles. He concludes that no doctrine which claims to ground an ethical totality can achieve practical efficacy without ethical compromise. Chapters 4 and 5 discuss Weber's most diagnostic essay, the 'Zwischenbetrachtung' in the sociology of religion, in which this position is formulated with an oft-neglected theoretical rigour.[13] This essay, on the conflict between religious ethics and non-ethical values, is interpreted both as a thesis about modern 'fragmentation', and as a statement of the universal tragedy of culture. Although Weber's account of value spheres is analytically pluralist, value spheres become interesting when they take on an exceptional status, become sites for the claim that the grounds of one practice are the grounds of all others. The special position of science here is that it provides a secular universalist rhetoric in support of such claims. This turns out to be more science's vulnerability than its strength. If, as the essay suggests, this tragedy is intensified in the modern world with an increase in the number and persuasive force of these claims, this is as much the contemporary confirmation of a historical truth as a theory of modernity.

Chapter 6 treats *PV* as both a defence of the autonomy of the political and the elaboration of a theory of personality first sketched in the so-called methodological writings. But it is more. The political has an exceptional status in Weber's work, not in the normative sense that the state is the highest form of human association, but because the political cannot be defined in terms of an ultimate value which grounds it. And it is just because the political is not a value sphere in the neo-Kantian sense that it is here that the ordeal of the valuing subject is displayed most directly, that Weber's account of the tragedy of culture is vindicated.

Weber's theory of tragedy, such as it is, is not a 'relativist' theory of society. His work lacks a 'theory of society' in the strong sense. Many of the contemporary debates between theorists of communication and desire, rationality and power, order and domination, universalism and pluralism, would have appeared to him as so many forms of sterile excitation. What makes what he calls culture interesting is that it is a means of expressing the tensions between these principles, what becomes of those whose striving for ultimate values can never meet with complete success, and what becomes of them when they are made aware of it. The task of a cultural science is to deepen this acquaintance. It does not ask fundamental questions, but states the conditions of action for those who act on the basis of purported answers to those questions.

Weber is a poorer guide to his work than Marx, Durkheim or Freud are to theirs, and cared less about his legacy. I suspect this has led many non-Weberian readers away from the question of how, to that of whether to read him. For those for whom the difficulty or weight of Weber's texts places them in this position, there is perhaps only the following consolation. During the last twenty years it has become fashionable to add, to extend the scope of the political far enough to warrant talk of a 'politics of reading' or a 'politics of interpretation'. The 'political' writing of those who use these phrases is often suffused with metaphors of 'play' or 'dance', and in its affirmative moments is hard to distinguish from mysticism. But while it prides itself on its 'difficulty', this remains the easily imitated difficulty of an orthodoxy.[14] Weber described politics as 'the slow boring of hard boards'. The development of the forces of ideological production knows no progress, or if it does, the boards harden with the alleged sophistication of our drills. But since this is a message for which few have the ears, Weber not only said it, he showed it. His writings are difficult, and sometimes wilfully so, because and in the way that the world is difficult, his texts hard boards because and in the way that the world is hard boards. The product of any engagement with Weber is usually little more than a few blisters. But it is also the anticipation of more.

# Chapter 1

# The coherence of the concept of modernity

The modern age ... in contrast to the middle ages, is not present in advance of its self-interpretation, and while its self-interpretation is not what propelled the advance of the modern age, it is something that the age has continually needed in order to give itself form. . . . This makes the concept of an epoch itself a significant element of the epoch.

(Hans Blumenberg)

the discontent of modernity with itself exists only on the basis of historical consciousness, of the knowledge of other and 'better' times.

(Karl Löwith)

The other way around: historical consciousness is a *result* of the discontent of modernity with itself.

(Leo Strauss)

## INTRODUCTION

Is there anything left to say on the subject of modernity which hasn't already been said or implied in the mountain of literature which has appeared in the last ten years? Aren't the main theoretical and political positions by now so entrenched that everyone knows roughly what the stakes are? Can't the remaining work in this area be divided into that which pushes the birth of the modern world as far back as possible, and that which pulls it in the other direction, or into that which views modernity from a pre-modern, a post-modern, or an 'intra-modern' perspective? And can't those who push the line back, and who adopt a pre-modern or post-modern perspective be called conservatives, and those who pull it forward but remain committed to the recent project that line defines be called radicals? Haven't the debates between Habermas and Gadamer, Habermas and Lyotard, MacIntyre and his critics, Derrida and Foucault, Rawls and his critics exhausted the main lines of argument over what constitutes the modern age, what it entitles us to know and to hope for?

The answer is probably yes, but in all of these debates, the name of Max Weber has hovered in the background, asking those who believe they have solved the problems they set themselves to think again, and reminding them that what they think are their own problems were his too. In the last ten years, his significance has begun to increase, not only as a figure without reference to whom talk about the nature of the modern world makes no sense, but as someone whose work the participants in those debates increasingly wish to claim as their own.

To take one example. In the early sixties the debate between critical theory and neo-Aristotelianism in Germany took the form of an argument for or against the Enlightenment, for the idea of an ethics binding on all human beings or for the 'rehabilitation of practical philosophy', grounded in a concrete ethos.[1] For both sides Weber was an enemy. For Habermas and Marcuse he was a decisionist whose work contained no hint of the possibility of binding norms,[2] for political scientists like Voegelin and Wilhelm Hennis his conception of the state as a power organisation with no inherent purpose meant that the political science which accompanied it was inadequate to treat questions of the good life for human beings and of the concrete practices in which that life might be embedded.[3] Since then, with the exhaustion of the Habermas-Gadamer debate, the positions have remained largely the same, but Weber has been rediscovered, in Habermas's case as the analyst of the institutional consequences of the 'splitting apart' of reason,[4] in Karl-Otto Apel's case as one whose ethic of responsibility is the standard against which his and Habermas's discourse ethics must measure itself[5] and in Hennis's as someone whose science after all fulfils an Aristotelian function – the education of the judgement of members of a political community.[6]

I am not sure that these authors have done Weber the favour they think they have. It is one thing to rediscover an author, another to treat him/her as a recruit in one's own campaign. Hennis's interpretation in particular, though the most spectacular to appear in recent years, would have us believe that it is an act of devotion which at the same time wrests Weber from the clutches of those – particularly American sociologists – who don't deserve and haven't understood him. But the plea to pay Weber 'complete attention' rings hollow.[7] To let Weber speak to us directly is to become acquainted, indirectly, with Hennis's own neo-Aristotelian project. At least Habermas makes his instrumental reading of others, including Weber, fairly obvious.

On the other hand, a criticism of these readings merely for being instrumental hardly grasps their specificity. Instead, I want to try to show why these newer interpretations are wrong by asking two questions, only the first of which critical theory and neo-Aristotelianism take seriously. Firstly, what was Weber's account of modernity? Secondly, what theoretical status did he believe this account was entitled to claim for itself in the very light of its findings? For the distinctiveness of modernity consists not only in the empirically observable emergence of the modern state, a modern understanding of self, modern capitalism, modern science, but in our very need to define the modern epoch.

## HUMAN FINITUDE AND THE CAESURAL NEED

Odo Marquard has suggested that modernity be understood in terms of the transformation of a limit, the substitution of one version of human finitude for another.[8] Here, secularisation consists in a decline in the significance of a power boundary between human beings and God, and a concomitant increase in that of the spatial and temporal boundaries between human beings. And as globalisation undermines the significance of the spatial boundary, that of the temporal increases further. Hence an epochal consciousness, an increased sensitivity to historical trans-formations and to what distinguishes one epoch from another, becomes central to the modern epoch. In terms of an anthropology of finitude, the importance of modernity lies not so much in a transition to a new age, worldliness as opposed to unworldliness, the substitution of immanence for transcendence, but more in the fact that the very formulation of that epoch's substantive charac-teristics is the satisfaction of a secularised, temporalised, *caesural* need. The most obvious temporal caesura is the medieval–modern break, either in its pro-modern, enlightenment version, or in the form of a romantic or classicist anti-modernism. But as

Marquard notes, there is also the 'futurised antimodernism' of the modern–post-modern distinction, which embraces the utopian elements of Marxism, Nietzsche's philosophy of the future and those contemporary theories which claim that we already live in a 'postmodern age'.

For Marquard the caesural demand is such that it cannot be met in two places at once, or rather, at more than one temporal threshold. So for a classicist like Leo Strauss, the dramatic character of the pre-modern/modern distinction, the myth of the modern's origin, has to be secured by the reduction of the middle ages to antiquity, while what Marquard calls futurised anti-modernism, by emphasising the modern/post-modern threshold, necessarily deprives the pre-modern/modern threshold of its threshold character, 'de-dramatises' it, leaving historical research into that threshold free to discover new (pre-modern) indices of modernity or to alter significant dates: 'how much has changed where almost nothing has changed, and how little has changed where almost everything has changed'.[9]

Max Weber never presented the medieval/modern distinction in especially dramatic, caesural terms; for him there was no 'breakthrough' to the modern world. If Marquard is right, then part of the explanation is perhaps that for him the power boundary between human beings and god had never completely lost its significance, but more importantly that he insisted on the continuing relevance of spatial boundaries, expressed most forcefully in his emphasis on the distinctions between 'value spheres' and in the centrality of territoriality to his definition of the modern state. Weber's account of modernity has far more to do with the question of what, 'today', is possible and what is not, with the conditions of contemporary historical action.

It is perhaps no accident that the sharpest critics of Weber's ethics and politics are those for whom the pre-modern/modern break has precisely the dramatic character which Weber's version of it lacks. For romantic and classicist anti-modernists he cannot see the significance of the pre-modern/modern caesura and is in thrall to the modern, for critical theory and especially Habermas he cannot see the pre-modern/modern caesura and therefore fails to recognise the connection between modern rationality and human emancipation. What these critics object to is less Weber's philosophy of the human sciences, his mistaken account of the relationship between meaning and cause or the theory of charismatic leadership, than the fact that these individual features of his work are all indices of a degenerate modernity. Weber himself could never have had an adequate theory of modernity because the only possible version of such a theory implies either a critique of the modern age as a whole, or an acknowledgement of the modern 'project'. Conversely, if Weber believed neither in the rehabilitation of Greek political thinking, nor in a link between enlightenment rationality and freedom, it was hardly incumbent upon him to develop a thoroughgoing theory of the the modern 'epoch'. What would have been at stake for him had he done so?

Given the assumed centrality of 'the modern' in Weber research, especially in the last ten years, it is surprising how little attention has been given to the question of whether and how one ought to construct epochal thresholds. To be sure, the variety of senses in which the terms modernity, the modern and modernism are used does not inspire confidence in the belief that the concept of modernity has any coherence. In particular, there seems to be a series of incommensurabilities:

1 between participants' accounts of the criteria (political, aesthetic, economic, cognitive, etc.) according to which the concept of 'modernity' is to be defined;
2 between participants' understandings of the type of concept 'modernity' is (i.e. between individual, generic and ideal typical concepts);
3 between those features of an individual participant's account in which (i) an object is being described; (ii) a characteristic of an object or set of objects is being employed in its description; (iii) a term is being used, nominalistically, to collect a series of objects or characteristics of objects; (iv) a critical or endorsing stance towards a set of objects is being recommended.

In Weber research modernity tends to be theorised in two senses: as the contemporary Western epoch; and as newness or innovation *per se*, regardless of the historical time or culture in which it occurs. The first sense resolves itself into an alternative between the idea of modernity as a subject lying behind appearances, a backstage area housing the director of front-stage social and political activity, and the predicative exercise of discovering ever new spheres of cultural life to which the label 'modern' can be attached. The second is expressed most explicitly in Mommsen's charisma–rationalisation schema, according to which world-historical innovation is the product of periodic charismatic 'eruptions'.[10]

Yet most epochal, caesural accounts of modernity depend upon the extrapolation from one set of predicates to the set of all possible predicates, upon the globalisation of a local phenomenon, in which the onesidedness of a specific problematic becomes the universality of a general problem. The substantive criteria which define an object domain define the point at which the modern age as a whole breaks with the pre-modern. The tendency today to talk of 'modernity' rather than of 'capitalism', 'industrialism', 'ascetic protestantism', 'bureaucracy', '*Gesell-schaft*' or 'organic solidarity', tends to obscure this, especially when the greater abstractness of the concept 'modernity' is taken for greater depth of insight. Not that modernity is a mere word. If an insistence on the onesidedness of all historical inquiry is a legitimate part of a 'war on totality',[11] the spoils do not have to include abandonment of the term altogether. But in Weber's case we should be especially wary of the concept of an epoch, firstly because his explicit references to 'modernity' and 'modern culture' are disparate and inconsistent. The 'modern world' is bureaucratic, capitalist, intellectualist, Christian, post-Christian, 'worldly' or 'a tremendous tangle of cultural values'.[12] Weber never attempted seriously to unravel this tangle, for which reason his 'theory of modernity' will remain largely a commentator's reconstruction – or construction.[13] But secondly, there remains not only the reflexive problem highlighted by Marquard, but the fact that Weber took one of the main consequences of the 'modernity' of his own science to be the impossibility of a science of modernity.

Weber himself was acutely aware of the cultural significance of his own scholarly work, and believed that there was an ineradicable split between the intepretive and legislative roles of a 'cultural science'. In the literature this is usually expressed as science's value neutrality, but I think it is more important to emphasise that the presupposition of all of the more muscular, theoretically up-front theories of modernity on offer today is that theory has a legislative role, too. Many of those theories feed on talk of 'crisis', in particular of a crisis of legitimacy, a discourse in which the voice of the legislator can always be heard.

## MODERNITY FROM A PRE-MODERN PERSPECTIVE

### Modernity as a crisis in theology

Perhaps the most popular totalising theory of modernity rests upon a distinction between religion and science, understood not as sets of social practices but as rival, societal ordering principles. Their significance lies in their legitimation function, in their capacity to 'hold society together'. Whether religion or science are themselves legitimate is less important than the question of their capacity to legitimate the activities which constitute a social or political order. The 'crisis of modernity' to which so many allude represents, or can be held to represent, the inefficient operation of an ordering principle.[14] For example, science cannot do the work of God, a causal mechanism founded on law-like connections between appearances provides a less stable account of the continuity between those appearances than does an account of the source from which they derive their meaning.[15]

The theoretical rationale for interpreting modernity as crisis is almost always pre-modern, a point made most forcefully by Hans Blumenberg.[16] Blumenberg argues that modern intellectual curiosity in particular and the 'modern age' as a whole display a definite discontinuity with the Christian tradition, and that therefore the content of their intellectual and political endeavours cannot be treated as merely the secularised form of an essentially Christian substance, in particular that 'progress' is not secularised eschatology. Yet they did inherit a set of absolutist questions posed by that tradition, and were thus subject to a 'pressure' to provide absolutist answers.

In *Meaning in History* Karl Löwith had argued that 'Marx sees in the proletariat the world-historical instrument for achieving the eschatological aim of all history by a world revolution'[17] and that Comte's leading idea of progress is theological, a Catholic system without a faith in Christ. And in 1966, the year Blumenberg's *The Legitimacy of the Modern Age* was published, Michel Foucault was writing of Comte and Marx: 'a discourse attempting to be both empirical and critical cannot but be both positivist and eschatological'.[18] But Blumenberg's point is that the idea of progress at the heart of modern philosophies of history is not a secularised eschatology, since the 'goal' which is history's telos is understood by those philosophies as immanent to the historical process, while eschatology entails a fundamental event introduced into that process from without. Nevertheless, 'progress' and 'providence' do have a functional identity.

In a sense, the epistemological break with a religious *Weltanschauung*, which the enlightenment promised, and which Blumenberg, in opposition to Eric Voegelin, summarises as 'the second overcoming of gnosticism',[19] is negated at the very moment at which the self-assertiveness of an autonomous reason dissolves into a crisis of confidence attributable to that very autonomy. Reason is recaptured by that which it was thought to have denied, precisely because it attempts to 'empower' rather than assert itself. For it seems that the only models of self-justification available are absolutist ones. The scientific self-assertion of Bacon's intellectual curiosity becomes the scientistic self-empowerment of the philosophy of history or positivism, modernity's 'wrong turning'.[20] This is not a process in which reason gradually throws off a series of fetters before forcing back its horizon until it encompasses the world. Rather, having chiselled out a domain of competence for itself and established cognitive criteria peculiar to that domain, reason accepts questions addressed from without, questions it is less equipped than Christianity to answer. Immanence will always be weaker than transcendence as long as the rules are absolutist ones, but it might hold its own if it can find a way of changing them. But the problem for immanence is that the rules appear fixed, the questions 'non-negotiable'. We could formulate this dilemma in Nietzschean terms. Reason's original potential as a noble mode of evaluation – i.e., as a form of human endeavour which does not have to legitimate itself – remains unfulfilled because it cannot accept its own finitude, and at the same time cannot ignore what is thought to lie beyond its limits. It allows that which lies outside it to set its own agenda, in the first place to the extent that it experiences a pressure to legitimate itself, secondly to the extent that the only source of that legitimacy is that the overcoming of which is supposed to be reason's most distinctive achievement. Reason's extension of its sphere of competence is a form of weakness and, like all legitimation processes, a form of *ressentiment*. The question of whether, as Weber – *contra* Nietzsche! – argued, this legitimation 'drive' is the product of a deeply rooted human need for self-justification, must remain open.[21] So, too, must the more difficult question posed by Blumenberg and answered by him affirmatively: 'Is a non-absolutist mode of legitimation by reason possible?'[22]

The problem is highlighted in Kant's essay 'What is Enlightenment?'. He writes that enlightenment:

> is man's emergence from his self-incurred immaturity. Immaturity is the inability to use one's own understanding without the guidance of another. . . . The motto of enlightenment is therefore: Sapere aude! Have courage to use your own understanding! [23]

'For enlightenment of this kind, all that is needed is freedom . . . freedom to make public use of one's reason in all matters'.[24] Marx reinterpreted this possibility and it became the demand that society be transformed consciously. And from a different perspective Nietzsche is able to remark.

> The problem I raise . . . is not what ought to succeed mankind in the sequence of species . . . but what type of human being one ought to breed, ought to will, as more valuable, more worthy of life, more certain of the future. This more valuable type has existed often enough already: but as a lucky accident, as an exception, never as willed.[25]

Yet all three exhibit the weakness of which Blumenberg speaks and compromise their version of the thesis that human beings make their own history. For Kant, 'a lesser degree of civil freedom gives intellectual freedom enough room to expand to its fullest extent'.[26] Foucault describes this as 'the contract of rational despotism with free reason'.[27] Marx hooked his emancipatory narrative onto a naturalistic-evolutionary societal schema, provoking Popper's claim that for Marx 'politics are impotent'.[28] And Nietzsche wrote that 'every strengthening and enhancement of the human type also involves a new kind of enslavement'.[29] 'I want to learn more and more to see as beautiful what is necessary in things . . . Amor fati: let that be my love henceforth'.[30]

The idea that 'modernity' can be defined in terms of universalist modes of legitimation is common enough. For the Lyotard of The Postmodern Condition, the legitimation of modern knowledge is secured through a metadiscourse which appeals to a 'grand narrative', such as the dialectic of spirit, emancipation, or the wealth of nations.[31] And Francois Bourricaud, following Parsons, defines modernity in terms of 'involvement with the issue of universalization'. There are numerous other examples. But the point here is that in functional terms grand narratives are indistinguishable from the Christian belief in providence, that in the very appearance of discontinuity with Christianity they have, in Blumenberg's terms, 'reoccupied' answer positions Christianity left vacant. And since those answer positions are pre-modern, 'the philosophy of history is counter-modernity'.[32] This reoccupation of a product of a pre-modern preoccupation is not, for Blumenberg, part of a dialectic of enlightenment. For example, if Comte's positive philosophy is caught up in a series of reflexive binds to the point where it finally fulfils the sort of mythic function in contrast to whose superfluity it proclaimed itself,[33] the explanation is not to be sought in the logic of philosophical positions, but in an interpretation of localised question-and-answer sequences which formed the condition of possibility of 'progress'.

   An incidental consequence of the Löwith/Blumenberg debate is that the justification for many uses of the term 'postmodernity' collapses. The de-dramatisation of the pre-modern/modern break is not simply a consequence of the emphasis on the modern/post-modern break, but derives from the fact that if that with which post-modernity breaks is a universalist mode of legitimation, 'modernity' is merely an example of such a mode, and cannot intelligibly be regarded as a distinctive epoch to which the prefix 'post-' can be attached.[34] 'Post-modern' philosophy which aims to deconstruct 'logocentrism', 'phallocentrism' or 'phonologism', or reanimate the question of the meaning of Being, but which at the same time topicalises Cartesianism, Kantianism, 'the age of the world picture' or the transcendental subject, can justifiably be accused of not taking its object seriously. While for Heidegger the 'modern age' is constituted through a series of essential phenomena – science, machine technology, art becoming the object of mere subjective experience, culture as the consummation of human activity, 'the loss of the gods' – that age remains just another form in which the forgetting of the question of the meaning of Being is expressed, in this case as 'nothing less than the making secure of the precedence of methodology over whatever is', as a consequence of which the Being of whatever is is sought in the objectivity of an explanatory representation.[35] Though the essential distinctions between ancient, medieval and modern interpretations of that which is are made very clearly, the rationale for such distinctions undermines their significance. If the average deconstructive critic's concern tends to be with modern texts, this perhaps indicates more a lack of interpretive nerve than a belief in the distinctiveness of 'modernity'. For the philosophical basis of deconstructive criticism is a set of dilemmas endemic to any effort to construct a meaningful 'discourse', not merely to a modern version of that effort. If now Lyotard suggests that post-modern *art*:

> is undoubtedly part of the modern. All that has been received, if only yesterday . . . must be suspected. . . . A work can become modern only if it is first postmodern. Postmodernism thus understood is not modernism at its end but in its nascent state.[36]

then this expresses less a doubt about the reality of the modern/postmodern caesura than the realisation that its sharpness might serve to blur the pre-modern/modern one. It seems that the distinctiveness of the modern epoch cannot be established at both ends simultaneously.

## Modernity as a crisis in political philosophy

Leo Strauss identifies the crisis of modernity with a crisis of political philosophy inaugurated by Machiavelli. The crisis of political philosophy consists, according to Strauss, in its being no longer possible. That impossibility takes two forms. Either fact and value are distinct, but the rational grounding for morality political philosophy requires is lost; or fact and value are united, but values no longer have the ahistorical status which is a necessary condition for political philosophy. The lowering of expectations represented by Machiavelli's political 'realism', in which 'virtue must not be understood as that for which the commonwealth exists, but virtue exists exclusively for the commonwealth',[37] in which political action has a purely instrumental status, contrasts with a classical idealism which aims at the best regime, in which there exists a language in which reasonable talk about the good is possible, and political action is understood teleologically. Machiavelli's version of ought is developed in an account of how a prince ought to act on the basis of how human beings actually live, not of how they ought to live. The primary consequence of the adoption of such a basis is that ideal and reality are more likely to coincide, not because human beings are better equipped to actualise the ideal, but because the ideal is desublimated. The Aristotelian concept of virtue gives way to that of *virtu*, which consists in the judicious alternation of virtue and vice. For classical philosophers the actualisation of an ideal was possible but improbable due to its dependence on *fortuna*. The point about Machiavelli is not simply that 'men are obstinate in their ways' while *fortuna* 'is a woman and if she is to be submissive it is necessary to beat and coerce her',[38] but that such beating and coercion are considered possible. The importance of this move is that the elimination of chance in human affairs generally and control over the future in particular is a central enlightenment motif, which leads Strauss to conclude that 'the enlightenment . . . begins with Machiavelli'.[39]

The condition of possibility of Strauss's interpretation of Machiavelli's thought as a 'beginning' or discontinuity is the level of abstraction which provides the logical sense of modernity, namely political philosophy and in particular a classical political philosophy under whose auspices the idea of a set of 'permanent problems' makes sense. Modernity would then be intelligible as a mode of addressing those problems. But what is distinctive about modernity for Strauss is not that those problems are addressed in a particular way, but that the very idea of them has disappeared, and with it the intelligibility of political philosophy. Not only that, the disappearance for which Machiavelli is responsible, the variety of political realisms which have followed in its wake and the relative absence of genuinely utopian thinking are now so familiar that it is difficult to appreciate the 'newness' of Machiavelli's or any other modernity.

Strauss distinguishes between what he calls 'three waves' of modernity.[40] The first wave is driven forward by Machiavelli and continued by Hobbes and Locke. Strauss argues that Hobbes' understanding of natural right derived from human beginnings – the 'pedestrian hedonism' of self-preservation and fear of violent death – rather than human ends. Locke maintained this theme by finding a substitute for morality in economic acquisitiveness. The second wave is inaugurated by Rousseau's counter-modern plea and his subsequent concept of the general will which provided a horizontal check on selfishness rather than an appeal to a transcendental principle, and thereby collapsed the distinction between natural and positive law. This was continued by German idealism and culminated in the philosophy of history, in Hegel's version of which the right order is actualised as a by-product of the pursuit of passion and interest, and not as a direct result of a human striving to achieve it. The third wave is provided by Nietzsche's rejection of the rationality of history and of the possibility of any harmony between society and the *genuine* individual.

But for Strauss's purposes this distinction is superfluous, since all three belong to the same tide which sweeps away the possibility of intelligible talk about the good. What is important is less an understanding of the distinction between the three waves of modernity, than of that between the first wave and the calm waters of antiquity.

> One cannot see the true character of Machiavelli's thought unless one frees himself from Machiavelli's influence. For all practical purposes this means that one cannot see the true character of Machiavelli's thought unless one recovers for himself the pre-modern heritage of the Western world, both Biblical and classical.[41]

> historical reflection . . . is an unavoidable means for the overcoming of modernity. One cannot overcome modernity with modern means, but only in so far as we are natural beings with natural understanding; but the way of thought of natural understanding has been lost to us . . . we attempt to *learn* from the ancients.[42]

Without that recovery we are unable to attain a viewpoint from which Machiavelli appears new. This classicist move has informed Arendt's *The Human Condition* (1958), MacIntyre's *After Virtue* (1981) and the attempted rehabilitation of practical philosophy in Germany.

The kind of politics Machiavelli 'defends' – guided by expediency, the unavoidability of warfare, dissimulation, well-used cruelty, the dependence of good laws on good arms and instrumentalism – 'is as old as political society itself'.[43] 'There is in Machiavelli not a single true observation regarding the nature of man and of human affairs with which the classics were not thoroughly familiar'.[44] What he is defending is nothing new – the main topic of the *Discourses* is Roman republicanism – but he *is* defending it. And this move, in which recognition is claimed for what has always been the case, is a common – perhaps the dominant – way of legitimating the revolutionary character of thinking.

It is crucial to an understanding of the complexity of the problem of 'modernity' to bear in mind that the transition or change – conceived of continuously or 'caesurally' – which provides for modernity is not necessarily a transition or change in a concrete set of human relations or procedures, but can be a change in the publicly dominant account of that in which those relations and procedures consist. The call for caution is an urgent one in view of the plethora of claims that we live in a Marxian, Nietzschean or Freudian 'age'. The effect of Marx, Nietzsche and Freud on our understanding of relations and procedures is undeniable, but the historical effectivity of 'class struggle', 'the will to power' and the Oedipus complex is another matter. These are *rhetorics of recognition*, historically appropriate and bounded treatises on the ahistorically constitutive features of human relations, 'new' only by virtue of a claim about what has always been the case. The extent to which talk of a Nietzschean, Marxian or Freudian 'age' makes sense is the degree of isomorphism between the hermeneutic and political force of ideas.

## Modernity as a crisis in moral discourse

A second example of a conservative concept of modernity is worked out in MacIntyre's *After Virtue*, whose analytic framework parallels that of Strauss at key points, incorporates a number of motifs central to critical theory,[45] but offers a way out of modern aporias which neither Strauss nor critical theory would be willing to support. *After Virtue* is a philosophical history of morality in which the self, social science and politics are mutually underwritten. The argument divides into two parts, a theorisation of 'modernity' not as a set of modern practices but as the philosophical and sociological presuppositions of such, and an account of the historical roots of such presuppositions; and a discussion of the Aristotelian moral tradition which, if it has not been wholly forgotten, has been only partially remembered, and whose characteristic features stand in opposition to 'modernity'. Despite this opposition MacIntyre argues for the pertinence of a coherent account of that tradition to the cultural dilemmas adumbrated in the first part.

The first dilemma is a conceptual one. The fact that 'there seems to be no rational way of securing moral agreement in our culture' is traced to a disorder in the language of morals. Contemporary moral disagreement has three characteristics: the absence of external criteria to which individuals can appeal in support of moral decisions; an impersonal mode of presentation of moral argument premissed upon the alleged existence of such criteria; and the employment of concepts uprooted from larger totalities in which they were once at home. Their combination results in a distinction between the meaning of the terms of moral discourse and the use to which they are put. What appear to be objective arguments are nothing more than the expression of personal preference. This historically specific state of affairs was reified by logical positivism's emotivist theory of ethics, by Sartre's existentialism, by the ethical theory of R.M. Hare, by Max Weber and latterly, by Goffman. Value conflict is interminable, adherence to individual values a matter of decision or choice, rather than reason, and the sphere of competence of 'rationality' restricted to the matching of means to predetermined ends. Bureaucratic rationality seems to be the only rationality available to a world whose value choices are arbitrary.

MacIntyre notes immediately that the argument for radical choice rests upon a claim about the irreducibility of individual conscience and hence on a particular – modern – theory of the self. Since the emotivist self lacks external criteria of judgement there is no limit to the field in which that judgement may be exercised. Modern moral agency is abstractly universalist, detached from the concrete particularity which would provide the boundaries without which human identity is impossible. The absence of external criteria not only undermines the possibility of commun- ally sanctioned decisions but threatens the temporal continuity which defines human biography and without which life degenerates into a form of hedonism. Durkheim had already hinted at this contradiction between egoism and narrativity.

A thirst arises for novelties, unfamiliar pleasures, nameless sensations, all of which lose their savour once known. Henceforth one has no strength to endure the least reverse. . . . The wise man, knowing how to enjoy achieved results without having constantly to replace them with others, finds in them an attachment to life in the hour of difficulty. But the man who has pinned all his hopes on the future and lived with his eyes fixed upon it, has nothing in the past as a comfort against the present's afflictions, for the past was nothing to him but a series of hastily experienced stages.[46]

But spatial and temporal continuity is the condition of possibility of any determinate mode of human conduct, any substantive self. Hence the paradox of liberalism: the formal, pre-social self of modern individualism is a constant threat to those liberal institutions which are appealed to in its defence. The very possibility of stable institutions presupposes a coherent set of continuities. MacIntyre argues that the defining feature of the 'modern project' is the absence of the supreme principle of coherence, the Aristotelian idea of the good life for human beings, of human purpose. The modern self and modern moral discourse *are* conceptualised teleologically, but the individual ends of human action are not referable to the (natural) end of any human community.

The radicality of the autonomous moral subject presupposes and engenders a third, scientific dilemma. In the *Groundwork to the Metaphysics of Morals* (1964) Kant proposes a radical distinction between the unconditional nature of those imperatives which confer on action a moral content, and those to which action is 'in fact' subject. It is to the mechanisms of that conditionality – and those mechanisms alone – which, so argues MacIntyre, positivistic social science addresses itself. The facts of human action with which science is concerned contain no reference to the facts of what is valuable to human beings because there are no such facts. The only facts which 'exist' are facts about the conditionality of action. And the conditionality of action is at odds with the idea of freedom. Practical anthropology denies the moral law. MacIntyre makes the speculative claim that the mechanistic human science proposed in the eighteenth century was turned not into a real achievement but 'into a social performance which disguises itself as such an achievement',[47] and attempts to show that those social scientific generalisations which have proved genuinely fruitful have co-existed with their own counter-examples, *and* have been subject to sources of 'systematic unpredictability', MacIntyre's version of *fortuna*.

MacIntyre's account theorises the link between the modern self, social science and politics in terms of what he calls

'characters', who are 'moral representatives of their culture'
'because of the way in which moral and metaphysical ideas and
theories assume through them an embodied existence in the
world'.[48] The key feature of the character is that it constitutes not
a culture's standard of moral excellence, but that culture's moral
definitions. The incoherence of modern moral discourse requires
a common framework within which it can be made intelligible.
That framework is constructed through three characters. The
bureaucratic manager treats ends as givens. The therapist does
likewise in order to produce well-adjusted individuals. What
makes MacIntyre's analysis distinctive is the third character of the
modern triad. The aesthete, the protagonist of individual liberty,
is seen by MacIntyre as a viable alternative to the regulated activity
of the bureaucrat/therapist, but for that very reason the 'other
side' of the modern coin. The modern world view is not that of
instrumental rationality, opposed to which is a pre-modern or
post-modern freedom, or impersonal functionalism to be opposed
by personal autonomy. Rather: 'the society in which we live is one
in which bureaucracy and individualism are partners as well as
antagonists'.[49] The philosophical roots of that partnership,
objectivism and subjectivism, have been traced numerous times,
notably by Nietszche, Heidegger and Arendt. The latter's thesis of
a twofold process of 'world alienation', on the one hand through
a shift in the natural sciences to a universal standpoint which
increases the power of human beings over the world but at the cost
of making the gap between world and standpoint unbridgeable,
and on the other through the emergence of a sphere of intimacy
as the seat of individuality and the consequent devaluation of the
political as an internally coherent, public realm, will have an
important bearing on my interpretation of Weber's politics.[50] For
that politics is Weber's attempted solution to the very problem of
bureaucratic individualism by which MacIntyre believes his work
is haunted.

   Within a culture of bureaucratic individualism there is no
possibility of a form of judgement which lies between obedience
to a universal law and unbridled freedom. This squeezing out of
judgement constitutes the political crisis which animated much of
Weber's work. That crisis could not be the object of policy
measures, since it consisted in a threat to the very possibility of
political action itself. For the freedom associated with liberal
individualism is a deontologically conceived negative freedom,

whose sphere is politically *oriented* action, rather than political action 'proper',[51] a negative protest at the threat to individual rights posed by collective utility.

Although MacIntyre's concern is with the problem of commensurability in moral discourse and political practice, and thereby contrasts with Strauss's emphasis on the possibility of political philosophy, the presupposition of both accounts is that 'modernity' can only be 'seen' as modern, or distinctively new, through the adoption of a pre-modern perspective. For both, modernity is the absence of what was once present, atrophy rather than hypertrophy, a loss rather than an addition. Aristotelian virtue, the good life for man, and teleological accounts of human action have been either abandoned or only partially 'inherited'. Fortune, on which the (remote) possibility of an actualisation of an ideal depended, and which was inviolable, is now subject to the human control of the Machiavellian politician or the scientist whose goal is general laws. Clearly, the options Strauss and MacIntyre propose are different. And while Strauss appeals to a concept of natural right with which MacIntyre will have little to do, and seeks to defend the permanent character of the problems he addresses, MacIntyre is historicist enough to attempt to render his Nietzsche/Aristotle choice a practical one. But they are both classicist accounts, an epochal understanding of modernity which maintains a faith in a set of fixed judgemental criteria and argues that modernity cannot furnish those criteria itself.[52]

## MODERNITY FROM A MODERN PERSPECTIVE

For both Strauss and MacIntyre Max Weber is the most important contemporary representative of the position they oppose. His 'individualism', 'historicism', 'emotivism', 'Machiavellianism' and 'Nietzscheanism' are the most obvious warrants for their claims that Weber believes all faiths and evaluations to be equally non-rational, that questions of ends are questions of values, that Weber's understanding of 'value' is chiefly indebted to Nietzsche, that Weber's theory of bureaucracy did not allow for the possibility that 'effectiveness' could be a masquerade for social control rather than a reality, that Weber has no Sophoclean sense of the tragedy of action,[53] and that, in the end, 'the contemporary vision of the world . . . , is predominantly . . . Weberian'.[54]

I will try to show that many of these criticisms are misplaced.

For now I make the observation that, if Arendt is correct to claim that 'Max Weber . . . is the only historian who raised the question of the modern age with the depth and relevance corresponding to its importance',[55] it is perhaps because his questioning was unclassical, and because his work is *not* the victim, still less the embodiment, of a rigid dualism between the inviolability of a personal freedom rooted in conscience and the impersonality of a mechanised, bureaucratised, rationalised 'world', a dualism in which a surprising number of avowed Weberians still believe his strength consists.

## Modernity as philosophical discourse

The distinguishing feature of pre-modern and post-modern theories of modernity is a claim about the impossibility of meeting or the pointlessness of attempting to meet the specific demand for legitimacy constitutive of modernity. Jurgen Habermas formulates this demand thus: 'Modernity can and will no longer borrow the criteria by which it takes its orientation from the models supplied by another epoch; it has to create its normativity out of itself.'[56]

For MacIntyre the enlightenment could not find a rational foundation for morality because it took nature – *natura* – to be a matter of causality, to which it opposed the freedom of a self wholly detached from nature. Coherent moral discourse requires a concept of nature – *physis* – which is teleological, an account of that towards which a thing's activity tends. For Strauss, the only binding morality is grounded in classical natural right, for which the Kantian moral law is a poor substitute. Habermas's position is of interest here since it appears to reject pre- and post-modern moves and recognise its own situatedness, to fulfil precisely Blumenberg's demand that the requirement that modernity 'create its normativity out of itself' be met by a form of self-assertion, not by an attempt at self-grounding.

The logical sense of modernity for Habermas is a philosophical one. The philosophical discourse of modernity begins around 1800 with the conceptualisation of the period in Western Europe after 1500 as an epoch, and with Hegel's understanding of philosophy as its time grasped in thoughts.[57] Habermas argues that all attempts to go 'beyond' modernity have to consider their relationship to Hegel's concept of modernity. The problem Hegel inherited and which his philosophy tries to solve is this. A competition exists between: the orthodoxy of 'positive religion' whose chief characteristic is a distinction between priestly and mass belief, and between private religion and public life; and the 'religion of Reason'[58] in which religion is binding on all only because it is authorised by human reason. For Hegel, both are abstractions at a remove from the public realm, and thus neither can shape religion into an ethical totality. The provision of such a totality depends upon a philosophy of the absolute based on the self-relation of a knowing subject which encounters itself as both a universal subject and as a particular I. But Habermas argues that the culmination of this attempted provision is the 'primacy of the higher-level subjectivity of the *state* over the subjective freedom of the individual'.[59] While the central claim of the *Philosophy of Right* was that it was possible to formulate the substantive, determinate character of human subjectivity, its embededdness within human institutions – 'objective spirit' – without at the same time violating the integrity of conscience, the formal, negative freedom of Kantianism was dissolved, rather than sublimated, in positive freedom. Because of this, Hegel's philosophy is no more adequate to the task of instructing the world how it ought to be than Orthodoxy or the religion of reason. Hegel has maintained a link between modernity and rationality, but severed that between rationality and an ethical totality. The theory of communicative action is another attempt to derive an ethical totality – or *substantielle Sittlichkeit* – from within a 'modernity divided against itself'. Its main validity claim is that the problems of the theory/practice distinction which has plagued all attempts at self-grounding from within a philosophy of consciousness can be solved, or more adequately addressed, at the level of a philosophy of language. 'The higher-level inter-subjectivity of an uncoerced formation of will'[60] with which he opposes the higher-level subjectivity of Hegel's state occupies a higher level to which all can aspire, and do, in the course of everyday speech. The theory of communicative action, unlike Hegel's *Philosophy of Right*, is not merely a philosophical theory, but an everyday theory held to implicitly by all who constitute a public. Even under conditions of distorted communication, it is analytically, and that means practically, recoverable as the immanent ground of speech. We might borrow a formulation of Althusser's here and say that for Habermas, 'of course, we have all read, and all do read *The Theory of Communicative Action'*. The public use of reason which for Kant defined the maturity he identified with enlightenment is transformed into the public presupposition of a formal rationality inherent in the structure of everyday, mature, speech. Enlightenment no longer refers to a reason which at best can provide a false (because non-democratic) version of an ethical totality, but to an ethical totality grounded in the intersubjectivity of argumentative reasoning.[61]

But the curious feature of this philosophical theory of modernity is that its central question, that of an ethical totality, is hardly a modern one, as Blumenberg has pointed out. Habermas's statement that:

> Even on methodological grounds I do not believe that we can distantiate Occidental rationalism, under the hard gaze of a fictive ethnology of the present, into an object of neutral contemplation and simply leap out of the discourse of modernity.[62]

points up a tension within his own project: in warning against a leap forward he is in danger of falling backward.

The tension here stems from the difficulty of uniting a 'modernity divided against itself' without appealing to transcendental arguments. Moreover, those post-modern critiques of a philosophy of subject-centred reason he addresses are treated as inferior answers to the same problem. Thus Heidegger's Being, Derrida's *differance*/writing/general text, Nietzsche's Dionysus, all aim at providing binding judgemental criteria. Each represents an affirmative moment within what are often treated as pluralistic, nihilistic or relativistic forms of thought. It is not so much that Habermas wants to 'go back to Hegel and start again',[63] as that the post-modernist claim to have moved beyond the discourse of modernity amounts at best to a mythic restoration. But just as Habermas attempts to show that post-modernism is only comprehensible in relation to a Hegelian discourse and problematic it has failed to supersede, that if it has not reoccupied vacant answer positions it has attempted to take up that currently occupied by Habermas, Habermas himself plays into the hands of theologians or classical political philosophers to the extent that his answers could be read as poorer answers to *their* questions.

## Modernity as a mode of production

For a final version of a totalising theory of modernity I turn to Marx, for whom the capitalist mode of production cannot be, as it was for Weber, 'the most fateful force of our modern life',[64] since it is the founding principle of that life, its central generating mechanism. But as in the case of Habermas, Marx's work will be subject to two tensions: between the narrative structure of the account of the development of capitalism and the account of the narrative's final scene; and between two accounts of the nature of the final scene. If that scene is the present, Marx's historical sociology is one in which the present is a product emancipated from the process which produced it, yet in which the attempt is made to re-establish the continuity which that emancipation seems to threaten. As Alfred Schmidt writes:

> Marx would not have been successful in unfolding the content of the historical presuppositions of capital's emergence had he not first grasped the essence of capital theoretically. He would not have known where and how they were to be found.[65]

In order for an epoch to regard itself as the culmination of a developmental process from whose previous constituents it is different, it must first establish its identity. As Marx himself has it:

> The Christian religion was able to be of assistance in reaching an understanding of earlier mythologies only when its own self-criticism had been accomplished to a certain degree . . . Likewise, bourgeois economics arrived at an understanding of feudal, ancient, oriental economics only after the self-criticism of bourgeois society had begun.[66]

Yet Marx's analysis of what is allegedly the last frame is haunted by his own futurised anti-modernism, by the possibility that he would not have been successful in grasping the essence of capital theoretically had he not been aware of the ethical presuppositions of capital's supersession.

## ETHICS AND ETHOS

In all of these accounts of modernity two themes are dominant, one ethical and the other scientific. The ethical problem is this. Regardless of the precise point of origin of modernity, the classicist critique and the Habermasian endorsement of modernity are both directed against a fundamental dualism which received its most consistent form in the philosophy of Kant. This is a dualism between the intelligible and the sensible, between the two worlds of which I, as a human being, am a 'citizen', the world of a freedom grounded in the relationship between conscience and the moral law, and a world of causality whose phenomena are held together by laws, 'the starry heavens outside me and the invisible self within me'.[67] In an epistemological sense Kant never thematised a 'third world' of social and political relationships in such a way that those relationships could be regarded as anything other than objects of a causal account or the activities of moral agents whose morality consisted solely in the intentions they brought to bear on those activities. To this there have been three main responses:

1   the neo-Aristotelian argument that the ultimate reference point for ethical reasoning is not a formal freedom detached from determinate practice, but a conception of the good life for human beings, a good life embedded in those practices themselves, not an ethics but an ethos;

2   the neo-Hegelian argument that moral agency only makes sense in relation to what Hegel called 'Sittlichkeit', which, in contrast to the formal, negative freedom of the Kantian moral law, is, as the embodiment of reason, the positive freedom of the membership of a modern political community, a community whose modernity consists precisely in the fact that the claims of conscience – one of the 'achievements of the modern world'[68] – are sublimated, not destroyed, in determinate conduct. What Dilthey called the *Geisteswissenschaften* and what Weber and Simmel took to be the object of an interpretive sociology were only possible on the basis of Hegel's category of '*objektiver Geist*';

3   Habermas's and Apel's discourse ethics, according to which both the neo-Aristotelian and the neo-Hegelian views fail to respect the integrity of a Kantian *Sollen*, and with it the integrity of a universalist ethics. Both ethos and *substantielle Sittlichkeit* are taken to be coterminous with the factually given, and the task of a communicative ethics is to conceive of the Idea of a communicative community in such a way that that Idea provides grounds for a critique of the conditions of its applicability, that is, is not simply the categorical imperative 'act

as if you were a member of a communicative community', but is consistent with what Max Weber called an ethic of responsibility. In effect, communicative ethics is the attempt to reconcile Kant and Hegel, it is the belief that it possible to reject the formalism which grounds ethics in the conscience of the individual without reducing intersubjectivity either to neo-Aristotelian convention or to another subjectivity – Hegel's state. Thus Apel:

> In contrast to Kant's epistemological reflection on the unavoidable necessity of the unity of the object of consciousness and self-consciousness, that is of the trancendental unity of the subject–object relation, transcendental–pragmatic reflection leads immediately to the transcendental unity of the subject–cosubject relation of linguistic communication.[69]

The scientific problem consists in the fact that all of these accounts link a strictly ethical theory to a diagnostic account of modernity as an epoch. The problem of the moral law, of nature as a causal mechanism, of the state as an ethical totality, of the possibility of an intersubjective community of argumentative reasoners, is at the same time a problem of the nature of the modern epoch – the modern idea of conscience, modern science, the modern state and a 'postconventional' stage in the ethical evolution of the species as a whole.

## A TRAGIC CULTURAL SCIENCE

In many ways Max Weber's work lives in the tension between Kant and Hegel which the classicist critique sees as a symptom of a degenerate modernity and which discourse ethics believes it can overcome. His work contains an account of personality which is reducible neither to the claim that personality consists in the integrity of individual conscience and the moral law, nor to the claim that it is identifiable with integrity of the life of a political community. It is decisionistic, yet the concept of responsibility is central to it. It is individualistic, yet contains passages which could have come straight out of Hegel's *Philosophy of Right*. Weber's account of ethical reasoning is often formulated in terms of what it is possible for ethical reasoning in the modern world to be, in terms of the historical appropriateness of, for example, an ethic of responsibility and ethic of conviction.

Yet Weber's science, while taking modern phenomena for its object, is acutely aware of the limits of its own activity, and is, as a result, and in comparison with those accounts sketched above, surprisingly timid in its formulations of the character of the modern epoch. He once said that 'there are two ways, Hegel's and our own approach'.[70] This was less a repudiation of objective idealism than a reminder that either is a choice. That choice is a tragic one, and tied to the cultural location of a science – based on *Verstand* – which can know its own limits because it knows what lies beyond them – speculative *Vernunft* or mysticism. It is truly tragic because it recognises the equal validity of cultural science and speculation and, unlike Hegel, refuses to view *Verstand* and *Vernunft* competitively (or even dialectically). 'Our own approach' is different from Hegel's not least because it believes Hegel's to be just as valid. The tragedy of Weber's science stems from the impossibility of a systemic and at the same time practically effic-acious concept of culture. The cultural sciences are located within a culture whose tragic character ironises the systematicity promised by its singular formulation. To fulfil that promise would be a denial both of that location and of locatedness in general.

It is primarily for this reason that it would be premature to attribute to him a 'theory of modernity', however extensive and profound his insights into modern 'life conditions'. For the theories of modernity discussed in this chapter all belong to what Weber called 'the speculative view of life'.[71] Weber's own work, as a *Wirklichkeitswissenschaft*, is too deeply rooted in empirical history for him to have achieved a comparable level of abstraction. In addition, his work is remarkable for the extent to which he eschews both classicism and a philosophy of the future. To be sure, although his work contains not a hint of a philosophy of the future, it is peppered with nostalgic references to the Puritan sects, to the life style of the medieval knight and 'warriordom'. But this nostalgia never assumes a systematic character.

It might be objected that Weber's tragic view of history is in fact his theory of modernity, an expression of modern 'fragment-ation', loss of unity, ethical plurality, 'polytheism', that he treats a science of order or the attempt to grasp one's time, synthetically, in thoughts, as historically inappropriate. It is true that, although Weber claims that 'today' anyone wishing to practise science must specialise, his own cultural science displays a constant tension between specialisation and the synthesis without which it seems impossible to announce specialisation's unavoidability. Perhaps this is why he was considered such a giant, and why Jaspers said of him what Nietzsche said of Goethe – that he held together the conflicting forces of the age without being torn apart by them, yet lacked the charisma required to integrate them.[72]

If we want to understand both Weber's account of personality, which receives its sublimest expression in *Politics as a Vocation*, and the fact that he developed a science of the modern world in the face of his own belief that the concept of an epoch was unscientific, I think we have to understand a concept Weber's own use of which unites these themes – culture. Weber's concept of culture goes a long way to explaining why many of the participants in contemporary moral and political debate find him neither ethically nor politically nor theoretically satisfying. For Weber, we are not, as Straussian political philosophy requires, natural beings with a natural understanding, but cultural beings with a cultural understanding. But while the absence of both a caesural concept of modernity and a political philosophy is attributable to Weber's concept of culture, it is this very concept which helps explain the link between his account of modernity and his defence of the integrity of the political. Above all, given the tension and at times opposition between culture and politics within the German *Bildungsbürgertum* at the time, Weber's understanding of culture is remarkable for the extent to which it *is* consistent with the view that to be a political animal is to lead a truly human life. It is to that understanding that I now turn.

# Chapter 2

# The theory of culture

Culture stands at the mid-point of intellectual work; all oppositions of modernity take part in the struggle over it.

(Rudolf Eucken)

He seeks the whole man and enjoys his uniqueness. He asks not
so much what one achieves, of what one is capable, as what one
is . . . our friend . . . is very unmodern.

(Werner Sombart)

## INTRODUCTION

To attribute the lack of an epochal Weberian theory of modernity
to his understanding of 'culture' is to invite at once the question
of the 'modernity' of that understanding. For if the emergence of
the modern epoch can be constituted theoretically in various ways,
so can a modern concept of culture. The definition of that concept
depends partly upon an account of the opposition of which it is
held to partake. Were there a unitary conceptual history of 'culture',
it would be one whose stages were defined by culture's 'others'.

Culture's other may be nature, understood as radical evil; as
drives which have to be mastered; as a golden age from which
culture is a fall; as a causal mechanism to which an infinite reality
is reduced; as the counter-factual ground of the necessity of
political society; or as a state towards which the progress of a fallen
culture nevertheless aspires. The usual story told by conceptual
historians is one of the move from a continuous to a discontinuous
relationship between culture and nature, of the transformation of
'culture' from its pre-modern sense, as the cultivation *of* nature in
Cicero's *cultura animi*, in which the idea of culture is inseparable

from agri-culture, in which the cultivation of the soul is analogous to the cultivation of the soil, to everything which is added by human beings *to* nature by virtue of their own efforts, or as everything which contributes to the denial, repression or overcoming of a *status naturalis*, or barbarism.[1] Culture's other may be civilisation, understood as forms of outward behaviour having no reference to the inwardness of the personality, as the self-expression of a French middle class entitled, unlike its German counterpart, to participate in the life of the court in the latter half of the eighteenth century,[2] or as a synonym for decadence.[3] It may be life, as the subterranean source of a liberating dynamism, discovered in the nineteenth century by Schopenhauer, Nietzsche, Dilthey and Bergson, and whose channelling into rational forms is the task of culture.[4] It may be religion, as the only source of meaning for worldly human activity. Here, culture is nothing other than that activity, and the distinction between culture and civilisation collapses.[5] It may be enlightenment, whose universal ethical promise contrasts with the particularity of individual cultures. It may be society, as an economic, political and technological base with a cultural superstructure; it may be '*Bildung*', as the only true way to the freedom of the personality.[6]

Weber invokes all of these oppositions with varying degrees of explicitness throughout his work. The next chapter will be concerned with the neo-Kantian distinction between culture and life as the ground for the object domain of an empirical, historical science, the following two with that between religion and culture. But what is culture for Weber, and how does he arrive at the concept of it he in fact adopts? What is its intellectual–historical provenance? An understanding of it enables us to understand at least the following aspects of his work:

1  his account of the relationship between the onesidedness and allsidedness of the personality;
2  his account of modern polytheism and its relationship to the division of labour;
3  his account of the relationship between the claims of the personality and the demands of determinate action, in particular, political action;
4  the significance of the fact that he combines an insistence on the centrality of *Beruf* with a rejection of corporate theories of the state based on that same centrality;

5  the paradoxical fact that to understand culture is to understand both Weber's account of the modern age and the difficulty of ascribing to him a theory of modernity.

## KULTUR, BILDUNG AND BRAUCHBARKEIT

If there are two concepts which to the English-speaking world encapsulate a specifically German idea of selfhood, they are *Bildung* and *Kultur*. The fact that the six-volume encyclopedia project, *Geschichtliche Grundbegriffe*, edited by three German historians,[7] contains an entry for *Bildung* but not for *Kultur*, might lead us to assume their equivalence. And indeed, (still) the most significant attempt to account for those concepts' historical emergence, Elias's *The Civilizing Process*, placed them on one side of an opposition whose other side is a (French) concept of civilisation in relation to which they were held to define themselves. For Elias, *Kultur* and *Bildung* are the means with which a late-eighteenth-century German intelligentsia, excluded, unlike its French counterpart, from the life of the court, legitimates itself. While 'civilisation' refers to a universal process of increasing mastery over barbarism, the identification of the destiny of a nation with the fate of humanity, 'culture' is bound up with the forging of a particular national identity. And while the one implies propriety, decency and external appearance, the other refers to concrete achievement (*Leistung*) as a mark of personal distinction: 'On the one hand, superficiality, ceremony, formal conversation, on the other, inwardness, depth of feeling, immersion in books, development of the individual personality'.[8]

And personal development is to be sought in books, music, art, and philosophy, in a realm 'situated beyond economics and politics'.[9] To be sure, that inner enrichment is dependent upon human achievement rather than manners or specific codes of outward behaviour, upon a style of life which has not degenerated into mere style. Yet, as Goldman has recently shown, an understanding of Weber's account of personality requires a distinction between *Bildung* and *Kultur*, a distinction made by many of those Elias discusses. Weber's insistence that *Kultur* is *the* object of his empirical historical inquiry is what distances him from this German tradition of self-cultivation,[10] and more specifically from a *Bildungsideal*. For neither Herder nor Kant nor Schiller nor Wilhelm von Humboldt nor Schleiermacher nor Fichte, all of whom Weber had read as a boy, is *Kultur* the highest form of human endeavour, the ultimate goal of human existence. At most, it is the necessary means for its achievement.

## *Bildung* and the division of labour

For the tradition to which Elias refers the concepts of *Bildung*, *Kultur*, *Aufklärung* and *Zivilisation* were all employed for the purpose of distinguishing the inner from the outer human being, the person from the conditions of his or her activity, and usually it was *Bildung*, not *Kultur*, that expressed the former. If *Kultur* implied a relation to the inner human being which *Zivilisation* or *Aufklärung* lacked, if solid achievement was valued more highly than the external forms, the wigs and fripperies, the pregnancies of word and gesture charactersitic of the French court, there remained the possibility that those achievements might themselves develop a life of their own which detached itself from any relationship to the inner personality of the producer, and that even if they did not, the price to be paid for a harmony between external achievement and inwardness might be a lack of harmony between different realms of achievement and therefore between different 'provinces' of the soul. There is a twofold tension here between the superficial allsidedness of 'civilisation' and the solidity of *Kultur*, and between the onesidedness which this demand for solidity brings with it, and a *Bildung* which combines multiplicity and depth. In the Germany of the late-eighteenth century it is expressed in that between two educational ideals, the classical–idealist–humanistic conception, and one tied to the particularities of *Beruf* and *Stand*. Put another way, to what extent does the completion or perfection of the individual threaten his/her usefulness to society, and to what does the idea of usefulness undermine personal identity? This tension, between *Bildung* and *Brauchbarkeit*, received its fullest lamentary expression during the 1790s. Schiller writes:

> everlastingly chained to a little fragment of the whole, man develops himself into nothing but a fragment; everlastingly in his ear the monotonous sound of the wheel that he turns, he never develops the harmony of his being, and instead of putting the stamp of humanity upon his own nature, he becomes nothing more than the imprint of his occupation, of his specialised activity.[11]

The Hölderlin version of this occurs at the end of *Hyperion*.

It is a hard thing to say, but I do so because it is the truth; I can-not imagine a people as divided as the Germans. You see craftsmen, but no human beings, priests, but no human beings, masters and servants, boys and men, but no human beings – is that not like a battlefield in which hands, arms and limbs lie about and the spilled blood dissolves into the earth?[12]

The same thought is expressed famously by Goethe's Wilhelm Meister.

What use is it to me . . . , to bring order to an estate, if I am divided within myself . . . ? I do not know how it is in other countries, but in Germany a general, dare I say, personal edu-cation is possible only for the aristocrat. A bourgeois can earn merit and develop his intellect . . . but he forsakes his person-ality, do what he will . . . he must train individual capacities, in order to be useful, and it is already assumed that there neither is nor ought to be a harmony in his being, because in order to make himself useful in *one* way, he must neglect everything else.[13]

It is this problem, of the division of labour, of fragmentation, of the seeming impossibility of committing oneself to what Weber called 'the conditions of all technique' without becoming entangled in the conditions of this rather than that technique, of the relationship between the unity of the personality and the differentiation of its spheres of activity which, initially, lies at the centre of Weber's engagement with the problem of culture. It is implicit in his remarks on perspectivism and organicism in the cultural sciences, and on education, bureaucracy and the relation-ship between science and politics. It culminates in his attempt to save the meaning of *Beruf* from its degeneration from calling to profession.

## Culture and civilisation

In the December 1783 edition of the *Berlinische Monatsschrift*, the priest Johann Friedrich Zollner asks: 'What is enlightenment? This question, which is almost as important as the question: what is truth? needs to be answered before we begin to enlighten.' In the September 1784 edition Moses Mendelssohn took up this challenge, and began by noting that the words *Aufklärung*, *Kultur* and *Bildung* are of recent origin, belong to the world of books, and are scarcely understood by the common herd. Despite this, they describe something perfectly familiar. Mendelssohn formulates the relationship between *Bildung*, *Kultur* and *Aufklärung* hierarchically. The more the state of sociability of a people is brought into harmony with the determination of man, the more *Bildung* it has. *Bildung* consists in a combination of *Kultur* and *Aufklärung*. While *Kultur* tends towards the practical, for example, in craftsmanship, arts and 'ethics of sociability', *Aufklärung* tends towards the theoretical, in an objective sense towards rational cognition, in a subjective sense towards a preparedness for a rational consideration of human affairs according to their influence on the determination of man. And this distinction corresponds to that between the determination of the human being as a human being and as a citizen: 'the human being as human being does not need culture: but he does need enlightenment'. Culture is identified with a sphere of social particularity, with that which contrasts with the cosmopolitan demands of enlightenment. That sphere is not the political community or state, but the *Stand* or vocational group.

> Status group and vocation in civil life determine the duties and rights of each member, demand, in accordance with those rights and duties, different skill and accomplishment, different tendencies, drives, ethics of sociability and habits, a different *Kultur* and *Politur*. The more these, throughout all estates, correspond to their vocations, i.e. to their respective determinations as members of society, the more culture the nation has.[14]

The link between culture and vocation is provided solely by a set of rights and duties which a vocation ascribes to an individual, whose culture is the degree to which he/she conforms to them. Vocation is not the result of individual choice grounded in ultimate values. That which transcends the particularity of a vocational ethos is that enlightenment which corresponds to the determination of the human being as human being. A state in which culture and enlightenment, the particular and the universal, combine, is one with *Bildung*.

Unhappy the state which must concede that in it the essential determination of man is not in harmony with that of the citizen, that the enlightenment which is indispensable to humanity cannot extend across all estates without placing the constitution in danger of collapse.[15]

The link between *Kultur* and the determination of man as a citizen is not that between *Kultur* and a citizen of the state, but between *Kultur* and membership of an estate. The constitution of the unhappy state is a feudal constitution which cannot endure the existence of an enlightenment which transcends the differences between its orders and powers. But the constitution of the happy state is a feudal constitution which can.

For Kant, the superiority of *Kultur* to *Zivilisation* remained tied to a cosmopolitanism expressed in the idea of '*Weltbürgertum*'. In the same year as but in ignorance of Mendelssohn's essay he writes

We are cultivated to a high degree through art and science. We are civilised to the point of excess by all social courtesies and proprieties. But we are still a long way from being entitled to call ourselves morally mature. For the Idea of morality belongs to culture; but the use of this idea, which extends only to that in love of honour and external propriety which resembles ethics, constitutes mere civilisation.[16]

If culture is somehow superior to civilisation, it is because it meets a demand which civilisation cannot, the reconciliation of the human being with itself, the achievement of a human state *beyond* a state of culture, a state which once again corresponds to the (natural) determination of man. The gesture of Kant's 'Idea of a Universal History' is not a return to nature, nor a mere development of a natural potential to its logical conclusion. Culture and nature are both *eigengesetzliche Ganzheiten*, totalities with their own laws. The idea of the full development of the laws of culture is the idea of their full development to the point at which culture accords with the laws of nature. If both an original state of nature and a final state of freedom are standards with which to judge all hitherto existing societies, they remain external to the historical process. *Weltgeschichte* is not yet *Weltgericht*. Kant's account of culture is still short of making a link between culture and Germanness. Or, if there is one, *Kultur* remains subordinate to

*Bildung*. The 'vain and violent' application of the powers of the state to schemes of expansion is a hindrance to the slow development of the '*Bildung*' of its citizens, the ulitmate aim of which is a '*weltbürgerlicher Zustand*'[17] in which the original capacities of the human species as a whole might develop. For Herder, too, a concern with the centrality of culture and the idea of cultural diversity had as its ultimate aim the overcoming of an opposition between nature and culture. At the top of Herder's conceptual hierarchy stands not culture, but humanity.[18]

A hierarchy between *Zivilisation*, *Kultur* and *Bildung* reappears in Wilhelm von Humboldt, for whom *Zivilisation* is 'the humanisation of peoples in their external institutions and customs and the inner disposition which relates to them'. *Kultur* 'adds art and science to this enoblement of the human condition'. And *Bildung* 'is something higher and more internal, namely the conviction which, out of the knowledge and feelings of an entire spiritual and ethical striving, pours forth harmoniously into feeling and character'.[19] 'The true goal of man . . . is the highest and most proportionate formation of his powers into a whole.'[20] The *Bildung* of an individual is a development outward from within.

But whereas for the cosmopolitan classics of the late German enlightenment *Bildung* referred to the perfection of the species as a whole, a perfection reconcilable with the limited or partial development of the individual through *ständisch* or vocational activity (Kant's account of citizenship is still not free of this idea), for Humboldt it had become the *Bildung* of the individual which is the purpose of social and political institutions. The years around 1800 in Germany had witnessed a transition from accounts of culture which combined the particularity of *ständisch* or vocational conduct with a cosmopolitan ideal of the development of humanity, to ones in which the particularity of culture referred increasingly to the identity of the nation and 'development' meant the development of the individual personality.[21]

When this connection between culture and Germanness is invoked, it is invariably tied in turn to the idea that the emphasis on 'personality' is essentially a-, anti- or at best pre-political. And the political failure of German liberalism in the first half of this century is often attributed in part to the prevalence of the distinction between culture and politics among members of the German *Bildunsbürgertum*. In 1907, Werner Sombart asks

How is it that in Germany the interest of precisely the educated stratum in everything known as politics becomes ever smaller, that the cleft that opens between *Bildung* and politics expands to an abyss which seems no longer bridgeable?[22]

The idea that culture, too, signified something at once peculiarly German and anti-political had been a pervasive feature of Nietzsche's thought. 'Culture and the state . . . are antagonists: the 'cultural state' is merely a modern idea. . . . All great cultural epochs are epochs of political decline: that which is great in the cultural sense has been unpolitical, even anti-political.'[23] The link between culture, Germanness and inwardness found its most extreme expression in the wartime writings of Thomas Mann, in which some have attempted to seek a comparison with, or even clearer expression of, Weber's own account of culture.[24] For Mann, World War I was not only a war waged against Germany, but a war waged by civilisation against culture, by the 'Ideas of 1789' against those of 1914.

No more of Schopenhauer's denial of the will, let intellect dominate will and let it create paradise. No more of Goethe's ethos of personal culture: society rather. . . . The imperialism of civilisation is the last form of the Roman idea of unification against which Germany is protesting.[25]

Yet 'The German will never elevate social problems above moral ones, above inner experience. We are not a social nation and not a bonanza for psychologists.'[26] For our purposes, Mann's 'nationalism' is less important than the fact that his concept of culture is to be legitimated through accomplishments in art, music and scholarship, but not in politics or economics, in which, by implication, problems of morality and 'inner experience' cannot arise. What Elias takes to be true for a late-eighteenth-century German middle class is undeniably the case for Mann in 1914–18.

But the exclusivity of the referent of the concept of culture continued in the work of Lukács and the Frankfurt School, particularly Marcuse, and persists today in the critical theory of Habermas. Shortly after his conversion to communism in 1919 Lukács writes: 'The concept of culture (in contrast to civilisation) embraces all those valuable products and capabilities, which for the immediate maintenance of life are dispensable.'[27] Culture is only possible outside the realm of production, of necessity. What

Lukács called the 'old culture' of feudalism was the culture of the dominant classes who were free to devote themselves to it, it 'consisted in the fact that once ideology and the order of production were in harmony, the products of culture could develop organically out of the soil of social being'.[28] This entailed a harmony between 'ideology and *Lebensführung*', a harmony which capitalist society destroys through the fact that the dominant class is as tightly bound as the proletariat to the realm of necessity. Thus, 'the culture of capitalism could consist in nothing more than the relentless critique of the capitalist epoch', whereas culture 'in the true sense of the word' is 'the natural harmony and beauty of the old culture'.[29] The new culture which the revolution is to bring with it is the emancipation of humanity from the priority of production, the liberation of culture from civilisation.

> For culture is as much the internal domination of the human being over his environment as civilisation is his external domination. As civilisation created the means for this domination over nature, so this means for the domination of society is created by proletarian culture. For precisely civilisation and its most developed form, capitalism, has developed furthest the bondage of man to society, to production, to the economy.[30]

If the precondition for culture is the human being as its own end, the Idea of the humanity of human beings, then feudalism – the old culture – made it available to the dominant classes, capitalism to no-one, and socialism – the new culture – will make it available to all.

Marcuse's more pessimistic 'Remarks on a Redefinition of Culture' of 1965 ties culture to the power of negation in the face of civilisation's success – i.e. its failure to fit the schema of Lukács' philosophy of history – but it employs the concept of culture in the same restrictive sense, while claiming to derive it from Weber.

> I take as a starting point Weber's definition of culture, according to which culture is to be understood as the complex of specific modes of belief, achievements, traditions, etc. which form the 'background' of a society[!] . . . In the centre of my discussion will be the relationship between background and ground.[31]

The relationship between culture and civilisation becomes that between purposes, the setting of which falls to art, religion, philosophy and literature, and means – dominant institutions. In the following table Marcuse forces home the point

| Civilisation | Culture |
|---|---|
| Material work | Intellectual work |
| Working day | Holiday |
| Work | Leisure |
| Realm of necessity | Realm of freedom |
| Nature | Spirit |
| Operational thinking | Non-operational thinking |

Technical progress collapses these distinctions and leads to the integration of culture in society. It *'puts an end to the alienation of culture from civilisation* and thereby levels the tension between *"Sollen"* and *"Sein"* (which is a real historical tension)'.[32]

With Habermas's borrowing of Parsons' distinction between social, cultural and personality systems, the critical theoretical restriction of culture was complete, a restriction which remains even when it falls to culture to establish society's purposes.[33] Of the possible criticisms of Habermas's most sustained engagement with Weber, *The Theory of Communicative Action*, the most significant is less its utilisation of Weber for its own evolutionary purposes than the account of culture such utilisation presupposes. This affects not only the account of rationalisation, but, as we will see, that of Weber's theory of 'value-spheres' too.

## WEBER AND THE AMBIGUITY OF CULTURE

Any attempt to tie Weber to this tradition, in which critical theory and bourgeois thought have a peculiar affinity, is likely to founder on the fact that it is only in the light of his very concept of culture that it makes sense to talk of spheres of human endeavour at all. As long as we talk of the relationship between culture 'and' politics, culture 'and' economics, between a realm of culture which pertains to human inwardness and a social realm which does not, we will miss this point completely. 'Culture' *is not a sphere at all*. Weber's concept of culture should be interesting to us because through it we can gain an understanding of his vision of the human condition without making that understanding dependent upon this or that feature or dimension of it.

And yet, it is true that when Weber writes that we *are* cultural beings he means that we are not natural, living, social, religious or political beings. The tendency to think of the Weberian concept of culture as one side of an opposition, or as a polemical concept, is not wholly unfounded. While culture and the *Kulturmensch* ought to be interesting to us for formal reasons, as the ground of Weberian cultural science in general, it is clear that for Weber himself they have a substantive historical referent. Moreover, Weber's empirical historical work contains two senses of the *Kulturmensch* which are wholly inconsistent. As his forthright appeal to the idea that we *are Kulturmenschen* goes hand in hand with the contradictoriness of its substantive sense, an attempt at clarification is called for.

In the '*Zwischenbetrachtung*' in the sociology of religion[34] – the object of Chapters 4 and 5 – Weber invokes an opposition between religion and culture, and does so in order to point out the *modernity* of the *Kulturmensch*. Yet in his scattered remarks on education, he speaks of what he calls an 'old *Kulturmenschentum*', with which he contrasts the modernity of the object of modern specialised training, the *Fachmensch*.

As we saw, at the end of the eighteenth century, the opposition between the allsidedness and onesidedness of the personality was expressed through that between *Bildung* and *Brauchbarkeit*, between the idea that the purpose of human institutions was the development of the whole human being and the idea that a lasting human achievement in one sphere was worth more than a dilletantish all-round cultivation. The replacement of the first view by the second is the story of Goethe's Wilhelm Meister. Weber's work contains two versions of this opposition.

The first is expressed in *The Religion of China* and scattered remarks in *Wirtschaft und Gesellschaft*.[35] What Weber is trying to do here is not simply to distinguish between a humanistic allsidedness and onesided specialisation. There is a correct and an incorrect, or a true and a degenerate interpretation of both. In the China essay Weber constructs a threefold educational typology which he claims corresponds to the typology of domination. He identifies two opposed poles. On the one hand, it is the task of education to *awaken* the charisma of the pupil, manifested in the possession of heroic qualities or magical gifts.[36] This type of education corresponds to a charismatic structure of domination. At the other stands the provision of a specialised schooling. Here the aim of specialised education is to *train* the pupil for practical *usefulness [Brauchbarkeit]* for the purposes of administration – be it in the management of an authority, an office, a workshop, a scientific or industrial laboratory, or a disciplined army.[37]

Specialised training corresponds to a rational–bureaucratic structure of domination.

Between these two poles lie 'all those types of education . . . which wish to *cultivate* in the pupil a particular type of *Lebensführung*, which can be temporal or spiritual, but which is in all cases *ständisch*';[38] a pedagogy of cultivation 'wishes to *educate* [i.e. neither awaken nor train] a *'Kulturmensch'*, that means here, a human being with a certain internal and external *Lebensführung*,[39] or way of leading one's life. Within this third category, the similarity between what Weber calls the universality of a Confucian *Bildung* and occidental humanism consists in the fact that both provided entry into the offices of civil and military administration, and in the western case shaped the pupil, socially, as belonging to the estate of *'Gebildeten'*. In the Occident, according to Weber, an ideal of universal education, an education of the whole human being, has largely been replaced by one of rational, specialised training.

If on this basis we formulate the problem in terms of allsidedness versus onesidedness, we miss the deeper significance of Weber's remarks on specialisation. What Weber means by the cultivated individual, at least in this context, is as general as what he means by the *Kulturmensch*. The cultivated individual is not, as we are perhaps inclined to believe, a universal sophisticate, developing him- or herself in a series of different directions, but simply the object of education, breeding, upbringing *rather than training*. As examples of the settings in which the cultivated man in this sense was the goal, Weber cites feudal, theocratic and patrimonial structures of domination, the English administration-by-notables, the ancient Chinese patrimonial bureaucracy and the demagogy of 'the so-called hellenic democracy'.[40] In short, forms of *traditional* domination. The particular type of traditional domination and social conditions upon which membership of a ruling stratum depended would determine *the type of cultivated individual* for which education aimed.

Weber then speaks of an opposition between the emerging trained specialist *Fachmensch*-type and 'the old *Kulturmenschentum*'.[41]

So on this account, the supersession of a concern with the education (*Erziehung*) of the whole human being by the training (*Abrichtung*) of that human being for a specialised activity is the supersession of the *Kulturmensch* by the *Fachmensch*. The training of the *Fachmensch* has no intrinsic relationship to the manner in which he leads his life, save perhaps that successful training entails a refusal to put the question of the leading of one's life. The key to the distinction between *Kulturmensch* and *Fachmensch* is that the *Lebensführung* of the former is only understandable through the category of '*Stand*'. And in so far as Weber makes *Lebensführung*, not ideas or doctrines, the object of what he insists is a science of culture, that science contains a built-in nostalgia.

But as the next chapter will make clear, there is a second sense in which the *Kulturmensch* is the object of science. Here, to be a *Kulturmensch* is not simply to be a being with a distinguishable *Lebensführung*, but to be capable of taking a position on the 'reality in which we move', of adopting a standpoint, not allowing one's activity 'to run on as an event in [second] nature'. Culture refers less to *Lebensführung* than to its conscious ground, conviction based upon an ultimate value, upon an abstraction from the conditions of determinate action.

The difference between the old and the new senses of culture is that in the first case, the onesidedness of modern specialisation is contrasted with culture as the *Lebensführung* of a *type of human being*, while in the second, it is contrasted with culture as the value-related activity of one who remains a specialist but whose limited activity is the product of active choice, not custom. The implicit substantive referent for an allegedly formal condition of inquiry gives either of these concepts of culture a polemical character. On the one hand, the opposition between the old *Kulturmensch* and *Fachmensch* makes it difficult to conceive of the (modern) bureaucrat/specialist as the object of an avowedly cultural science. On the other, the idea that culture is constituted by human beings capable of taking a position makes it difficult to conceive of either the Hindu Brahmans or the Confucian literati as cultural beings, since in both China and India the idea of 'taking a position' was, according to Weber, *absent* from the Hindu or Confucian '*Lebensanschauung*'.[42] And this despite the justification for taking such strata as objects of cultural science being Rickert's concept of the 'historical centre', those groups in which certain *values* are 'truly vital'.[43]

Because the concept of culture, quite apart from the endless discussion of the substantive question of '*Kultur*' during Weber's lifetime, is polemical, both the neo-Kantian and neo-Aristotelian camps of Weber research have a point. If the first is right, the old concept of *Kulturmensch* cannot include modern specialisation under its rubric, cannot appreciate the fate of the bureaucrat who could take a position but doesn't. If the second – e.g. Hennis – is right, the new, neo-Kantian concept of *Kulturmensch* treats the whole of world history not simply from the point of view of the modern *Kulturmensch*, but as if it were the world to which that *Kulturmensch* belonged.[44]

## CULTURE, PERSON AND CONDITION

This ambiguity in the concept of culture recalls, and indeed expresses perfectly, the tension discussed in the last chapter, between the embeddedness of ultimate values in concrete practices, and their having, as Schiller put it, retreated into the human breast. In Lukács' terms, between a state of affairs in which ideology and *Lebensführung* implied one another, and one in which they do not.[45] It reminds us, too, of the legacy of Kantian ethics, the idea that I inhabit two worlds, the world of my invisible self, my personality within me, and the world as a causal mechanism without. Kant's attempt to find a solution to the problem of the division between the intellectual and the sensible realms foundered on his ethical rigorism, on the detachment of the claims and responsibilities of the personality from the context of determinate action: 'the moral law has no other cognitive faculty to mediate its application to objects of nature than the understanding (not the imagination); and the understanding can supply to an idea of reason not a schema of sensibility but a law'.[46]

Schiller's *Letters on the Aesthetic Education of Man*, published in 1795, are an attempt to find that solution in the category of the aesthetic. Instead of standing alone and suppressing the sensible, the intellectual should take it up and transform it. The personality is not something whose unassailability ought to be protected, but rather something which can only be enriched and developed by outward, determinate activity. 'Only as he changes, does he *exist*; only as he remains unchanged does *he* exist'.[47] Human beings must be more than 'mere *world*', more than the conditions of their action. But they must also be more than mere formality. The human being is pulled in two directions, on the one hand by the need to give form to matter, which Schiller called the *Stofftrieb*, on the other by the need to give matter to form, the *Formtrieb*. Schiller took these drives to be unifiable precisely because the first does not demand the extension of change to the person, who remains essentially the same throughout the course of an action, and because the latter is not reducible to the demand that all sensations be the same.

> To guard over this, and to secure to each one of these drives its limits, is the task of culture. . . . Its business is two fold: firstly, to guard sensibility against the encroachments of freedom; secondly: to secure the personality against the power of sensations.[48]

If, then, it is possible to talk of the culture 'of' an individual, this can be expressed in the following form: the more culture a person has: (a) the greater is the *passivity* of the receptive faculty, which ensures a multiplicity of contacts with the world; (b) the greater the *activity* of reason, which ensures the highest degree of independence for the individual. If either of these drives begins to do the work of the others, if the receptive faculty exhibits the intensity appropriate to the formal and does all its work, and if the determining faculty exhibits an extensity appropriate to the receptive, and does all *its* work, then, 'in the first case he will never be *himself*, in the second he will never be *anything else*, and for just this reason in both cases he will be *neither one nor the other* – nothing'. Culture for Schiller is that which prevents the mutual annulment of person and condition. But while it is not bound up solely with concrete human achievement, but rather expresses a harmony or balance between a commitment to the conditions under which human achievement is possible and the integrity of the human being who carries it out, in the end culture is *not* that which expresses a unity between them. It keeps apart those which should be kept apart. It is to *aesthetische Bildung* that the task of uniting, of synthesising them, falls.

This depends upon the existence of a transitional stage from feeling or sensation to reason. While the physical state is that of sensual determination and the logical/moral state is that of rational determination, the aesthetic state is one of 'real and active determinability'. While everything capable of phenomenal manifestation has a particular character related to its specific sphere, realm or function, it can also have an aesthetic character, which 'can refer to the totality of our various powers without being a particular object for any one of them'.[49] This 'middle disposition' (*mittlere Stimmung*) tells us nothing about conviction (*Gesinnung*), and beauty accomplishes no particular purpose: 'Through aesthetic culture the personal worth of the human being remains wholly undetermined'. And yet aesthetic freedom remains the precondition for that in which personal worth might be held to consist. Finally:

> One of the most important tasks of culture is to subordinate man, even in his physical existence, to form, and, as far as the realm of beauty extends, to make him aesthetic, because it is only out of the aesthetic, not out of the physical state, that the moral can develop.[50]

Aesthetic culture is the reconciliation of the intellectual and the sensible, of Idea and experience, of the universality attached to the personal worth of human beings and the particularity of their phenomenal existence. But that personal worth, rooted in conviction (*Gesinnung*), is not reducible to culture. While the whole point about aesthetic culture is its mediating function, that function itself is not that in which human dignity or human freedom consists.

Two years before Schiller's letters, in his *Beitrag zur Berichtigung des Publikums über die Französische Revolution*, Fichte writes:

> enjoyment has no value in itself, it acquires one, at most as a means to the revival and renewal of our capacity for culture . . . Culture means the exercise of all powers for the purpose of complete freedom, of complete independence from everything which is not ourselves, our pure self.[51]

Once again, culture is not the highest purpose of human existence. It is only formulable in terms of a relationship between form and that which is not form, and it is in form alone that the essential dignity and freedom of the human being resides. The pure form of the self is unchangeable, and even that which we call the education of the spirit or the heart pertains to sensibility. Only *'in so far as he is a part of the sensible world'* is the ultimate purpose of the human being "*Kultur zur Freiheit*" '.[52] What Fichte calls the culture of sensibility is a process of cultivation, of *Bildung*. But as the purpose of this process is independence from everything which is not the pure form of the self, from the realm of sensibility in which that process itself occurs, that process is not a passive one in which the human being 'becomes' cultivated. Rather, 'Cultivation occurs through self-activity', and the object of this self-activity is the whole of the external world. Everything which is not form, that is, everything which pertains to determinate existence, must be turned into a servant of the self. The human being is called upon, through culture, to work for the highest purpose of all *moral* beings. And 'to be able to do that, he/she must be able, above all things, to live in the world of appearances'.[53]

But for neither Kant nor Fichte nor Schiller can this living in the world of appearance compromise the integrity of the self, either as that 'personality' which 'elevates man above himself . . . which connects him with an order of things which only the understanding can think and which has under it the entire world of sense',[54] or as that which is rooted in conscience. Marianne Weber wrote that for Weber:

> 'self-determination' of the personality by a *Sollen* remained a basic law for him all his life. . . . Another conviction that remained with Weber all his life was also expressed by Kant and the early Fichte . . . namely, that the purpose of political and social institutions is the development of an autonomous personality'.[55]

This is more an attempt to protect Weber than an accurate account of his ethics. While it is true that Weber never abandoned the idea of a firm anchorage for the self, the 'personality' was never, as it was for both Kant and Fichte, anchored in that which makes human beings identical. For Kant, the radicality of the opposition between self and world is the radicality of an opposition between two modes of human connection, between my belonging to a world of phenomena and to the world of those subject to the moral law. The 'personality' lies at the centre of Kantian ethics because it is the origin of *duty*. To abstract from the conditions of all action is, in this sense, not to find oneself alone.

Weber's thought does not belong to the tradition of *Sollensphilosophie* whose chief representatives are Kant and the early Fichte, for two reasons. Firstly, because the conscience in which personality is anchored is a conscience which has, so to speak, shrunk to its pre-Kantian dimensions.[56] Secondly, Weber, like Hegel, insisted that the idea of personality anchored in a

*Sollen*, or even a conviction or ultimate value, was unintelligible in isolation from the means to the realisation of such an idea which human institutions are. When Odo Marquard described Hegelian philosophy as 'mediation research' he meant that Hegel's critique of Kant consists in a rejection of *Sollensphilosophie*'s refusal to bind a universal purpose for humanity to its mediation. The idea of freedom through self-determination makes no sense apart from the Greek and European city, freedom through mastery of nature no sense apart from the development of modern science and technology, freedom through inwardness no sense apart from the development of Christianity, freedom through equality no sense apart from the development of the modern state.[57]

A description of human institutions as a means does not imply that their ultimate purpose is the integrity of the individual personality. There is no Archimedean point outside culture from which to make a demand on it. Yet Weber he is also far from what Scheler described as Hegelian cultural pantheism, for which nothing with its own independent value can appear,[58] and which would sublimate Kantian morality (*Moralität*) in ethical life (*substantielle Sittlichkeit*) Weber is not interested in an abstract, formal freedom, but is concerned with the problem of how to give ethical imperatives a content without (a) making them non-universalisable; (b) embedding them so firmly in historical practice that they are in thrall to it. Near the beginning of the objectivity essay he remarks that the growth of the 'historical sense' in national economics has led to the second move, the attempt:

> to strip ethical norms of their formal character, to define them substantively through the inclusion of the totality of ultimate values in the realm of the '*Sittlichen*', and thus raise national economics to the dignity of an 'ethical science' on empirical foundations. While the totality of all possible cultural ideals was given the stamp of the 'ethical', the specific dignity of the ethical imperative evaporated, without anything having being gained for the 'objectivity' of the validity of those ideals.[59]

On the other hand, Weber's aim was precisely not to protect that imperative's dignity, but rather to expose its vulnerability.

## SIMMEL: THE UNITY AND DIFFERENTIATION OF THE SOUL

What in the end gives this tension a certain theoretical coherence and makes it rather more than a worthy attempt to avoid two extremes without saying anything distinctive, is Weber's encounter with Simmel, and in particular with Simmel's distinction between subjective and objective culture. A comparison between Simmel and Weber will reveal, however, that Simmel is tied more closely than Weber to the late-eighteenth-century tradition of self-cultivation, and that many of his sociological formulations lean upon it.[60] For that tradition, if culture was radically separate from nature, cultivation entailed the overcoming of this opposition, the promised reconciliation with the laws of its own nature of a being forced to follow laws of its own creation, of the actions of that being in the social and political world with its pre-social constitution. The reinterpretation of those actions which involve the employment of impersonal means as actions which flow unproblematically from the source of the self which employs them, is the task of a being capable of perfection, of completion, of the fulfilment of a natural potential contained within it from the start.

In his first attempts at an explicit formulation of culture, Simmel immediately ties it to a concern with inwardness and personal development. Simmel does not treat nature as a set of drives whose denial or suppression is the meaning of culture, nor is it reality understood as a causal mechanism. Rather, it is:

> a period of development of a subject – namely, that in which those drives peculiar to him unfold, and which ends as soon as an intelligent will employing *means* takes over these drives and leads the subject to a state it could not have achieved if left to them alone.[61]

This break between nature and culture is not an opposition, since 'cultivation of an object leads to the completeness which determines it in accordance with the actual tendencies rooted in its being'.[62] And the only being which can develop in this way is the human being. The human being is the only object of culture, is *the* cultural being, because and in so far as it contains within it a demand for perfection: 'That he ought to and can develop completely is indissolubly bound up with the being of the human soul.'[63]

How does such a process of perfection or completion take place? The key to personal development for Simmel is that it makes no sense without the individual's including within himself something taken from outside himself: 'certainly cultivation is a state of the soul, only one which is achieved via the exploitation of purposively formed objects'.[64] We might achieve a relationship to transcendental forces which is rooted deep in the soul, but as long as it entails no engagement with the world, it is still not culture. Yet it is in the course of precisely the purposive formation of objects that the individual creates for himself not only a world via which he becomes cultivated, but a barrier to that which human purposiveness was supposed to achieve. In the very act of engaging with the world in order to reappropriate it I create it anew – that which takes forms beyond their natural development to their teleological one is *capable* of functioning as a form which can be reappropriated, but it is as likely to develop its own logic, its own completeness. Neither the perfection of the self in isolation from the world nor the perfection of a part of the world amounts to culture.

> Where the developmental process of the subjective soul does not include an objective form, where it does not return to itself via such forms, as a means and stage of its completion, it might realise values of the highest rank *within and without itself*, but this is not the way to culture in its specific sense.[65]

The most important consequence of the need to act in the world is that the world which is a product of this need's recognition becomes a world with its own independent logics or laws, laws which can be followed *without* their being so followed contributing in any way to the development of the personality. For Simmel, the fact that the eighteenth-century pedagogic ideal of the formation of personal, internal value was replaced by a nineteenth-century concept of education as a body of objective knowledge, is a reflection of the preponderance of 'objective' over 'subjective' culture. At the turn of the twentieth century, it seems that the enrichment of the mind's forms and contents, its development, can be achieved only at the cost of an increased distance from objective culture. The presupposition of the insistence that the self only takes on an identity through recognising its finitude in determinate conduct still assumed the graspability of the world in which it was to occur. The presupposition of Simmel's account of culture is the radicality of a new distance between self and world. A modern 'psychologism' which would seek the development of subjective culture in a manner wholly divorced from objective culture makes perfect sense in an age of objective culture's preponderance. Yet Simmel argues that even in the face of this growing distance, the soul can only be said to assume a reality through determinate conduct.

For Simmel there is a distinction, not only between the claim of the self to perfection and determinate activity, but between the *significances* which that activity can take on. In so far as an objective product of human activity is reappropriated by the individual, amounts to a stage via which the self returns to itself, it has a cultural significance. In so far as it resists such reappropriation, it has an objective significance. Thus: 'The insignificance or irrationality of the individual's share [subjective culture] leaves the *substance* and *dignity* of mankind's ownership [objective culture] unaffected.'[66] Only Hegel's category of 'objective spirit' made it possible for Simmel to thematise this distinction, a fact he himself acknowledged.

> By establishing this category of objective spirit as the historical representation of the valid intellectual content of things in general, it becomes clear how the cultural process that we recognise as a subjective development – the culture of things as a human culture – can be separated from its content. This content, by entering that category, acquires, as it were, another physical condition and thus provides the principal basis for the phenomenon of the separate development of objective and personal culture. The objectification of spirit provides the form that makes the conservation and accumulation of mental labour possible; it is the most significant and most far-reaching of the historical categories of mankind.[67]

Simmel suggests that our tendency to treat the 'great series' which constitute our cultural life as 'cultural values' obscures this difference. For the activity defined by any one of those series may have a purely objective significance, may completely lack a cultural significance. An appreciation of this difference will be central to an understanding of Weber's account of the '*Eigengesetzlichkeit*' of cultural 'value spheres', and of the fact that this has a wholly different meaning for him than it does for Simmel.

For Simmel as for Schiller, the early Goethe and Humboldt, the self-development of the personality is at the same time allsided development, culture implies a balance and harmony of the soul. This seems to imply an outdated Renaissance–humanist ideal. But it is because of the distinction between cultural and objective significance that the charge would be misplaced. The Rennaissance Man is not what he is simply by virtue of his allsidedness, but by virtue of an isomorphism between the cultural and the objective significance of his activity. He not only develops himself in different directions, but in each one of those directions he achieves something of lasting, human, objective, significance, a significance independent of the other dimensions of his being. He is not a specialist, not because he is a dilettante, but rather because he achieves a multifarious immortality. Simmel expresses his distance from this tradition when he writes that a social form may be objectively insignificant, yet fulfil precisely that function which the soul's need for harmony demands of it. This was Humboldt's view, too. Onesidedness is overcome when the individual strives to unite not the *objects on which* she works, but the powers *with which* she works.[68] Conversely, today, the most impressive works and thoughts 'are too much lord within their own province to bow to the category of service under which they would have to place themselves as cultural factors, as means for the formation of the unity of the soul'.[69] While the whole point about culture is that it gives us an account both of human inwardness, and of the allsided harmony of the soul, the depth implied by the first is achieved at the cost of the objective superficiality of this or that concrete achievement. Culture for Simmel is a zero-sum game.

Although Simmel had formulated the difference between objective and subjective culture, between the world of concrete human achievement and the portion of that world reappropriated by a subject, as early as *The Philosophy of Money* (1978 (1900)), and insisted that personal development depended upon a path from the self via a reality interpreted in terms of cultural values, and back to that self, he did not make full use of either of two possible accounts of the dynamic character of that process – Hegelian dialectics and vitalism. But by 1912 the book on Schopenhauer and Nietzsche had appeared and he had read Bergson's *Creative Evolution*. This led to a reformulation of culture in terms of life philosophy. In his classic 'On The Concept and Tragedy of Culture' Simmel writes that 'all movements of the soul, such as willing, doing one's duty, being called, hoping, are the spiritual continuation of the fundamental determination of life'.[70] The source of all values is the human soul, and all meaning, value and significance are not only created by subjective dynamic life, but it is in this alone that they can be said to *have* a life. On the other hand, even the idea of personality only makes sense in relation to the impersonal. The subject's relationship to cultural values is expressed thus: the subject 'must include *these* in itself, but must include them in *itself*'.[71] The becoming objective of the subjective and the becoming subjective of the objective is the 'metaphysical form' of the cultural process. The meaning of culture is this synthesis.

But the objective form of culture as such is the impossibility of this synthesis. Sombart had already formulated this as the tragedy of culture:

> The innermost essence of the problem of culture is tragedy: it is the cleft between our drive towards the most highly personal, free shaping of our life and that which compels us from without as necessity, and often enough, as hated necessity.[72]

But in so far as the tragedy of culture is its necessity, is the very need to overcome the distinction between the life of the individual and objective spiritual products, it is already contained implicitly in the *Philosophy of Money*.

It is also contained in his use of the category of objective spirit. What he wants to grasp is not a relationship between subjective and objective spirit in terms of spirit's return to itself in the absolute, *à la* Hegel, but the relationship between objective spirit and the human soul. The path of the soul from unifferentiated unity to differentiated plurality – the soul's engagement with spheres of culture – and back to a differential unity, in which the unity of the soul consists in its being 'this and that, rather than this or that, trait',[73] is quite different from the path along which spirit returns to itself, a journey in which, so to speak, nothing gets lost on the way. Moreover, the differential plurality of which Simmel speaks is not the soul's division into its universal and particular moments, but rather its connection with various spheres of culture. This expresses the multidimensionality of a development which can take place at varying speeds and in varying directions. The 'path' which takes the soul from itself to obective spirit and back is in (theoretical) reality a series of paths beginning always at the same point, and presupposing what Simmel called the soul's 'enigmatic unity'. The enigma consists in the fact that while personal development depends upon the multifarious cultural significance of objective spiritual products and contains within it the possibility of an imbalance or disharmony between the soul's dimensions, its 'parcelling out', it is always possible to assert, in the face of, rather than as a result of an engagement with, objective spirit, the *integrity of the soul's predifferential unity*. Thus, while synthesis corresponds to the soul's demand for unity, it is not the only form of unity there is.

> Only an age as analytic as the modern could see in synthesis the deepest, the one and all of the relationship of form of spirit to the world – while there remains an original, predifferential unity; in so far as it allows these analytical elements to emerge from it like the organic seed branches out into the multiplicity of its particular members, it lies beyond analysis and synthesis.[74]

An individual encouraged to believe that the source of the self lies *inside* him/herself, but whose identity depends upon determinate conduct in a society whose division of labour threatens to pull him/her now this way, now that, experiences the conflict between internal unity and external division as a conflict which continues within herself. Simmel employed this Nietzschean motif, which he formulated as a capacity of the human mind as fundamental as our ability to grant complete externality to its products, on numerous occasions, including his account of the tragedy of culture: 'In general we call a relationship tragic – in contrast to merely sad or extrinsically destructive – when the destructive forces directed against some being spring forth from the deepest levels of this very being.'[75]

The tragedy of this relationship consists in the fact that the real conflict between the demands of the personality and the demands of society is a conflict between two entities defined by the same principle – that of an organic totality.[76] The unity of the soul depends upon the co-ordination of those parts of the soul into which the soul must divide itself in order to have a life. The unity of society depends upon a co-ordination of those functions of which it consists and which individuals must fulfil in order to have a place in it. While the differentiation of the soul is the differentiation between practices in terms of cultural significance, the differentiation of society is a differentiation between practices in terms of objective significance. The division of labour threatens the unity of the soul in two ways, by forcing activity into one sphere, and by reducing cultural to objective significance within that sphere.

## WEBER AND ONESIDEDNESS

Simmel's account of culture is significant for an understanding of Weber's because its problem is that of the relationship between the claims of the self and the fact that those claims are only redeemable through determinate conduct. Like Weber's, it does not appeal to a distinction between culture and civilisation, a distinction which, within the German tradition of self-cultivation, often resolved itself into the mere preference of some modes of determinate conduct over others. If it was true, as Wilhelm Meister complained, that as a bourgeois one was what one was by virtue of what one did rather than what one 'was', the importance of inwardness could be saved by the argument that the claims of the personality are more likely to be redeemed through this rather than that activity, a concession to *Brauchbarkeit* which didn't wholly sacrifice *Bildung*. Analytically, Simmel seemed to avoid this restrictive theory of culture, and make available the idea that there is no sphere of human endeavour in which the problem of culture is more urgent than in others. But he could only do so by an appeal to allsidedness, to the idea of a harmony of the soul ensured by the existence of a pre-cultural *core*, a fixed confluence for those forces which make up the personality. Here, the difference between cultural and objective significance is itself significant only to the extent that an activity with cultural significance contributes to that harmony. Weber rejected the idea that there is a conflict between personality and onesidedness, between 'be yourself' and 'specialise'. The question is not how to overcome onesidedness, but how to accept it. Here, everything hangs on the question of whether one's unavoidably limited activity has a cultural or an objective significance.

Theoretically it is through the concept of value that Weber expresses this. The personality is not a pre-cultural, pre-evaluative core, but a self which has found an anchorage for itself in a value, a value which not only mediates between self and world, but defines the meaning of that self's activity. More than this, it is through this relationship to value that individuals are able to *take a position* towards the world. The significance of the fact that onesided activity can be a calling, not just a profession, is that the values which define it can define the meaning of human conduct as such. The self which for Simmel is defined by a potential harmony is for Weber locked into a context of conflict from the start, a conflict between rival perspectives from which the whole of reality might be justified.

When Weber says that we are cultural beings, culture is not a culture of sensibility understood in relation to a self which stands above it. Its ultimate purpose is not a freedom which exists beyond it, in a realm in which all are subject to the same (natural or moral) law or one in which the self exists for itself alone. Culture for Weber will not be a process of cultivation which follows from the demand that an already-existing personality take on a concrete content, act in the world. Goethe's 'demands of the day', which Weber was fond of invoking, are not demands made upon a self conceived of prior to their being confronted. Rather, to have to *be* a personality, to have to take oneself to be a self independent of the world but needing to act in the world in order to take on an identity, is itself to meet one of those day's demands. Weber's concept of culture should be interesting to us less because it tells us about his world view than because it suggests to us how we ought to think about what becomes of modern human beings thrown into a world in which one might have to ask *oneself* what one's world view is, human beings set free from feudal ties, standing on their own two feet yet not knowing in what direction and how far they might carry them.

It is this individual, who has no choice but to make choices, who is the object of a cultural science. It is no accident that he saw in neo-Kantian value philosophy, and not the life philosophy of Dilthey or Nietzsche or the later Simmel, the means by which he could express this epistemologically. And as he rejected the idea of the harmony of the soul in favour of the calling and the incommensurability of value spheres, so he rejected the reduction of the relationship between those spheres to a harmony between elements of an epoch. To do justice to the fate of the modern human being it seemed necessary to reject the idea of the modern age. The next chapter tries to show how he arrived at this conclusion.

# Chapter 3

# The illusion of the epoch

You would indeed have to discover that single word which would contain everything that it is to express; else one simply reads – a *word*.

(Johann Gottfried Herder)

## INTRODUCTION

We saw in Chapter 1 that the need to establish a point of discontinuity between the pre-modern and modern epochs was the product of an increased sensitivity to historical transformations. It seemed that this could be met most successfully by the conscious adoption of a pre-modern perspective, be it the classicism of Strauss or the theological argument for which modern worldliness now reveals the sinfulness of the world more forcefully than theology ever could.[1] On the other hand, a theory of modernity which claimed that one cannot step outside the modern, but at the same time identified modernity with a 'crisis of legitimacy',[2] 'fragmentation',[3] or the belief that 'everything is permitted',[4] appeared to presuppose a continuity between the pre-modern and modern in the very act of announcing that they were distinct. The certainty with which fragmentation is announced is often as great as that which is alleged to have characterised the unity which has now been lost, forgotten or split apart. A theory of the crisis of legitimacy which is held to be a consequence of, say, the collapse of a Christian world view, attempts to answer questions the 'crisis' ought to have rendered unintelligible. The suggestion that in the modern age legitimation through divine revelation or nature has been 'replaced' by 'mere convention'[5] claims for itself an authority which is more than conventional.

## A SCIENCE OF HISTORY

### The coherence of the concept of an epoch

A theory of modernity-as-crisis seems to find support in Weber's account of modernity, in particular in the view that the claim that reality can only be justified as a religious phenomenon has been replaced by a proliferation of mutually irreducible claims of a similar type. But this account of 'modern polytheism' is a provisional and tentative conclusion to a series of historical investigations each of which adopt a specific problematic. Weber himself was always wary of the equation of this with one of the modern epoch as a whole. His most extended reference to the human need to consider the world a 'meaningful totality' is in the section on religious intellectualism in *Wirtschaft und Gesellschaft* and in the introduction to the 'Economic Ethic of the World Religions'.[6]

There are numerous passages in which Weber accepts, quite conventionally, a distinction between Antiquity, the Middle Ages and Modernity, and offers remarks on the defining character of 'the modern'. Although in many of these remarks the modern is defined in terms of specific substantive criteria – 'exchange' or 'specialisation' or 'the quest for experience' or 'constitutionalism' – the generalising diagnostic tone is unmistakable. But there are several in the *Wissenschaftslehre* in which the concept of an epoch is associated with two unscientific procedures, the intuitive grasp of a whole or the gratuitous collection of examples. Here, Weber's concern is: can history be considered a science? What is the logical basis for the distinction between generalising and individualising modes of concept formation, and can the latter be considered scientific? The logical consequence of his answer is that the concept of 'modernity' has an instrumental rather than a teleological status, that it is a heuristic device for rather than the goal of historical inquiry, and that therefore any reconstruction of his 'theory of modernity' on the basis of his substantive remarks is premature unless their status of those remarks has been established.

A discussion of this problem will show: (a) that Weber's hesitancy over the methodological utility of the concept of an epoch derives from a theory of subjectivity which was part of the response to the logical question; (b) that the neo-Kantian value philosophy to which Weber appeals for the solution of problems of concept formation both contributes to and is dependent upon a conception of 'personality' which extends well beyond the horizon of those problems; and (c) that the problem of a Weberian theory of modernity is complicated by the presence within Weber's writings of a metatheoretical problem: what follows from the fact that the science of which that theory is a part cannot be self-grounding? If science is implicated in the polytheism it claims to be able to announce, where does it go to announce it? To philosophy? Or ideology?[7]

## Schopenhauer, Nietzsche and the problem of historical selectivity

Conventional accounts of Weber's theory of concept formation begin by treating it as a response to problems raised by the *Methodenstreit* in economics.[8] That these did play a major role in the *Wissenschaftslehre* is undeniable – the first page of the essay 'Knies and the Problem of Irrationality' refers explicitly to Gustav Schmoller and Carl Menger, the debate between whom sparked off the *Methodenstreit*.[9] And the essays on Roscher and Knies taken together are subtitled *'die logischen Probleme der historischen Nationalokonomie'*. But although Weber attempted to establish a clear distinction between his science of culture and a science of nature on the basis of the logic of concept formation, another way of reading his 'methodological writings' is to see his appropriation of neo-Kantian value philosophy as a response to the implications of remarks on the scientific character of history found in the *Lebensphilosophie* of Schopenhauer, Nietzsche and Dilthey. It was just as important for him to distinguish between culture and life, not least because *Lebensphilosophie* itself contained an account of the logic of historical inquiry.

Schopenhauer writes that history:

> lacks the fundamental character of science, the subordination of what is known; instead of this it boasts of mere coordination of what is known. Therefore there is no system of history, as there is of every other branch of knowledge; accordingly it is rational knowledge indeed, but not a science. For nowhere does it know the particular by means of the universal, but it must comprehend the particular directly, and continue to creep

along the ground of experience. . . . As the sciences are systems of concepts, they always speak of species; history always speaks of individuals. History would accordingly be a science of individual things, which implies a contradiction.[10]

The nearest history comes to the subsumption of a particular under a universal is the relation of a particular event to its historical 'context'. But context is merely another particular. The relationship between event and structure cannot be compared with that between case and law. The elaboration of any structural context, however complete, is a forlorn attempt 'to make up for depth by length and breadth'. This process of making up, this 'work of fiction', is an endless narration of forms which will never attain to the (philosophical) truth that 'the really essential content is everywhere the same'.[11] 'Just because [history] is so transitory, the human mind should select for its consideration that which is destined never to pass away'.[12] It should reject the optimism and eudaemonism of 'glorifiers of history' such as Hegel, and instead adopt the motto: 'The same, but otherwise.'

The glorification of history which forms the object of Nietzsche's second untimely meditation of 1874 is founded on *'the demand that history should be a science'*,[13] on what he refers to as the 'historical sense'. Although Nietzsche interprets 'science' in the opposite manner from Schopenhauer – science being understood in empiricist terms – his account, too, is directed against historical inquiry which creeps along the ground of experience. The rise in the nineteenth century of history as a yardstick of individual cultivation is treated by Nietzsche as the emergence of a promise which is not only incapable of fulfilment but generates the opposite of its intended goal. History – as means – is treated by those with the historical sense in such a way that the end it is to serve is obscured. The historical science Nietzsche depicts lacks criteria of historical *selectivity*. Knowledge of the past is a boundariless, unlimited striving, an infinite quest in which 'memory opens all its gates',[14] in which 'we moderns have nothing whatever of our own; only by replenishing and cramming ourselves with the ages, customs, arts, philosophies, religions, discoveries of others do we become anything worthy of notice, that is to say, walking encyclopaedias'.[15] The ultimate effect of this is a form of indigestion in which the individual, far from being cultivated through history, is weakened by it.

The truly cultivated individual understands that 'culture is the child of each individual's self-knowledge and dissatisfaction with himself'.[16] The individual who is 'consecrated to culture'[17] is capable of experiencing this dissatisfaction without lapsing into the apathy prompted by an overdose of history. Instead, the experience is accompanied by a striving for 'a higher self as yet concealed'.[18] The development of the individual is dependent upon the transformation of the outside world through historical knowledge, which is impossible as long as the historical sense prevails. For history as science sees history as an infinite, flat terrain across which the individual is encouraged to travel so quickly that his/her 'sense of strangeness' is quickly muted. The result can only be a form of cognitive agarophobia, which causes the individual to retreat into interiority, into 'the smallest egoistic enclosure'.[19] An objectivist account of objectivity goes hand in hand with a subjectivist account of subjectivity, fear of not being oneself leads to the need to be nothing but oneself. Culture for Nietzsche depends upon the transformation of the outer world by an individual who acts upon it, whose dissatisfaction does not degenerate into *ressentiment*. The 'culture' championed by the historical sense is 'a false and unfruitful conception of culture' whose goal is not the free, cultivated man – there are none to be seen, 'only muffled up, identical people'[20] – but the *scholar* and *scientist*.[21] It is not culture – which is an active engagement with an independent but manipulable world – but *knowledge* of culture – which is contemplative.

Nietzsche is opposing two modes of cognitive democracy and their levelling effects. The first is Cartesian. Descartes' conception of method is intended both to be available to each individual and to guarantee a binding morality. The knowing subject and the moral subject are one. The second is Baconian. Here,

> it was sufficient if the combination of everyone's theoretical accomplishments guaranteed a state of domination over . . . reality, a state of which the individual could be a beneficiary even without having insight into the totality of its conditions. The subject of theory and the subject of the successful life no longer need to be identical.[22]

The encyclopedia radicalises this split to the fundamental and unendurable discrepancy between an accumulated and ordered corpus of knowledge and the fraction of it susceptible to individual appropriation. The historical sense is the attempt to overcome the discrepancy by appropriating as much of this corpus as possible. If successful, it produces a scholarly or scientific standard of cultivation. If it fails, it leads to a retreat into 'subjectivity'. But in both cases, the result is *knowledge* of culture. Nietzsche argues that the discrepancy is endurable only if it is not perceived as a discrepancy. And the condition of its not being so perceived is 'active forgetting', what he later called 'measure'.[23] Nietzsche demands a standard of selectivity for historical knowledge, a bounded horizon, and finds it in 'life'.[24]

'Life', so often treated as a principle of becoming, which knows no boundaries, which constantly transgresses limits, which overflows the forms in which it is only apparently contained, as the unconditional which is denied but never destroyed by the conditional, is for Nietzsche a principle of cognitive finitude, a standard of discipline for historical inquiry. The claim that 'the essence of life' is '*its will to power*'[25] becomes a 'major point of historical method',[26] and provides for a form of practical asceticism. This practical asceticism contrasts with the ascetic *ideals* which form the object of Essay III of the *Genealogy of Morals*. Here, the ascetic ideal of modern science is linked to a faith in truth which, as a functional equivalent of the Christian belief in God, undermines science's secular credentials. This faith, argues Nietzsche, has to be 'experimentally called into question'.[27] But what Nietzsche does not call into question is the historian's ascetic need for a point of view without which he/she would be forced to surrender to or retreat from the infinity of possible objects of inquiry.

While Weber's stress on the onesidedness of historical inquiry is unthinkable without Nietzsche's second untimely meditation, his objection to it derives from the fact that although the concept of 'life', or, more accurately, the Idea of 'life', might avoid empiricist history, its capacity to generate empirical research was limited. Nietzsche overcame empiricism by means of a speculative rather than a critical philosophy of history. He sought the criteria of significance which empiricism lacked in an actually existing principle which lay behind the historical facts empiricists were to accumulate, rather than in the conceptual apparatus of the historian. The perspective of 'life' Nietzsche recommends the historian to adopt is, as it were, already there waiting to be adopted. Whatever Nietzsche's claim about the link between a correct understanding of historical inquiry and historical action, historical inquiry *as* action is threatened by theoretical vitalism. While Weber was rather agnostic on the question of whether a speculative philosophy of history was more likely than empiricist fact-accumulation to impair historical action – 'The most radical political innovators have been profoundly influenced by the Calvinist theory of predestination, the theory that man is a machine, and the Marxist belief in future catastrophe[!]'[28] – this was not true for science.

> There are ... 'subject matter specialists' and 'interpretive specialists'. The fact-greedy gullet of the former can be filled only with legal documents, statistical worksheets and question-naires, but he is insensitive to the refinement of a new idea. The gourmandaise of the latter dulls his taste for facts by ever new intellectual subtilities.[29]

## DILTHEY AND THE *GEISTESWISSENSCHAFTEN*

Dilthey appropriated Nietzschean life philosophy in order to formulate the substantive grounds of the *Geisteswissenschaften*. But whereas Nietzsche opposes 'life' to 'history-as-science' but leaves aside the question of the foundations of natural science, Dilthey distinguishes the *Geisteswissenschaften* from the natural sciences in order to argue that they be accorded the same cognitive status. While Nietzsche is opposing an empiricism which has intruded into and misunderstood the purpose of historical inquiry, Dilthey contrasts the proper approach to historical inquiry as a whole with a natural science he takes to be unobjectionable.

Dilthey's account of the *Geisteswissenschaften* provides a link between Nietzschean life philosophy and Weber's neo-Kantian contribution to the *Methodenstreit*. The concepts of 'life', 'lived experience', 'direct experience', are Nietzschean to the extent that they are substantive foundations for 'history', but neo-Kantian to the extent that they are logically provided for. For like the neo-Kantians Dilthey was not merely distinguishing natural and non-natural science in terms of their objects, and arguing that in the latter 'method and object are identical'[30] but distinguishing between two consciously adopted perspectives employing different categories.

In 'The construction of the historical world' Dilthey remarks that the *Geisteswissenschaften* 'work with abstractions, not with entities ... these abstractions are only valid within the limits imposed by the *point of view* from which they arose'.[31] 'Humanity seen through the senses is just a physical fact which can only be explained scientifically. It only *becomes the subject-matter* of the human studies when we experience human states, give expression to them, and understand these expressions.' On this basis Dilthey constructs a series of dichotomies between:

1  a system of laws and a system of value-laden or meaningful existence;
2  the unconditional validity of those laws and a validity of values which is neither unconditional nor entirely personal;
3  the indirect human experience of the natural world and the direct human experience of the world of social and cultural relations;
4  *Naturwissenschaften* and *Geisteswissenschaften*.

Dilthey refers to the expressions of human states whose understanding is the historian's task as 'objective spirit'. But the link betwen 'objective spirit' and the *Geisteswissenschaften* should not be allowed to obscure the hierarchical relationship between experience, expression and understanding. The expressions which belong to what Dilthey calls objective spirit, or objective spiritual products, and which form the object domain of a science whose task is to understand them, are not objectified spirit. What Dilthey calls 'spirit' does not pertain to the realm of experience. On the contrary, the direct experience of which the cultural artefacts which make up objective spirit are the expression, is designated by the term 'life'. There is an hierarchical relationship between a science of spirit and spirit, and between spirit and life. Expression is a condition of possibility of understanding, experience a condition of possibility of expression. When Dilthey describes understanding as a 'recreative experience' he does not argue that 'one has to be Caesar in order to understand Caesar', that the actually existing relationship between the historian and his/her object is 'empathic', but rather that the categories of historical understanding are derivative of or parasitic upon that of 'direct experience'.

Dilthey's use of the term 'objective spirit' to describe the object domain of the *Geisteswissenchaften* has few affinities with the Hegelianism from which it is borrowed. In Dilthey's work, the term only makes sense as the objectification and alienation of 'life'. The rigidity of objective spirit is to be overcome not by referring forward to the absolute, but back to 'life', not in the continuous process of thought, but in an eternal origin – direct experience. The responsibility of finite conceptual thought is towards the inexhaustibility of the 'life' from which it arises, not towards the infinity into which the concept is to develop. Art, religion and philosophy, which for Hegel belonged to absolute spirit and were self-validating, are part of 'objective spirit'.[32] It is only through this restriction, which implies their conditionality, that art, religion and philosophy could become the object of a *Geisteswissenschaft*.

And yet, although Dilthey draws on life philosophy in order to solve a particular problem – the conditions of possibility of historical science, there is a sense in which the oppositions outlined above are false. From the truly vitalistic perspective of 'life', the distinctions between inner and outer experience, between lived and sensory experience, between modes of relatedness to the social-cultural world and to the natural world, are post-experiential constructions which arise in reflection. If 'life' is prior to, or the grounds of, 'spirit', it is also prior to 'nature'. And if it is prior to both it is prior to the distinction between them. In any consistent life philosophy, 'Life' will designate, monistically, a primordial experience which is only subsequently 'split apart' into lived and sensory experience, into the conditions of possibility of specific sciences. The neo-Kantianism of Windelband and Rickert was not free of this move either, of the extrapolation from the grounds of one mode of inquiry to the grounds of all others.

## *GEISTESWISSENSCHAFT* AND *KULTURWISSENSCHAFT*

### Dilthey versus neo-Kantianism

Seen in the light of Nietzsche's solution to the problem of historical selectivity, the difference between the *Geisteswissenschaften* and Rickert and Weber's *Kulturwissenschaften* is less obvious than might be assumed. Firstly, Dilthey accepts that there is no such thing as a science without presuppositions. The *Natur*- and *Geisteswissenschaften* are underwritten by points of view.[33] The categories with which Dilthey would construct a science of the concrete are not immanent to the object. Secondly, it is false to attribute to Dilthey a form of mentalism, or the argument that 'inner states' are the object of the human sciences. The primary object of both natural and human sciences is not the physical and the psychical 'worlds', but different modes of relatedness to a world, one of which is mediate, one of which is direct.[34] Thirdly, although they argue that they are concerned solely with the logic of general- ising and individualising concept formation, in contrast to Dilthey's ontological perspective, neither Rickert nor Weber can avoid an appeal to substantive criteria in order to ground their concepts of 'culture', and hence their understanding of historical inquiry.

The real bases of neo-Kantianism's opposition to life philosophy are: (i) Dilthey's opposition between causality and meaningfulness is false, and undermines any attempt to attribute causal efficacy to meaningful phenomena;[35] (ii) so is his oppo- sition between the unconditional validity of laws and the con- ditional validity of values. Values are as unconditional as laws; (iii) Dilthey conflates the difference between two perspectives or intellectual procedures with the difference between two disciplines;[36] (iv) by tying meaning to the categories of 'direct experience' and 'life', Dilthey turns it into a vitalistic category. For the purposes of science, there can be no such thing as 'direct experience'. The difference between modes of relation to the natural and the socio-cultural worlds is one between modes of mediate experience. Hence, the addition of meaning has to be understood as a rationalisation process. The concept of 'value' is supposed to ensure this.

Theoretical vitalism generates what Nehamas has called trans- cendent perspectivism, but not the immanent perspectivism demanded by an empirical science.[37] Transcendent perspectivism is the formulation of *the* perspective of the human sciences – for instance, 'life' – immanent perspectivism the formulation of that perspective in such a way that it is at the same time the formu- lation of the internal differentiation of those sciences themselves. Rickert and Weber object to life philosophy because it is limited to the provision of a single, unifying principle for the human sciences. As a result, it generates a homogeneous concept of culture in which cultural forms are only explicable in relation to the same, vitalistic content. The neo-Kantian theory of 'value spheres' aims to disrupt this homogeneity. In order to do so it has to establish the primacy of 'value' over 'life', and *Kultur* over *Geist*.

## Culture and value

In the 'Objectivity' essay Weber writes:

> The concept of culture is a *value-concept*. Empirical reality is 'culture' for us because and in so far as we relate it to value ideas. It includes those, and *only* those segments of reality which become *significant* for us through this relation. Only a small portion of the individual reality observed at any one time is coloured by our value conditioned interest and it alone has significance for us. It has this significance because it reveals relationships which are important for us due to their connection with value ideas. Only because and to the extent that this is the case is it worth knowing in its individual peculiarity. We cannot discover, however, *what* is significant for us by means of a 'presuppositionless' investigation of the empirically given. Rather, the establishment of what is significant is the presupposition of something's becoming an *object* of investigation.[38]

It could be argued that this passage contains everything which is fundamental to Weber's philosophy of social science – the distinction between concept and reality, the selectivity of empirical science, the grounding of that selectivity in values, the transcendental status of values, the apparent rejection of all forms of realism. Yet it prompts a number of questions. What is meant by values and what is their analytic status? What is meant by 'for us'? Does the fact that no investigation is free of presuppositions make it the product or vehicle for the expression of, a set of ethical or political commitments? Even if the significance of that small portion of reality is a presupposition of something's becoming an object, does not the establishment of significance imply culture's preconstitution? Is Weber attempting to ground the cultural sciences formally or substantively?

An answer to these questions requires an account of neo-Kantianism's critique of vitalistic accounts of the substantive foundations of the 'human sciences'. Perhaps the key feature of the 'Back to Kant' movement in the middle of the nineteenth century, embodied in Lotze's *Microcosmus*,[39] is the abandonment of the good as the highest systematising power which, so to speak, holds the world together.[40] The good loses its metaphysical status and becomes a term confined to what becomes known as the 'realm' or 'province' of the ethical. Whereas for Kant morality stood at the peak of a conceptual hierarchy, for South–West German neo-Kantianism science, morality and art are each 'governed' by and grounded in an equally valid claim to universality. This claim was embodied in *values*. These values were said to have 'validity' but no existence. The practices we call 'science', 'art' or 'morality' are each grounded in values which are transcendental to them but without whose acknowledgment they would not be possible. 'Pure and true being is, either in virtue of appreciation of value or the postulates of conceptual thought, what *ought to be*, yet is no part of empirical reality'.[41]

In his *Introduction to Philosophy* Windelband begins by drawing a clear distinction between 'theoretical' problems – questions of knowledge – and 'axiological' problems – questions of value. But if this distinction is held to with any strictness, the import of 'value philosophy' is undermined. And in fact, the distinction collapses when Windelband discusses ethical and aesthetic problems. For he argues that, if consciousness is to rise above the level of merely individual values or individual moral systems, it must postulate a 'normal consciousness' which is to do for axiological problems what the concept of 'consciousness in general' did for theoretical problems. He formulates this as follows: 'the value-in-itself points to the same normal consciousness which haunts the theory of knowledge as the correlate of the thing-in-itself'.[42] And he concludes that 'noetic problems themselves have something of the nature of the axiological in them and therefore represent a transition from the theoretical to the practical'.[43] Rickert makes the same point more clearly. 'Scientific knowledge may not only be dependent on a conceiving subject. On the contrary, it must further be determined that it depends on a valuing subject, in which we would have to see an even "more subjective" subjectivism.'[44]

Truth is a value, too, so that as well as a horizontal distinction between is and ought, description and prescription, the realms of the theoretical and of the axiological, questions of truth and questions of goodness, there is a vertical distinction between is and ought, or existence and validity, within every province of culture. In addition, the tripartite distinction between science, art and morality is expanded to include political, economic and legal cultural practices. For neo-Kantianism, culture is a mosaic of domains of normativity.

Central to neo-Kantianism's theory of knowledge is the distinction between the origin of a proposition and its validity.

The validity of a judgement, in which matter is subsumed under form in order to constitute an object, is independent of processes of consciousness. The neo-Kantians all interpreted Kant logically rather than psychologically. The origin of knowledge was a matter of fact which proceeded according to psychological laws, and turned on the distinction between empiricism and rationalism, the validity of knowledge was a matter of value which proceeded according to logical norms, and turned on the distinction between aposteriorism and apriorism.[45] 'The unity of the object depends on the subject–predicate unity of a judgement which necessarily acknowledges a value.'[46]

The irreducibility of value spheres, the transcendental status of values and the distinction between origin and validity play a crucial role in Weber's critique of vitalism. The clearest statements of the value philosophy by means of which Weber distanced himself from Dilthey and attempted to ground empirical historical inquiry are contained in the following two passages. The first comes from Rickert:

> Dilthey confuses the nonreal, meaningful content of culture that is situated in the realities of history with the real psychic existence that actually occurs in the mental life of single individuals. Thus it remains concealed that it is not the real spirit, but, rather, the nonreal meaning that forms the genuinely decisive factor in *substantively* distiguishing history from every natural science.[47]

The second comes from Simmel's *Philosophy of Money*.

> the two series constituted by reality and value are quite independent of one another . . . value is never a 'quality' of the objects, but a judgement upon them which remains inherent in the subject. And yet, neither the deeper meaning of life of the individual, nor the practical social events and arrangements based upon it, can be sufficiently understood by referring to the 'subject'. The way to a comprehension of value lies in a region in which that subjectivity is only provisional and actually not very essential.[48]

Both Rickert and Simmel construct a tripartite distinction between value, reality and the subject which is fundamental to Weber's account of both historical inquiry and, as Chapter 6 argues, political action.

Rickert accepts that there is a link between 'mental life' and historical inquiry, but rejects Dilthey's claim that the relationship between experience, expression and understanding is direct. On the contrary, 'real' mental life in itself contains nothing which would imply that it ought not to become the object of a natural science whose task is to establish laws. The fact that a being is a mental being rather than a physical being cannot tell us why it ought to be the object of an 'empathic' understanding. The move which Dilthey fails to make is to argue that mental beings are also – but not necessarily – *valuing* beings, and that it is their status as valuing beings which warrants a distinctive mode of inquiry into the phenomena their evaluative activity brings about.[49] For Rickert, and Weber, too, the meaning of a phenomenon – that which for Dilthey distinguishes natural from non-natural science – is dependent upon its relatedness to a value. It is not 'inherent' in a real process. As long as 'value' does not play this mediating role between mental life and historical inquiry, there is no discernible reason why that inquiry should not be a generalising and, in neo-Kantian terms, natural science.

Dilthey, Rickert and Weber accept that the historian's object domain is the 'realities of history', that historical science is a *Wirklichkeitswissenschaft*. The difference between them is that while Dilthey interprets real history as the expression of 'real psychic existence which actually occurs in the mental life of single individuals', and calls it 'objective spirit', Rickert interprets real history as the embodiment of 'nonreal meaning configurations' born of values, and calls it 'culture'. While neither accept that the presuppositions of historical science or the 'human studies' are immanent to the realities of history, Rickert presupposes the non-real *validity* of values which operate, so to speak, 'above' those realities, while Dilthey presupposes the real *existence* of a mental life which operates below them.

Rickert's concept of culture and the account of subjectivity which accompanies it attempts to capture an ambiguity and differentiation which, he alleges, Dilthey's concepts of *Geist* and of mental life cannot.

by culture we understand, first, real historical *life* to which a meaning is attached that constitutes it as culture. In addition, we can also understand by culture the nonreal 'content' itself, conceived as the *meaning* of such a life that is detached from all real existence and is interpreted with reference to cultural values. In 'meaningful life' itself, both of these senses interpenetrate. In the theory of such a life, they must be distinguished.[50]

This ambiguity is expressed in the fact that something can both be a value and have a value, that value can inhere in it or adhere to it. The naturalness of 'meaningful life' – the immanence of human values – is undermined by the fact that its meaning derives from a realm of value which is both external to it and non-real. For this reason, the statement that culture is the embodiment of values is ambiguous in a way in which the statement that spirit is the embodiment of life is not. For the manner in which spirit is the embodiment of life is never subject to intervention by mental beings. The idea that the artefacts and processes studied by the historian are the product of a human effort to embody 'life' makes no sense. 'Mental life' can never be the ground of human commitment.

Rickert does not want to argue that culture is the embodiment of something wholly different from and unrelated to mental life. It *is* the embodiment of mental life. But only in so far as mental beings are valuing beings. Which means: mental beings whose relationship to culture is mediated by values in which human commitments are grounded. Although 'it is doubtless correct that life is a condition of *all* culture, and all tendencies hostile to life, such as Tolstoy's absolute chastity, are to the same extent hostile to culture',[51] life remains nothing more than a condition, and 'only he who is able to suppress mere animation can be called a cultural being. In other words, one must to a certain extent "kill" life in order to arrive at goods with their own values.'[52]

Rickert's relationship to Weber is usually understood solely in terms of problems of concept formation, at the expense of that of why the problem was thought worth addressing. Hennis and Scaff in particular have stressed Weber's distance from Rickert in order to point out that the methodological writings are far more than an instruction manual for historians. This is true, but Weber was also convinced that the war against vitalism should be conducted on all fronts, and that Rickert was a sound ally.

Whoever attempts to equate scientific truth biologically with its usefulness for life, not only commits a gross conceptual error, but would, were he successful, lead us back to that state which dominated Europe before the Greeks generated that theoretical attitude to the value of truth and of science which turned away from mere life.[53]

Might it not be for this, as well as purely logical reasons, that Weber found Rickert 'very good'?[54]

## WEBER'S SCIENCE OF CULTURE

### The valuing subject

Weber's 'Knies and the Problem of Irrationality' is a critique of a number of philosophies of the human sciences which attempt to establish their distinctive problematic by means of a 'Diltheyan' account of experience. It culminates in a definition of 'personality' which recalls those sketched more tentatively in the quotations from Rickert and Simmel above.

> the 'freer' . . . an action is, that is, the *less* it bears within itself the character of a 'natural event', the more there comes into force that concept of 'personality' which finds its essence in the stability of its inner relationship to certain ultimate 'values' and 'meanings' of life, which are forged into purposes and thus translated into rational–teleological action. At the same time, there is a concomitant decline in that romantic–naturalistic use of 'personality', which by contrast seeks the essential sanctuary of the personal in the diffuse, undifferentiated and vegetative 'underground' of personal life, i.e. in that 'irrationality' which rests on the entwining of an infinity of psycho-physical conditions for the development of temperament and mood, an irrationality which the 'person' *shares* with the animal.[55]

The philosophies of social science of Wundt, Munsterberg, Lipps, Croce and Knies amounted to the same mistake: that of attempting to found the human sciences on something so radically opposed to naturalism that the result was a mirror image rather than something truly distinct. By distinguishing the human sciences purely ontologically, and doing so by recourse to the category of 'immediate experience', these theorists were forced to insist on the identity of method and object in such a way that object dictated method. The consequence was the claim that social scientific knowledge was an intuitive, or 'recreative' psychology, that the identity between scientific knowledge and scientific object could only be secured if both were founded in an immediate experience of real historical processes, processes which were only intelligible in so far as they *could* be immediately experienced.

For Weber, an undifferentiated account of subjectivity will, as an ontology with pretensions to provide the foundations of a science, produce an undifferentiated account of scientific method, a doctrine of the Same. He makes use of value philosophy in order to provide for the logical possibility of such differentiation. Without the idea that the personality is a valuing being and not simply a mental being, it is impossible for human beings to produce the cultural artefacts they do. For it is only 'ultimate values' that can provide criteria of significance with which to make sense of and differentiate the infinite heterogeneous continuum of experience.[56] And they can do this only if they are accorded a 'transcendental' status. The idea that personality consists in a stable relationship to ultimate values which are then forged into purposes implies this. Cultural experience is defined by a *distance* between self and world, and between value and world, a distance to which Weber attached enormous ethical as well as logical significance 'the widespread talk of "intuition" conceals nothing other than a lack of distance [*Distanzlosigkeit*] towards the object, which should be judged in the same way as a similar attitude towards human beings.' [57]

As with Simmel, the concept of distance has a twofold meaning. Personality consists in a stable *relationship* to ultimate values. The personality is not consumed by or absorbed in the values which make possible the mediate character of cultural experience, nor are those values merely a constituent of the personality. To be a personality capable of cultural experience and cultural action is to be a valuing subject, but not wholly a valuing subject. For Weber, distance towards values which are held to be valid is as important as distance towards the object. As a result of this second sense of 'distance' neo-Kantianism has been called an 'idealism without a subject'.[58] The validity of knowledge is separate from the origin of knowledge because values are independent of processes of consciousness.[59] As Simmel puts it: 'The subject who comprehends all objects is different from the subject who is confronted with objects'[60] In meeting the demands imposed upon us by values, 'we sense that we are not merely satisfying a claim imposed upon ourselves, or merely acknowledging a quality of the object'.[61]

Chapter 6 will show that 'Politics as a Vocation' culminates in an account of personality at the centre of which lies this concept of distance.

The origin/validity distinction holds for both cultural actors and historical scientists. Or rather, for both the historical scientist and the cultural actor constructed by the historical scientist. Both relate 'existence' to values which have validity and thereby render significant a segment of the 'meaningless infinity of the world process'. The actor performs an *evaluation*, takes a position, adopts a standpoint which is necessarily particular and implies the existence of other conflicting standpoints derived from other valid values.

By contrast, the concept of significance acquires a threefold meaning for the historian. Weber brings this out in the 'critique' of Eduard Meyer, in a discussion of the interpretation of Goethe's letters to Frau von Stein. What is true for a biography of Goethe will be true for the treatment of any 'fact' of cultural life. The sentiments expressed in Goethe's letters – the relevant historical 'facts' – may be significant: (a) as real links in an historical causal chain, i.e. in their 'historical effectiveness'; (b) as heuristic means for the disclosure of (i) the particular features of a composite phenomenon, which latter – such as Goethe's *'Lebensführung und Lebensauffassung'* or that of similar social circles – would be the real causal link; or (ii) the general features of such phenomena, features which are either common to *all* cultures or are 'non-cultural' features of interest to psychopathology. Such features would be expressed by class concepts; (c) as an object of evaluation.[62]

The third type of significance, argues Weber, outweighs the first two. Why? Because the fact that the historical fact in question can be significant as an object of evaluation is what makes it a cultural, rather than a natural, fact, an historical individual rather than the exemplar of a law. We *'are* cultural *beings'* endowed with the capacity to lend the world meaning through relating concrete reality to values. English translations of the *Wissenschaftslehre* have a tendency to ignore his treatment of this *constitutive* trans-formation. For instance, the two passages in which Weber writes: 'Empirical reality *becomes* "culture" to us because and in so far as we relate it to value ideas,'[63] 'viewpoints in the light of which reality becomes "culture" through being significant in its unique character'[64] (emphasis added) are, in the original: 'Die empirische

Wirklichkeit *ist* für uns '*Kultur*', weil und insofern wir sie mit Wertideen in Beziehung setzen',[65] 'Gesichtspunkten . . . unter denen die Wirklichkeit für uns jeweils '*Kultur*', d.h. in ihrer Eigenart bedeutungsvoll war oder ist.'[66]

The translation implies that the reality which confronts the historian or the historical actor is concrete reality, which only becomes 'culture' once 'we' relate it to 'value ideas'. In fact, what Weber (and Rickert) wishes to convey in these passages is that the 'reality' which the historical scientist relates to values is already constituted as 'culture'. 'From the standpoint of *human beings* "culture" is a finite segment, endowed with meaning and significance, of the meaningless infinity of the world process'.[67] When Weber writes that culture is the object of a *Wirklichkeitswissenschaft* he does not mean that it is the object of a *Realitätswissenschaft*. The use of this distinction is a deliberate concession to Hegel, whose science of spirit was a science of actuality – *Wirklichkeit* – a philosophical science. But whereas for Hegel actuality is the actualisation of the Idea, for Weber *Kultur* is the result of a human striving to embody values. It is one mode of rationalisation of an irrational, infinite manifold – *Realität*. Nature is another. This rationalisation process is in itself as infinite as the reality it orders. Yet the actuality in relation to which cultural beings in fact take a position – culture – is a product which has emancipated itself from the practical rationalisation process which produced it. All processes of cultural scientific concept formation are empty without this pre-logical structuring.

Rickert's and Weber's overemphasis on the logic of concept formation as the foundation of a cultural science can be explained by the fact that they needed to provide for the fact that culture is always the product of the attempt to embody values. Any such concession to a philosophy of *Sollen* will push immediately in a Kantian direction, towards the idea that the human being lives in just two worlds, that of causality and that of freedom. And to the extent that it does, it will appear unable to thematise the 'third world' of human institutions, for it will conceive of every such account as being unable to provide, logically, for that in which human freedom consists, namely, the possibility that the world might be otherwise, that one's life does not 'run on as an event in nature'. Yet the nature to which this refers is second nature, or custom.[68] Cassirer made just this point in *Zur Logik der Kulturwissenschaften*. Life is lifted out of the immediacy of drives through language, which establishes a system of significances, symbolic *forms* or *styles*, a common world, the proper science of which is a phenomenology of perception.

There is a fundamental difference between style concepts and value concepts. That which style concepts represent is not an Ought [*Sollen*] but a 'being' – even if here it is a case not of physical things but the existence of 'forms'. If I speak of the form of a language or of a particular artform, this in itself has nothing to do with a 'value relation'.[69]

The point of the *Wissenschaftslehre* is to show that ought cannot be reduced to is, that all human action must be capable of being understood in terms of a value which animated it, even if it is a value which none of us interpret in precisely the same way. As we saw, for Weber the neo-Hegelian attempt to sublimate *Moralität* into *Sittlichkeit*, could never succeed without impairing the integrity of ethical imperatives.[70] And if cultural science itself rests upon an Ought – belief in the value of truth – then the only way in which to respect the integrity of the object of this science – the fate of beings capable of taking a position towards second nature – was for *science to thematise itself*. Weber's account of the logic of concept formation in the cultural sciences is the means by which he, as a cultural being, prevents his own activity from 'running on as an event in nature'. If we want to understand that the *Wissenschaftslehre* is something more than a dry methodological treatise, we must understand the manner in which this is so. The point is not to search for moments of relief from the turgidity of its style, for asides in which Weber expresses a 'social philosophy', but to see that that philosophy is expressed through the very concern with the logic of concept formation.

### Empathy and the actualisation of values

The object domain of the 'cultural sciences' is the continually emergent product of a human striving to embody values. The object of any particular historical inquiry is always a historical individual selected from an infinity of historical individuals which are no less 'real' or 'unformed' for being 'actively forgotten'. The choice of which historical individuals to select is 'determined by the value ideas which dominate the investigator and his age'.[71] Once the selection has been made, in accordance with a scientific community's understanding of 'what everyone wants to know', of what is existentially relevant, a process of value *interpretation* can take place. Value interpretation ' "suggests" . . . various possible *relationships of the object to values*',[72] various possible positions historical actors can adopt and cannot avoid having to adopt in relation to an historical individual.

The most famous example of a historical individual in this sense is 'the spirit of capitalism'. It is in accordance with the claim that the selection of historical individuals is determined by criteria of general significance, by the values which dominate the investigator and his age, that Weber writes: 'The Puritan *wanted* to be a man of vocation – we *must* be.'[73] This is not an expression of pessimism or indeed of any diagnosis, but rather the relatively modest claim that no contemporary individual can live his/her life without taking a position on those practices which 'embody' the idea of vocation. This is what makes the spirit of capitalism worthy of historical – i.e. causal – interpretation, interpretation of its being 'so and not otherwise'. In the same way, the political historian may view the practices which fall under the term '*Rechtsstaat*' as the embodiment or attempted embodiment of a particular set of 'liberal' values. In so far, and only in so far, as the *Rechtsstaat* is an unavoidable condition for the action of historical actors, the value it embodies will be a 'value for everyone'.[74]

Weber goes further than this, and suggests that not only is an historical individual selected in accordance with its general existential relevance or 'universal significance', and its possible relation to values outlined, but that 'the inexhaustibility of its "content" as regards possible focal points of our interest is the characteristic of the historical individual of the "highest" rank'.[75] This inexhaustibility confronts both actor and historian. For the historian the extensive infinity of cultural actuality is mastered by the selection of a historical individual, the intensive infinity of that historical individual is mastered by selecting those sides which, according to our criteria of essentiality, are worthy of causal explanation. Once this selection has occurred, a further selection of relevant causes takes place. The difference between actor and historian is that, while the historical actor's values are normatively *valid* for the actor 'when the normatively valid is the object of an *empirical* investigation, it loses, as an object, its character as a norm. It is treated as "existent", not as "valid" '.[76]

By stressing two parallels between the actor's and the

historian's conduct, Weber was able to make concessions to Dilthey's concept of empathic understanding. Formally, while the scientist cannot empathise with the mental life of another, he/she, as Rickert put it, *can* 'get the feel' of another's values:

> Whoever wants to accomplish purely empirical, art-historical tasks, requires the capacity to 'understand' artistic productions, and this is clearly unthinkable without the *capacity* to evaluate. Naturally, this holds accordingly for the political historian, literary historian, historian of religion or of philosophy'.[77]

It is this capacity which makes possible value interpretation. But this 'empathic experience' is

> *still* no 'historical' work, but it is certainly the completely unavoidable 'forma formans' for the historical 'interest' in an object, for its primary conceptual formation as an 'individual', and for the causal work of history which thereby becomes meaningfully possible.[78]

In other words, empathic understanding is merely a condition for historical interpretation. It is not that interpretation itself. Substantively, the historical actor's capacity for valuation may be enhanced by value interpretation, which:

> broadens his own inner 'life', his 'spiritual horizon', makes him capable of grasping and thinking through possibilities and nuances of lifestyle as such, of developing his own self in an intellectually, aesthetically, and ethically (in the widest sense) differentiated way, of making his 'psyche' – so to speak – 'more sensitive to values'.[79]

In Rickert's work, the similarity between the actor's and historian's (mediate) mode of relatedness to the world supports his concept of the 'historical centre': '*those* persons become preeminently important for history who themselves have taken a real value position on the normatively general social values of the state, law, the economy, art, and so on'.[80] And in order to express his distance from life philosophy, Rickert again employs its terminology: 'Those persons (whether as individuals or groups) are included in the historical centres of a historical material of the past in whom cultural values of their time were 'truly vital'. This is why they become historically essential'.[81] Weber says the same thing in the Knies essay:

The 'valuations' in which 'historical interest' is anchored . . . are components of the immediate experience with which we can 'empathise'. Consider, therefore, the viewpoint of a science the object of which, philosophically formulated, constitutes 'the actualisation of values'. From this point of view it will follow that the individuals who themselves perform acts of 'evaluation' will invariably be conceived as the 'bearers' of that process of the actualisation of values.[82]

Weber's decision to focus on the Brahmins in India and on the Literati in China is rooted in statements such as these. As 'exponents of the unity of culture' these groups constituted the 'historical centre' without which the idea of unity of culture would make no sense.[83] In actual historical investigation Weber would insist, implicitly, that the concepts of 'historical centre' and 'actualisation of values' be used ironically. The latter expression 'is not meant to refer to a cosmic process, 'objectively' 'tending' to the 'actualisation' of an 'absolute' as an *empirical fact*. This expression is not meant to have any metaphysical status at all.'[84] The values which are 'truly vital' in a stratum of genteel intellectuals, Brahmins or clergy can never be actualised fully. In order for cultural action to be possible, ultimate values have to be forged into purposes, in the process of which their purity is irrevocably tarnished. The object of empirical historical science is constituted as 'culture' through a logical–psychological difference, between ultimate values and the purposes into which those values must be forged for action to be possible. Weber stresses this at numerous points.[85]

## Subject and epoch

Weber's critique of intuitionist theories of personality is a critique of theories which treat the self as an undifferentiated unity. But the wider implications for historical research in general and for the 'concept' of modernity are clear. Because what is true of 'personality' is true of 'epoch'. Of the personality Weber writes: 'It is *not true* – as has been claimed – that the "personality" is and should be a "unity" in the sense that it is, so to speak, injured if it is not visible on every occasion.'[86] The unity of the personality is not the transcendental unity of apperception, nor is it the unity of 'life'. The infinity of reality is overcome by a process of selection the criteria for which are not only variable but often mutually irreducible. The unity of personality is not a result of the fact that the 'same' personality performs different acts of evaluation, but consists at best in a coherent relationship between the different points of view, grounded in ultimate values, which the individual adopts in order to carry out this selection. Without this selection, experience remains in a state of 'leaden diffuseness', and the difference between artistic, economic, political and erotic experience is elided. Anti-naturalistic philosophies of social science such as those of Dilthey, Munsterberg, Lipps, Croce and Knies, which rest solely upon the category of 'immediate experience', and provide experience with no genuinely substantive predicates, are restricted to a transcendent perspectivism. If it amounts to more than a demand to surrender to the infinity of experience and generates abstract concepts for the purposes of historical inquiry, these concepts will be general rather than individual.

In the light of the distinction between Weber and Simmel's concepts of culture introduced at the end of the last chapter, it may seem paradoxical to introduce here the idea of a coherent relationship between points of view, a concession to the kind of organicist thinking Weber rejected. But the point is that Weber had to find a way of providing, analytically, for the unavoidability of modern specialisation and the ordeal of subjectivity which went with it. And in order to do this, he had to provide both for the mundane fact that in the course of my existence I am thrown into a series of 'value spheres', and for the idea that if the specialisation I cannot avoid is to amount to a calling and not a profession, it must entail a devotion to an ultimate value which grounds it. The development of the psyche then consists in an increase in sensitivity towards value differences, in an appreciation of 'possibilities and nuances of life-style as such', not in the enrichment of the personality by means of their exploration. Weber's culturalism is a theory of the *differentiated* personality only in this sense.[87] But he needed it in order to be able to ask, implicitly: is the ideal personality the one who achieves a harmony between activities; the one who retreats into interiority in the face of the impossible demand this entails; the one who restricts him/herself to one sphere but merely follows the intrinsic logic of the activity germane to it; the one who while restricting him/herself to one sphere devotes him/herself to the ultimate value which defines the activity germane to it and thereby gives his/her life a meaning; or the one who goes further and sees in the ground of his/her own activity the standard with which to judge all others? Organic unity; mute interiority; submission to the demands of a profession; devotion which defines the calling; or fanaticism?

In the Knies essay Weber is quick to spot the parallel between 'emanationist' theories of personality and emanationist theories of the 'total character' of a 'Volk', in which this total character 'is *the* entity which provides the ground for all its single elements. . . . Knies makes no attempt to analyze the nature of this mysterious power. It is analogous to the 'life force' of 'vitalism" '.[88] This objection to vitalism could be extended to Dilthey's concept of an epoch. *He* writes:

> It is the task of historical analysis to discover the *consensus* which governs concrete purposes, values and ways of thought of a period . . . every action, every thought, every common activity, in short, every part of the historical whole, has its significance through its relationship to the whole of the epoch or age.[89]

There could be no clearer statement of the conceptual hierarchy at work in theoretical vitalism. The key concepts of Weber's philosophy of social science – concrete purpose, value, significance – only make sense in terms of the holistic concept of an epoch. Of such a concept Weber writes: 'A representation of the "cultural contents" of an era, even if it is very comprehensive, is always an illumination of its "experience" under a plurality of different points of view which in their turn are oriented to values.'[90] Later in the Knies essay, Weber writes:

> Historical intuition carries with it the eminent danger of repressing the analysis of causal connections in favour of a 'collective character' which corresponds to a 'feeling of totality', and, where the demand for a formula which reproduces a 'synthesis of feeling' replaces the demand for empirical analysis, sticks to the 'epoch' like a label.[91]

The nearest Weber comes to such a comprehensive representation is the 'Author's Introduction' to the sociology of religion. Although the 'experience of modernity'[92] sketched there is frequently, and in a sense justifiably, interpreted as one of increasing rationality, rationalisation, disenchantment or impersonality, Weber deliberately attempts to disrupt this certainty by articulating a series of 'points of view' – scientific, musical, architectural, educational, political, economic, legal – from which that experience could and should be illuminated. Even if in all these cases 'it is obviously a question of the specifically formed "rationalism" of Western culture',[93] the task of historical inquiry is not to grasp the totality of that experience either by intuition, by an holistic concept, or by the simple omission of historical material. Historical inquiry may employ the idea of such a totality as a heuristic device, but the inquiry itself will concern the relationships between the specific forms that experience assumes. Or, if this still implies that 'rationality' is the essential content of those forms, a thing is never rational or irrational in itself, but only from a particular point of view.[94]

## CONCLUSION

Despite these anti-holistic strictures, it might still be argued that the neo-Kantian theory of the irreducibility of value spheres was, in Weber's hands, the self-consciousness of the total character of the modern age,[95] an age of increasing social differentiation, fragmentation and the mutual irreducibility of life's orders and spheres. But to the extent that this philosophy pushes to its limits the implication that a demand for synthesis is itself a localised affair, it might be taken as theoretical support for an opposition to the idea of such a character. In employing value philosophy in the way he does, is Weber arguing that an age in which the concept of 'direct experience' made sense is irrevocably lost, or defending, nostalgically, the idea of 'distance', 'vocation' and scientific 'specialisation' in the face of the 'modern quest for experience'?[96] Is vitalism simply the theoretical expression of what Simmel, following Baudelaire, called the 'blasé attitude', in which 'the feeling for value differences' 'is completely lost'?[97]

More explicitly, since Weber does make numerous remarks on 'the modern age' or the modern personality, what precise theoretical status should be accorded them? Are they dramatic asides or can they be read as the building blocks of a theory of modernity? A discussion of the 'Zwischenbetrachtung' in the sociology of religion is the most obvious way of addressing this question.

# Chapter 4

# The *Zwischenbetrachtung* I
## Theory of modernity or theory of culture?

## INTRODUCTION

Chapter 3 established a link between the idea of a cultural science and neo-Kantian value philosophy. It was suggested that Weber's appropriation of that philosophy meant that the concept of an epoch was too monolithic to be of value to historical science except as a heuristic device. Much was made of the idea that the claim that 'we *are* cultural *beings*' is tied to a differentiated concept of 'personality', and that there is a connection between this differentiation and the mutual irreducibility of cultural 'value spheres', that the theory of value spheres is both a theory of the world and a theory of the self. But while the account of the differentiation of culture and personality is an expression of Weber's objection to totalising philosophies of history and those which appeal to the concept of an epoch, this very account could be seen as an implicit theory of the modern epoch. An obvious place in which the suspicion arises is the '*Zwischenbetrachtung*', the 'Intermediate Reflections' essay in the sociology of religion, which is both Weber's only explicit and sustained substantive use of the value-spheres argument and shares with the 'Author's Introduction' a diagnostic tone which his other writings lack. In many ways it is the most interesting and the most unsatisfactory thing he wrote.

## THE PERSPECTIVE OF THE *ZWISCHENBETRACHTUNG*

Perhaps because of this, it has engendered a certain confusion in the literature, some of it purely terminological, much of it the product of the attempt by some scholars to press it into the procrustean bed of their own theoretical problematic.[1] In a sense the terminological confusion is understandable. There was never a consensus among neo-Kantians over the precise manner in which the cultural continuum was to be internally differentiated, over how many 'value spheres' there are, and what the relationship between them is or ought to be.[2]

The essay is not a systematic account of 'culture' in general or 'modern culture' in particular, though it purports to be 'a contribution to the typology and sociology of rationalism. . . . Therefore it sets out from the most rational forms which reality can assume'.[3] To be genuinely systematic it would require an Archimedian point, a centre about which 'culture' revolves. But even if, as is often assumed, this typology is established by means of the statement that different spheres 'follow their own laws', culture is not a federation, there is no cognitive house of representatives, no higher theoretical principle regulating the relationship between them. It was already established in Chapter 2 that Weber's account of the relationship between *Bildung* and *Brauchbarkeit*, between the onesidedness and allsidedness of the personality was such that culture has no outside, that the personality has no pre-cultural 'core'. The same is true of the world.

The scope of the essay, despite its imposing erudition, is limited. Weber divides 'culture' into six value spheres: religion, economics, politics, aesthetics, the erotic sphere and the intellectual sphere (which includes both science and philosophy). He does not examine the relationship between value spheres as such, but in accordance with Rickert's claim that the empathic understanding of the cultural scientist enables him/her to 'get the feel' of the values of others, does so from the perspective of one of them: religion, or more accurately, a salvation religion which rests upon a dualism between the otherworldly and the inner-worldly, between religious ethics and the world. The reason is hinted at in the second paragraph of the essay.

> The theoretically constructed types of conflicts between 'life orders' merely signify that at certain points these internal conflicts are *possible* and 'adequate', but *not* that there is no standpoint from which they could be held to be resolved in a higher synthesis [*aufgehoben*].[4]

A standpoint from which the conflicts which do arise could be held to be resolved remains possible as long as the human mind retains the capacity to conceive the world as a 'meaningful totality',[5] in effect, to claim access to a point beyond the boundary of culture.

The world can only be viewed as a meaningful totality if a distinction is drawn between the world and the source of the world's meaning, between the world as it is and the world as it would have to be to correspond to its meaning. Expressed in neo-Kantian terms, between the world as (real) existence and as (non-real) validity. For a religious rejection of the world, from the point of view of which Weber will construct the clashes and tensions between value spheres, religion is not simply one value sphere among others, but denies its own perspectival character and claims universal validity. The tensions which result from the attempt to redeem this claim reach their height precisely when the same claim is made on behalf of non-religious values.

By setting up the problem of value spheres in this way, in granting religion an exceptional status, Weber is echoing a theme perfectly familiar to Windelband, Rickert, Simmel and the Protestant Social Congress. As Windelband wrote:

> We are accustomed to count religion as one of the great cultural forms together with science, art, morality, law and the state, but . . . there can be no question of the complete co-ordination of religion with other forms. These others have their peculiar kind of value in the content which they realise in the life of humanity, but religion has no such special province of values. It consists in the metaphysical tincture and relation which all these values may assume.[6]

The same point was made by Max Scheler in his review of Rudolf Eucken's *Der Wahrheitsgehalt der Religion*.

> Just as Kant shows that experience is only possible on the assumption of transcendent binding functions which do not stem from experience, Eucken shows that culture is only possible when one treats it as a work which draws the creative forces which work themselves out in it from a realm beyond its empirical form.[7]

And at the end of one of his attacks on *Lebensphilosophie*, in the course of an account of the different 'degrees of distance' between 'life' and various cultural values, Rickert writes:

> In the end religion extends not only beyond all natural life, but

also beyond all cultural life . . . to all thisworldly life there is opposed an 'eternal life', which is what is meant when life is accorded a religious reverence.[8]

But in analytic terms, in order to render coherent the account of tensions between value spheres, religion had to be reduced to the status of 'one value sphere among others'. Once again, Simmel was an indispensable resource, in particular his *Die Religion*: '*each* of the great forms of our existence must be capable of expressing the *totality* of life through its language'.[9] While Simmel's ideal of personality may have been one of organic harmony between different 'spheres', the constitution of those spheres is also that of a plurality of worlds. Simmel pushes this as far as the suggestion that: 'Reality is in no way simply *the* world, but rather just one, next to which the world of art and that of religion stand, brought together out of the same material according to other forms and presuppositions.'[10] Each world 'is created by the soul'. And a cultural *Wirklichkeitswissenschaft* constitutes that reality as just one world, in this case, the world of world-making. But while this plurality of worlds may be an expression of human finitude, 'like the logic of science, so often does that of religion claim to grasp or dominate all others'.[11] This is just what Weber's science seems to have to eschew in order to make the same point: 'The sole purpose of the constructed schema [of directions of world rejection] is to be a *means of orientation*, but not to teach a philosophy of its own'.[12]

For the secularisation thesis contained in the *Zg* the historical collapse of what Weber calls a 'universalist ethics of brotherhood' does not mean that non-religious practices are simply left to follow their 'own logics' (*Eigengesetzlichkeit*), but rather that tensions arise when the values which hold validly for particular cultural practices are sublimated into values which are held to hold validly for *all* cultural practices. When this sublimation occurs, the distinction between culture and nature collapses, one cultural value sphere is no longer simply a cultural value sphere but the values grounding it are both unconditional and universally valid. The *Kulturmensch* becomes a *Naturmensch*.[13] So the whole thrust of the value spheres argument is that value spheres only become interesting when one of them assumes an exceptional status, loses its status as a value sphere and becomes the ground or the character of all others.

The influential interpretations of the *Zg* by Habermas and

Schluchter have obscured rather than clarified this. The analytical particularism of the critical theoretical concept of culture was pointed out in Chapter 2. In *The Theory of Communicative Action*, Habermas writes that the capitalist economy, the modern state and formal law are 'constitutive for the rationalisation of *society*',[14] and with it the explananda in Weber's 'explanation' of modernity. Modern science, technology, autonomous art and a 'religiously anchored ethic guided by principles'[15] are cultural value spheres which, if Habermas is to be believed, became differentiated between the sixteenth and eighteenth centuries and began to follow their own logics. They are Weber's explanans.

The shortcomings of this approach are made clear in Habermas's interpretation of the following passage in the *Zg*.

> the rationalisation and conscious sublimation of our relations to the various spheres of goods – internal and external, religious and secular – have pressed towards making us *conscious* of the *inner autonomous logics* [*innere Eigengesetzlichkeiten*] of the individual spheres and their consequences, thereby allowing them to develop those tensions with one another that remain hidden in the originally naive relation to the external world.[16]

Habermas gives us only a partial sense of what Weber means by the 'inner logics' of spheres of goods. He appeals to Weber's distinction between ideas and interests and argues that 'so long as we view ideas in themselves, they form *cultural value spheres*; as soon as they are connected with interests, they form *orders of life* that legitimately regulate the possession of goods'.[17] Habermas is correct to stress that to each cultural value sphere there corresponds a 'life order' as a specific locus of interests that value generates.[18] But he maintains a distinction between cultural action systems – the scientific enterprise, the religious community and the artistic enterprise – and social action systems – the economy and the state. Problems of '*Innerlichkeit*' and 'personality' are at stake in science, morality, art and religion, but not in politics or economics. Habermas considers the relationship between personality and life orders for a restricted range of life orders, and a discussion of this relationship in the political and economic spheres is curiously shelved in favour of the tabulatory exercise at the end of Part II, Chapter 3 of *The Theory of Communicative Action*.[19]

Schluchter's *The Rise of Western Rationalism*, on which Habermas draws for his discussion of the *Zg*, and which was partly inspired by Habermas's earlier work, attempts to reduce Weber's account of the relationship between value spheres to a distinction between science, morality and art. Schluchter argues that Weber's historical studies are 'anchored' in a theory of rationalisation based upon an 'open value scheme[?!]' which:

> distinguishes between cognitive, evaluative and expressive symbolism. Moreover, the scheme subdivides the evaluative sphere. There Weber deals with the possible conflict between other-wordly and this-worldly values and within the latter, with the conflict between the values of the various spheres of life.[20]

Schluchter's acknowledgement of the generality of the neo-Kantian concept of value gives him seven values: 'cognitive values, religious (otherwordly) values, ethical (thisworldly) values in politics, economy and family, aesthetic values and, enlarging the expressive sphere [!], eroticism'.[21] He then introduces the concept of a 'partial order' and argues that in the *Zg* 'Weber addressed primarily seven partial orders related to value spheres: the family, religion, the economy, politics, art, sexuality and eroticism, and the realm of cognition, 'science" '.[22] Yet on the next page, he writes:

> I believe that I do not distort Weber's reasoning . . . if I assume that he focused on four partial orders in his analysis of society: the 'natural' order, which is tied to natural reproduction, especially family and kinship, and which is at the core of a much larger order, the educational order; the economic order, which meets the recurrent, normal wants of everyday life [?]; the cultural order, of which religion is the most important element [!]; the political order, which protects social life on a territorial basis internally and externally.[23]

Four features of this interpretation are noteworthy. Firstly, it treats 'religion' as one value sphere among others and fails to acknowledge either the exceptional status neo-Kantian value philosophy was prepared to grant it, or that it is from this perspective, and this perspective alone, that Weber addresses the problem of the conflict between value spheres. Secondly, it refers to 'ethical values in politics, economy and family'. But in Weber's classification, the 'ethical' sphere is nowhere to be found, and Schluchter's formulation appears to be an attempt at repair work.

For the purposes of the *Zg* Weber equates 'ethics' in the sense of ethical doctrine with religious ethics. 'Ethics' and 'religion' are not separate spheres, as they are for Schluchter and as they were in a different way for Rickert and Windelband.[24] Thirdly, Schluchter suggests that to 'partial orders' there correspond 'partial world views'. In my view this is a crucial insight without which Weber's account is incomprehensible. Unfortunately, Schluchter does not develop this idea. Finally, his reference to the 'cultural order' represents a move away from Weber's culturalism, in which culture is not a value sphere or life order, but precisely the formal and substantive ground for talking in terms of value spheres or life orders at all.

## TRIUMPHALISM AND THE CONSTANCY OF THE WORLD

Weber's conflation of 'religion' and 'ethics' gives him a series of oppositions between 'religion' and five orders and powers of 'the world'. The tension between religion and 'the natural sib community' is considered purely historically, at the beginning of the section of the essay on 'Directions of World Rejection'. Weber considers this tension solely in order to establish his major concern in the essay, the relationship between a universalist, specifically Occidental religious ethic of brotherliness, and 'the world'. We will return to the details of this tension.

For now, I highlight a metatheoretical tension which emerges on the essay's sixth page. Here Weber writes that the rationalisation and conscious sublimation of our relationship to the various spheres of goods 'has pressed towards *making conscious* the inner lawful autonomy of the individual spheres', and that the tensions he will discuss 'remain hidden to the originally naive relation with the external world'.[25] Weber's formulation of those tensions is ambiguous. At times he argues that 'polytheism' is a modern phenomenon, that '*today* something can be sacred not only in spite of its not being beautiful, but because and in so far as it is not beautiful',[26] that 'we live as did the ancients when their world was not yet disenchanted of its gods and demons', that 'today the routines of everyday life challenge religion. Many old gods ascend from their graves; they are disenchanted and take the form of impersonal forces'.[27] Yet at other times Weber's formulation is far closer to Simmel, in so far as it proposes a universal concept of culture.[28]

It is the fate of our culture to be more clearly aware of these struggles once again, after our eyes have been blinded for a thousand years – blinded by the allegedly or presumably exclusive orientation towards the grandiose moral fervour of Christian ethics.[29]

The problem is illustrated by Weber's use of James Mill's argument that if one begins with pure experience one ends with polytheism.

In *'Der Sinn der Wertfreiheit'* and in the wartime essay *'Zwischen zwei Gesetzen'* Weber uses it triumphalistically. In the first he refers to the possibility of a non-ethical sphere of value 'claiming its own immanent dignity in the most extreme sense of the word',[30] a dignity residing precisely in the refusal to buttress action by appeals to the good or the sacred. Everyday existence is such that 'persons who are caught up in it *do not become aware*, and above all do not wish to become aware, of this partly psychologically, but pragmatically conditioned motley of irreconcilably antagonistic values'.[31] In the latter he writes:

> In fact; whoever stands in the 'world' . . . can in himself experience nothing other than a struggle between a plurality of realms of value, of which each, considered for itself, appears binding. He must *choose* which of these gods he wants to and should follow, or when one and when another. But always he will find himself in the midst of a struggle against one or several of the other gods of this world and above all always far from the god of Christianity – at least from that preached by the Sermon on the Mount.[32]

At times in the *Zg* Weber's aim appears to be, in 'reliving' the experience of an individual committed to a universalist religious ethics (of any description), to argue that that individual, precisely because of the universalist character of his/her ethical standpoint, will continually run up against the specific autonomous powers of 'the world' and that that ethic is therefore unactualisable and historically inappropriate. If this was Weber's argument, he would have had to assume that 'the world' is a historical constant, a permanent reality against which the specific capabilities of the various modes of rejecting it can be assessed.

Weber's work often implies that the world does possess this permanent character. For instance, in the introduction to 'The Economic Ethics of the World Religions' he states that:

for the empirical student, the sacred values, differing among themselves, are by no means only, nor even preferably, to be interpreted as 'otherworldly'. . . . Psychologically considered, man in quest of salvation has been primarily preoccupied by attidudes of the here and now,[33] with solid goods of this world . . . health, wealth, and long life.[34]

On this account the distance between a salvation religion and the world varies solely with the degree of 'otherworldliness' of religious doctrine. The world remains in order as it is. The fact that its orders and powers follow laws irreducible to religious ethics is merely *made conscious* at a certain stage in the history of religion. Weber's normative and analytical use of 'worldliness' appears the illegitimate appropriation by empirical science of a primarily theological category, and does not seem to leave open the possibility that the 'world' with which world-rejecting religions are confronted only has any sense in relation to the specific manner in which those religions constitute the world as a world. As Blumenberg puts it:

there was no 'worldliness' before there was the opposite of 'unworldliness'. It was the world released to itself from the grip of its negation, abandoned to its self-assertion and to the means necessary to that self-assertion, not responsible for man's true salvation but still competing with that salvation with its own offer of stability and reliability.[35]

For Blumenberg, *contra* Karl Löwith, the manner in which a specific religion runs up against the world is dependent upon the manner in which that religion constitutes the worldhood of that world. The world is not a fixed domain. This assumption, for which he had been criticised by Blumenberg, had already been made in Löwith's existentialist interpretation of Weber: 'sober "reality" *now* stands in a secular light, and the principle for the interpretation of this sobered world is a process of rationalisation through which the world has disenchanted and sobered itself'.[36]

We might respond on Weber's behalf with the pragmatic defence that he is simply investigating, historical–sociologically, the inescapable 'world' of economic, political, artistic, sexual or intellectual relationships, or that the concern of a science which investigates the effect of doctrine on *action* thereby legitimates an indiscriminate use of the concept of a 'world'. As long as it can be shown that Weber consistently adopts a thoroughly secular, scientific perspective, that he opposes a 'religious conception of reality' for the purposes of an empirical science of reality, his use of the concept of a world would appear legitimate. But as I suggested above, the *Zg* is presented as the exhibition of the type of 'empathic understanding' we discussed in the previous chapter. It is a recreation of the relationship of an individual who adheres to an ethic of world rejection to the orders and powers of the world. This is the significance of the famous 'Ideas and Interests' quote in the *Einleitung*.

> The conception of the idea of redemption was in itself very old, if one understands by it liberation from need, hunger, drought, sickness and ultimately suffering and death. Yet redemption attained a specific significance only where it expressed a systematic and rationalised 'image of the world' a position [*Stellungnahme*] towards it. . . . Interests (material and ideal) not ideas directly dominate the conduct of human beings. But the world images, which were created through 'ideas', have very often, like 'switchmen', determined the tracks along which the dynamic of interests propels conduct. 'From what' and 'for what' one wanted to and . . . could be redeemed depended upon a world image.[37]

Weber's argument that the question of 'from what' one was to be redeemed depended upon a world image was intended to refute, or at least complicate, the accounts of religion given by Marx in the introduction to *The Critique of Hegel's Philosophy of Right* and by Nietzsche, most notably in *The Genealogy of Morals*. His claim that behind every type of redemption doctrine there lies 'a position towards *something* in the real world which was experienced as specifically "senseless" '[38] is intended to show that what Nietzsche called 'the metaphysical need' has its own dignity, and that the question 'for what?' should not be dismissed as nihilistic.[39] And with good reason. For experiencing something in the real world as 'specifically senseless' depends upon a prior capacity to 'take a position', to be the valuing subject of neo-Kantianism.

The *Zg* appears to provide the greatest scope for the claim that Weber fails to live up to these strictures and simply dismisses contemporary, outmoded forms of world-rejecting or universalist ethics in the name of the need to meet the worldly demands of the day. But Weber's point is that any salvation religion at whose centre lies a universalistic ethics and a distinction between the innerworldly and outerworldly will, in its encounter with the orders and powers of innerworldly relations, be forced into an ethical compromise, regardless of the particular status of the world. For example, the historical significance of Christian culture was in fact premissed upon an ethical compromise consequent on a recognition that the god of Christianity was far from the world. Unlike Judaism and Islam, Christianity was never strictly monotheistic – 'the supramundane God has not, as such, determined the direction of Occidental asceticism'.[40]

For Weber, the fact that the ability of a class, status group or party to secure worldly goods is dependent upon an ethical compromise is not sufficient to undermine the ethical beliefs or imperatives which act as the spur for worldly conduct. To believe that it is is to believe that empirical knowledge is commensurable with metaphysics, and that the former can be appealed to for a critique of the latter. The task of the empirical scientist is not to offer a critique of ethical compromise, but to assert its general inevitability and highlight its specific instances. The nearest empirical science comes to critique is the demand that the actor exhibit the 'intellectual integrity' required to recognise an ethical compromise for what it is. What it cannot demand is the actual abandonment of absolutist ethical positions, those 'impossibles' belief in which is a condition for the achievement of the possible.

> the rational, in the sense of the logical or teleological 'consistency' of an intellectual–theoretical or practical–ethical position, has and always has had power over human beings, however limited and unstable this power is and was in the face of other powers of historical life.[41]

On the other hand, there are passages in which the necessity of acting 'in the world' appears to cause Weber to forego the 'elementary scientific duty of self-control',[42] and to use enlightenment metaphors to characterise contemporary otherworldly positions as illusions. Here, the service rendered by science in enabling the actor to attain clarity about his/her position seems to give way to an ideological demand for a consistency, not of that position itself, but between that position towards the world and action in the world. The problem is addressed in the next chapter in the discussion of the clash between religion and science, and of the meaning of the concept of 'intellectual integrity'.

## THE POSITIONAL SIGNIFICANCE OF THE
*ZWISCHENBETRACHTUNG*

The first practical problem for English readers is that the only translation of the *Zg* is in the collection *From Max Weber* in the section on 'religion', while the section on 'social structures' includes extracts from 'Hinduism and Buddhism', and 'Confucianism and Taoism', in that order. In fact, the *Zg* is situated in *GARS* between the sections on the economic ethics of Confucianism and Taoism, and those of Hinduism and Buddhism, the latter being followed by 'Ancient Judaism'. For the tensions he is examining in the essay exist between religions of *salvation* and the 'world', and Confucianism is not – according to Weber – a salvation religion. Indeed, to the extent that it did not develop the cosmocentric or theocentric dualism constitutive of salvation religion, Weber concurs with Hegel that '*Chinese* religion . . . cannot be what *we* call religion'[43] since here, 'heaven has no higher meaning than Nature',[44] and individuality is not buttressed by anything akin to what 'we' would call conscience.

> The idea of salvation was naturally completely absent from Confucian ethics. The Confucian had a desire to be 'saved' neither from the migration of souls nor from punishment in the beyond (both of which were unknown to Confucianism) nor from life (which was affirmed) nor from the given social world, nor from evil or original sin (of which he knew nothing) . . . nor from anything other than the undignified barbarism of social rudeness.[45]

While for the panglossian Confucian the world is the best of all possible worlds, the problematic of the *Zg* only emerges with an ethical or ontological dualism, between 'the world' and a higher principle which is the source of the world's meaning. If Weber's only interest had been why rational capitalism failed to develop in China, the India essay would have followed immediately. The typological character of the *Zg*, and the sheer volume of the sociology of religion, suggests that we view the studies on China, India and Ancient Judaism as studies of historical individuals in their own right, and as neither 'control evidence' for the 'Protestant Ethic thesis',[46] nor as stages in an evolutionary or teleological schema of development.[47] Weber's corpus cannot be viewed as a 'history of the present' or a developmental history of the Occident. While Occidental rationalism is clearly at the centre of his concerns, in the studies in the sociology of religion transcend them, at which point Occidental rationalism becomes a reference point for comparative analysis, an unavoidable means of historical sociological orientation.

Although world-historical *interest* in the religions of China and India rests in the main upon the extent to which ethics of everyday conduct are imbued with magic and irrational quests for salvation, the construction of a unified world-historical process of rationalisation is, if it exists at all, at best a heuristic device auxiliary to the actual practice of the historian, the understanding of historical individuals. Weber himself does not always make this clear.

> the stage of rationalisation which a religion represents there are above all two standards of measurement which are in many ways internally related. On the one hand the degree to which it has divested itself of *magic*. Then the degree to which it has brought the relationship between God and world and, accordingly, its own ethical relationship to the world, into a systematic unity.[48]

But the scale constituted by these stages is logical rather than historical, the comparison between world religions it facilitates purely formal. Despite the similarity of the China–India–Judea order to Hegel's philosophy of history, Weber offers a disclaimer. 'The *sequence* of reflections . . . proceeds geographically, from East to West, only by accident. In truth, not the external spatial distribution but, as close reflection will perhaps show, reasons of expediency, have been decisive.'[49] And he makes the following remark about the 'relative autonomy' of antiquity and, by implication, of Chinese and Indian culture.

> A genuinely analytic study comparing the stages of development of the ancient *polis* with those of the medieval city would be welcome and productive. . . . Of course I say this on the assumption that such a comparative study would not aim at finding 'analogies' and 'parallels', as is done by those engrossed in the currently fashionable enterprise of constructing general schemes of development. The aim should, rather, be precisely the opposite: to identify and define the individuality of each development, the characteristics which made one conclude in a manner so different from that of the other. This done, one can then determine the causes which led to these differences.[50]

## MODERNITY, INCOMMENSURABILITY AND CONFLICT

### Forms of unconditionality

Despite these caveats, I read the *Zg* not only as an account of the experience of a universalist religious ethics which runs up against the orders and powers of the world, but as a rudimentary theory of modernity. My concern is less with the reconstruction of a developmental schema, at the end of which lies 'modernity' as a product which has emancipated itself, as an explanandum, from the rationalisation process which produced it, than with the manner in which Weber employs neo-Kantian value philosophy. For each value sphere he identifies both the intrinsic logic which governs a particular type of practice and the 'cultural value' which grounds that practice, what Schluchter calls 'partial world views'. He then drives these partial world views to the point at which they become 'sublimated' into total world views. The oppositions he establishes between religious ethics and the world then become significant, not as oppositions between a universalist ethics and a series of partial world views, but between different universalist principles.

Within any salvation religion the opposition between religious ethics and the world presupposes that a religious ethic is the only perspective from which the world's existence could be justified, the single means with which the specific senselessness of economic, political, artistic, sexual or intellectual relationships can be overcome. The meaning of the world, however differentiated that world might be, remains the same. Thus, an ethic of brotherliness is to apply not merely to the practices of a religious community but also to economic or political relationships. For Weber, the actualisation of such an ultimate value is hindered not by a series of intrinsic, circumscribed logics, but by a series of other ultimate values. His interest in the economic sphere is not in the practical unavoidability of economic relationships, but in economism; in the political sphere not the practical unavoidability of political relationships, but in warfare as the ultimate source of the world's meaning; and so on.

This approach gives him a theory of modernity as secularisation which remains peculiarly theological. For what he is arguing is not that 'modernity' signifies the inability of a universalist, Christian ethics to 'hold the world together', and that the result is a modern, pluralist culture in which different cultural practices follow their own immanent logics. This impression is certainly given in the passage in the essay on Eduard Meyer in which he writes of 'the total "modern" "culture", i.e. that Christian capitalistic constitutional [*rechtsstaatlich*] "culture" which "radiates" from Europe and is an enormous tangle of "cultural values" which may be considered from the most varied "viewpoints" '.[51] But the idea that there is a conflict between spheres of validity implies, in the language of contemporary cultural debate, that the 'grand narrative' of brotherly love gives way not to a series of local narratives, but to a plurality of alternative grand narratives which attempt to provide answers to the same absolutist questions raised by theology.[52] The existence of a variety of grand narratives is the existence of a variety of standpoints from which conflicts between value spheres, between forms of rationality, could be held to be *aufgehoben*.

And from the perspectives of these other, secular, modern grand narratives, religion comes to be regarded as one value sphere among others, a part of the world, possessing nothing more than its own immanent dignity. It is the analysis contained in the *Zg* which enables us to understand Weber's remark in 'Science as a Vocation' that 'precisely the ultimate and most sublime values have retreated from the public sphere [*Öffentlichkeit*] either into the netherworldly realm of mystical life or into the brotherliness of the immediate relationships between individuals'.[53] The cultivation of brotherliness, far from providing the grounds for the unity of culture, seems to be limited to its own sphere of jurisdiction.

But what Weber is also trying to express here is the idea of the secularisation of *Beruf*. The point is not just that *Beruf* has degenerated from calling to profession, from a religious anchorage for all non-religious activities to the pursuit of those activities on the basis of their own laws. Of course, for Weber this has largely happened. But through the distinction between validity and existence, cultural and objective significance, between values and the purposes into which they are forged in rational-teleological action, the concept of *Beruf* can be shown to have modern functional equivalents, embodied in the idea that the ultimate value which grounds my limited secular strivings might give a meaning to everything else, might be the only value worth holding. This is the reason that when Weber writes that the old gods ascend from their graves and take the form of impersonal forces, he does not conceptualise them in a truly polytheistic way. For Weber's version of neo-Kantianism, culture is not a pantheon. The incommensurability of which so much is made in the literature has nothing to do with pluralism or relativism, nor does it support an organic theory of culture. How could it? While modern polytheism is not the fragmentation of a substantial, original unity, or singular essence, the irrevocable loss of the alleged unity guaranteed by monotheism gives way to a series of alternatives all of which might provide the same guarantee. Because he believes that loss to be temporary, the classificatory exercise which makes up much of Habermas's discussion of the *Zg* in the *Theory of Communicative Action* misses this point. Modern culture is a tangle, not a table, of cultural values, a tangle whose increasing complexity is a product of the variety of attempts to unravel it, a tangle of the 'only' perspectives from which the world and the self can be justified. An empirical cultural science can at most disentangle a few fibres. This is part of the meaning of the research programme Weber set down at the end of *The Protestant Ethic*.

### The natural sib

The first tension is historical rather than logical, and merely establishes the perspective of brotherliness from which the essay will proceed. The decisive difference between the natural sib and the religious community founded upon prophecies of salvation is that the religious ethic of brotherliness 'has simply taken over the original principles of social and ethical conduct which the association of neighbours had offered'.[54] The neighbourhood association 'has known two elementary principles: (1) the dualism of in-group and out-group morality; (2) for in-group morality, simple reciprocity: "As you do unto me I shall do unto you" '.[55] The significance of a universalistic, as opposed to a particularistic ethic of brotherliness, for the development of European culture, is made clearer in *Ancient Judaism*. By 'the dualism of in-group and out-group morality' Weber means what he takes to be the decisive feature of Jewish ethics, that relationships with strangers, especially economic relationships, were a matter of ethical indifference. The world-historical significance of a universalist ethic of brotherliness, whose hour of birth for Weber was the community of the eucharists in Antioch, is that, in principle, no-one is excluded from membership of the community of faith it defines.

Because the ethic of brotherliness which lay at the heart of Christianity merely universalised a principle which was already operative within an exclusive group, the conflict between the two is not an essential feature of the *Zg*. In the interests of systematic completeness Schluchter mistakenly added the family to the sixfold classification, referring to the natural sib as if it had the same status as the other spheres. But the conflict between a universalist ethic of brotherliness and the natural sib is simply a difference between ranges of applicability of the same principle, between remaining within and transgressing limits. It is not a clash between rival principles or fundamental forces. Weber makes it clear, in the sentence directly preceding his discussion of the 'economic sphere', that it is this latter clash to which the essay is addressed.

> This religious brotherliness always conflicts with the orders and powers of the world, the more so the more consistently it is carried through. And indeed, the more these orders and powers are rationalised and sublimated according to their own laws, the more rigidly this division tends to hold true. And that is what matters here.[56]

### The economic sphere

A cursory reading of the *Zg* suggests that this tension reaches its height in 'the struggle in principle between ethical rationalisation and the process of rationalisation in the domain of economics'[57] and becomes qualitatively distinct under conditions of a (modern) market economy. For Weber, 'every purely personal relationship of man to man, of whatever sort and including complete enslavement, may be subjected to ethical requirements and ethically regulated'.[58] But 'where the market is allowed to follow its own autonomous tendencies, its participants do not look towards the persons of each other but only toward the commodity'. Therefore, the market is 'fundamentally alien to any type of fraternal relationship',[59] and stands outside the limits of ethical jurisdiction.

The link between depersonalisation and 'modernity' had been made more directly by Simmel in the *Philosophy of Money*: 'The general tendency . . . undoubtedly moves in the direction of making the individual more and more dependent upon the achievements of people, but less upon the personalities that lie behind them.'[60]

But there are two ways in which the bald statement of this link is likely to mislead. Firstly, the tension between an ethic of brotherly love and 'the inevitabilities of economic life' has existed as long as that ethic. It is not distinctively 'modern'.[61] This is why an account of Weber's theory of modernity which stresses the '*Eigengesetzlichkeit*' of different practices will never say enough. This is well illustrated in the medieval church's attitude to usury. The significance of the question of usury for Weber lies in its relation to 'the general and primordial dualisms of in-group and out-group morality'.[62] From the perspective of the medieval church's universalism of grace, the taking of interest from 'outsiders', for which an ethical dualism provides, was to be prohibited. Yet the demands constituted by material *interest*, combined with the inevitabilities of economic life, led the Catholic Church to allow the demand for the prohibition of usury to slacken through 'legalistic circumventions of all sorts'.[63] In so far as it did so it was forced into an ethical compromise. The second possible confusion derives from the equation of 'decreasing dependence upon persons' with 'increasing tension between ethics and economics', an equation which suggests that the term 'ethical' is inapplicable to forms of association founded on impersonality. If this were the case, Weber's most celebrated work, which traces the causal significance of religious ethics for economic practice, would be incomprehensible. Of this more below.

Weber constructs a tension between one (universalist) type of religious ethics and economics by driving their logics to their limits. At first this tension appears to be that between the radical personalism of brotherly love and the radically impersonal character of a universally valid – i.e. inescapable – market mechanism. But if we recall the distinction between cultural and objective significance, the importance of the opposition becomes clear. From the perspective of brotherliness, even if religious ethics is confronted with something more than the inevitabilities of economic life, namely, the market mechanism within which 'no personal bonds of any sort exist',[64] that market mechanism remains the economic sphere's intrinsic logic. It cannot be given the status of an 'ultimate value' with universal validity.

But, argues Weber, this is precisely the status it *can* be given. The impersonality of the market – an intrinsic logic – can become the personality of the market[65] – a cultural value. All ideologies which found human freedom on the freedom of the market, or turn the market into the analytical foundation for the unity of culture, make this move. And in another sense, Marxist economism, which founds the unity of culture on a mode of production, is as radically opposed to brotherliness as are ideologies of the market.[66] But at the same time, in religions of salvation 'there lay a tendency towards a unique depersonalisation of love in the sense of acosmism'. Which means, a tendency for the cultural value of brotherly love to collapse into the intrinsic logic of the institutions which were supposed to uphold it.

Since the meaning of Catholicism's institutional grace is that salvation is accessible in principle to all, 'the level of personal ethical accomplishments must ... be made compatible with average human qualities, and this in practice means that it will be set quite low'.[67] The levelling and depersonalising effect of a univeralist ethics of brotherliness which claims practical efficacy is embodied in the 'bureaucratic' character of the Catholic Church, which 'oscillated between a relatively magical and a relatively ethical and soteriological orientation'.[68] This refers to the 'fact' that the effect of sacramental and institutional grace, and the practices associated therewith, particularly confession, was that the ethical demands on the individual were less stringent than the ethic of brotherliness logically implies. The possibility of a periodical release of ethical pressure through confession conferred on sins the character of *discrete* actions to which discrete penances corresponded. The Catholic, as Weber has it, 'lived ethically from hand to mouth' because no bureaucratic institution founded on universalist principles can feasibly demand of the individual the type of *inner* conviction required for action in accordance with an ethic of brotherly love.[69]

To summarise, the distinctions between cultural value and intrinsic logic, and between brotherliness and the market, allows Weber to construct a conflict which is 'adequate' in so far as the universalism of brotherliness confers on it a paradoxically impersonal character which mirrors that of the commodity form, and the commodity form is 'reified' according to personalist principles which mirror those of brotherly love. But this adequacy is analytic rather than historical. Even if the conflict between an ethic of brotherliness and the market is a 'modern phenomenon', a definition of 'modernity' cannot be constructed on the basis of a conflict between 'religious ethics' and 'economics' as such.

In fact, the 'Protestant ethic thesis' is an account of one way in which the tension between religion and economics can be overcome 'in a principled and inward manner' through 'the paradox of the Puritan ethic of vocation'.[70] The world-historical significance of the concept of vocation is its renunciation of a universalistic in favour of a particularist grace, its specific contribution to 'the world dominion of unbrotherliness'.

*The Protestant Ethic* examines the capacity of 'an attitude towards life',[71] to generate a constant motivation, an attitude for which the 'conflict between individual and ethic (in Soren Kierkegaard's sense) did not exist',[72] and which provided for a reconciliation between 'ethics and economics'. The decisive difference between Catholicism and Puritanism lies in 'those psychological sanctions which . . . gave a direction to practical conduct and held the individual to it'.[73] For Puritanism, which Weber describes as a religion of virtuosos, a particularism of grace went hand in hand with the internal character of the psychological sanctions governing conduct. The devaluation of institutional grace and the absence of confession removed the possibility of momentary or intermittent relief from the burden of inner conviction. As the Church becomes invisible, so the sins of the individual are no longer discernible as discreet actions. Or rather, for Catholicism that which gives sense to and provides for the continuity between practices is institutional externality, for Puritanism it is personal inwardness, the 'total personality' of the individual. Precisely because salvation is not in principle accessible to all, the need to *prove* oneself saved in worldly activity becomes all the more urgent. For the Catholic, the combination of otherworldliness and the necessities of the 'world' confers on all worldly activity the status of an ethical compromise. For the Puritan, the need for proof, and for 'world mastery' makes possible 'the *religious* rationalisation of the world in its most extreme form'.[74] The paradoxical consequence of this will be that in contributing to the rationalisation of the economic sphere, Puritanism itself that sphere's logic to its limit, at which point 'victorious capitalism, since it rests on mechanical foundations, needs its support no longer'.[75] It stands at a distance from the Puritan idea of vocation and even further from the universalism of brotherliness.

One of the fruits of Weber's comparative studies was a comparison between the ritualistic character of the Catholic Church and that of the Chinese bureaucracy. Both make possible what Weber calls a rationalisation 'from without', but neither make possible a rationalisation of the 'world', since Catholicism's means of grace are otherworldly, and Confucianism's world-affirming character renders superfluous any rationalisation beyond that required for world adjustment. Ascetic Puritanism makes possible a religious rationalisation of the economic world because in its most rational form there is no distinction between individual and ethic. The constituents of the Puritan sect, unlike those of the Catholic Church, are not expected to perform a set of discrete acts, and unlike the Confucian – or the ideal Simmelian! – they are not 'a complex of useful particular traits'.[76] which accord with an external ethical demand placed on the individual. The absence of this distinction is not due to the fact that the individual has attained to the heights of an ethical ideal, or actualised an ethical potential. Ethics is understood in a different way. For the Puritan, the 'striving for unity from within',[77] 'the attempt to take the self by the forelock and pull it out of the mud, forming it into a "personality" '[78] means that life becomes 'a whole placed methodically under a transcendental goal'.[79] 'Ethics' here refers not simply to a theoretically rational demand placed upon the world, but also to a practically rational manner of acting in the world which ensures a *continuity* between activities which would otherwise remain discreet.

Weber himself employs the terms 'ethic of conviction' and 'ethic of responsibility'. But when he does so he writes not as an 'ethical rigorist enthusiastic about a formal, abstract freedom' but as one who believes that 'every human being, no matter how slightly gifted he is, no matter how subordinate his position may be, has a natural need to formulate a life-view, a conception of the meaning of life and of its purpose'. These are the words of Kierkegaard, whose influence on Weber remains virtually unex-plored but whose formulation of the relationship between the ethical and the continuity of practice, and of the idea of the 'total personality', finds its way into Weber's analyses at numerous points. It is difficult to read Weber's account of the relative discontinuity of practice of both Catholic and Confucian rationalism, and the difference between them both and Puritanism, without recalling Kierkegaard's distinction between the aesthetic and the ethical in *Either/Or*, a text of which Weber was surely aware.

For Kierkegaard the aesthetic is that by which a person immediately *is* what he/she is. The ethical is that by which a person *becomes* who he/she is. The conditions of possibility of enjoyment for the individual who adheres to the aesthetic view of life are external. They are not posited, but must be accepted as given. Therefore, the aesthetic self is a series of capabilities the selection from which will be a type of choice, but the capabilities which determine the individual as a result of this choice will do so only 'more or less'. The difference between capabilities is only a relative difference, as a result of which the individual may experience momentary pleasures, but will remain in a state of despair, since those pleasures have no internal connection. Choice for the aesthetic self is a choice between mere possibilities. By contrast, the ethical self knows only an absolute difference between good and evil, a difference which provides the self with a constant criterion for its choice. The ethical self chooses the good, and at the same time evil as its concomitant opposite, as a consequence of which choice between possibilities can never have the appearance of indifference, or of an enthusiasm the rationale for which is simply boredom with a previous choice. In choosing the ethical the personality is consolidated: 'to choose gives a person's being a solemnity, a quiet dignity, that is never entirely lost'.[80] To choose is to choose onself in one's 'eternal validity'. The route to this validity is traversed through despair. Ethical despair, unlike that of the aesthete, is despair turned to good account. Instead of despairing over the particular, turning to another particular, and despairing or negating it once again, and so on *ad infinitum*, thereby remaining in an immediacy which is external, the ethical individual chooses despair, carries it through and attains the absolute.

Kierkegaard insists that this critique of immediacy, and the idea that the absolute is attainable through a series of dialectical transformations, must be distinguished from Hegelianism by means of a distinction between doubt and despair. For Hegel, the doubt which provided for the negation of the immediate was a despairing doubt because it required the philosopher to point out to the consciousness engaged in negation that the negation of a previous truth was determinate, that it was the negation of that from which it results, that it was not the doubt of scepticism but amounted to a new positivity. For Kierkegaard, Hegel's doubt cannot be truly despairing, since the movement which results from the philosopher's doubt is a necessary movement, while despair has to be chosen. Doubt is only thought's despair, while 'despair is personality's doubt'.[81] Philosophic doubt can occur irrespective of its effect on the individual. Therefore, 'despair is an expression of the total personality, doubt only of thought'.[82] The difference between doubt and despair defines that between the partial and total personality.

Because Kierkegaard's ethical life is not an ethically rigoristic life, it preserves the aesthetic within it, rather than simply imposing a set of formal standards upon life. While the aesthetic individual sees *possibilities* engendered by forces which come upon him/her from the outside, the ethical individual sees *tasks* which express that individual's sovereignty. But in order to buttress this claim Kierkegaard must insist that this abolishes the distinction between individual and ethic. For if such a distinction exists, the tasks of the ethical individual remain duties whose origin is external, an externality indistinguishable from the aesthete's source of enjoyment, and therby merely co-ordinate with it. Once the ethical has been concretised, duty has an 'absolute significance'. The individual who chooses himself expresses 'his absolute dependence and absolute freedom in their identity with one another',[83] and is himself a task. And the aim of his/her activity is not an abstract, detached self, but one which exists 'in living interaction with these specific surroundings, these life conditions, this order of things'.[84] The difference between the ethical and the aesthetic resides ultimately in the fact that the dialectical character of the ethical provides a vector for identity which places the self in the world and relates its activities internally, while the aesthetic provides no such vector, and detaches the self from the world in proportion to the externality of the relation between its activities. This is why aestheticism often resolves itself into egoism. If life is a series of hastily experienced stages, events or actions, between which there appears to be no coherence, the only way to meet the demand that the world be a meaningful totality, a demand which will persist even in the face of this incoherence, is the type of egoistic retreat criticised by Nietzsche in his second untimely meditation, or the reserve which Simmel saw as the obvious response to the exhaustion of the senses in the modern metropolis.

Kierkegaard is significant here because of his formulation of the concrete character of the ethical and its link to the ideal of the total personality whose sense of duty derives from within. For it is only the concretisation of the ethical which makes possible the world-mastery associated with Puritanism. And it is only in this sense that Weber's remark that Puritanism overcomes the tension between religious ethics and the economic world with *inner consistency* is understandable. 'Ethics' here designates neither the universalism of brotherliness nor ethical rigorism.

The consequences for action entailed by the concretisation of the ethical in Puritanism have frequently been misinterpreted by commentators for whom any alternative to a universalist ethics is relativism or a radical, unprincipled, 'instrumental' individualism. Of course, for Weber the voluntaristic character of the sects 'formed *one of* the most important historical foundations of modern "individualism" '.[85] But 'the expression individualism includes the most heterogeneous things imaginable'.[86] And the central significance of 'individualism' associated with ascetic Protestantism, even as it is expressed in the idea of the 'total personality', is precisely that 'something more than a garnishing for purely egocentric motives is involved'.[87] 'Absolute and conscious ruthlessness in acquisition has often stood in the closest connection with the strictest conformity to tradition.'[88] Capitalist figures such as Pierpont Morgan, Rockerfeller or Jakob Fugger 'were not the creators and were not to become the bearers of the specifically Occidental bourgeois mentality'. Why? Because '*they* stood and they stand "beyond good and evil" ',[89] they lacked the peculiar *qualities* which were the distinctive criteria for membership of the Puritan sects and their secularised functional equivalents, the American business clubs. The conduct upon which a premium was placed in the Puritan sects was that which enabled one to prove oneself before God *and* other human beings. It was this combination of forms of 'holding one's own' which 'delivered' the 'spirit' of modern capitalism its ethos. 'Only the glory of God and one's own duty, not human vanity, is the motive for the Puritans, and today only the duty to one's calling.'[90] Even in Kierkegaard, the distinction between one's own duty and vanity provides for the possibility of *civic virtue*. For Weber too, 'world-mastery' requires a site for its exercise. And 'the cities, the seat of the middle class with its rational business activities, are the seats of ascetic virtue.'[91]

The centrality of the city as one condition for the development of an ethic of world mastery is implicitly ignored by those interpretations of Weber which point to Puritanism's 'absolute individualism'[92] or its 'egocentric *Berufsaskese* with its particularism of grace', a particularism which Habermas describes, inevitably, as 'the regression of the ascetic ethic of vocation . . . behind the level already attained in the communicatively developed ethic of brotherliness'.[93] The difference between Habermas and Weber is nowhere better expressed. His imagery is a repetition of Horkheimer's in *The Eclipse of Reason* (1947). As the object of an eclipse disappears only temporarily, the return of reason is the promised fruit of critical theoretical labour. The communicative, universalist ethic of brotherliness, which was never actualised institutionally – certainly not in the Catholic Church – having been superseded by an ethic which from the point of view of a communicative ethic amounts to a regression, returns and is actualised at the level of the formal properties of talk.

By contrast, Weber's interest in the concrete ethic of world mastery is in its capacity to generate voluntaristic forms of *association* premissed upon a distinction between duty and (egocentric) vanity, on the capacity, as Kierkegaard put it, to choose oneself into the world at the same time as one chooses oneself out of the world, to be 'in' the world but not 'of' the world. The peculiar tension between involvement and detachment which is the pervasive feature of sect membership, and of the everyday life of the Puritan, confers on Puritan 'individualism' its peculiar pathos. Chapter 6 will show that it provides the analytic framework for the second half of 'Politics as a Vocation'. Part of the explanation for Weber's undeniably nostalgic attitude towards the Puritan sects lies in the centrality of the question of the *qualities of the human beings* who constituted them. Weber's concern with the consequences of belief for *action* ties up with the substantive significance of 'accomplishment' for the concept of *Kultur*.[94] Habermas's theorisation of communicative rationality obscures this by equating *any* form of human association or solidarity which is not universalisable with a fall from grace. While Weber limits himself to the investigation of varieties of forms of intersubjectivity, Habermas attempts to formulate intersubjectivity itself, and to treat Weber's theory of intersubjectivity as inadequate, when it is non-existent.

Whereas Puritan asceticism escapes the tension between religious ethics and economics by moving in the direction of the world, to such an extent that the world no longer requires its support, mysticism escapes that tension by moving resolutely away from the world, towards contemplation. It is a genuine escape from the world. We can formalise the relationship between Catholicism, Puritanism and mysticism as follows. In Catholicism, the universalism of brotherliness clashes with the unbrotherliness of market relationships in such a way that Catholicism can be described as a failed escape from the world. In Puritan asceticism, the unbrotherliness of ethical particularism was already compatible with, and provided for the rationalisation of, economic relations which were conducted 'without regard for persons'. In contrast to the Catholic, the Puritan could view economic activity as significant for his 'personality', could engage in it on the basis of its cultural, not its objective, significance. In mysticism, ''benevolence', which does not at all inquire into the man to whom and for whom it sacrifices'[95] is already analytically compatible with impersonal economic relations, which makes mysticism a successful escape from the world.

### The political sphere

Weber formulates the tension between religion and politics in a manner parallel to that between religion and economics.

> The problem of tensions with the political order emerged for redemption religions out of the basic demand for brotherliness. And in politics, as in economics, the more rational the political order became the sharper the problems of those tensions became.[96]

The condition of possibility of this tension is the attainment of a stage of rationalisation higher than that represented by pantheism. As long as the systematisation of the God/world relation remained pantheistic, the type of tension to which Weber alludes could not develop. 'The emergence of a pantheon entails the specialisation and characterisation of the various gods as well as the allocation of constant attributes and the differentiation of their jurisdiction'.[97] And the idea of a political local god is in turn a special case of such specialisation.

The classical bearer of the important phenomenon of a political local god was the *polis*, yet it was by no means the only one. On the contrary, every permanent political association had a special god who guaranteed the success of political action of the group. When fully developed, this god was altogether exclusive with respect to outsiders. The stranger was ... not only a political, but a religious alien.[98]

The link between the scope of politics and religion, their shared particularity, renders a tension between them meaningless. More specifically, there is no tension between action subject to an 'ethical' interpretation, and the matter-of-factness of politics. The relationship between functional deity and world is natural rather than ethical. And 'the fact that a god was regarded as a local deity ... did not lead to monotheism, but rather tended to strengthen religious particularism. Conversely, the development of local gods resulted in an uncommon strengthening of political particularism.'[99]

The space within which a tension between religion and politics could develop was opened up by an ethic of brotherliness. Weber contrasts a universalist ethic of brotherliness and 'the pragma of violence which no political action can escape'.[100] Reasons of state – and here Weber refers to the modern, bureaucratic state apparatus, which like the modern economy, 'is less accessible to substantive moralisation than were the patriarchal orders of the past'[101] – 'follow, externally and internally, their own laws'.[102] The indispensability of violence is the 'intrinsic logic' of the political sphere, just as the market mechanism is the intrinsic logic of the economic sphere.

For a universalist ethics all forms of particularism are 'non-ethical', and the tension between religion and politics turns out, from the point of view of salvation religion, to be a tension between the ethical and non-ethical interpretation of human conduct. But once again, as in his interpretation of the economic sphere, Weber drives the intrinsic logic of violence to its limits in order to construct a tension between two universal validity claims. He writes: 'With the complete rationalisation of both religion and politics, their mutual strangeness becomes especially sharp ... *War*, as the consummated threat of violence, creates, precisely in modern political communities, a pathos and feeling of community.'[103] From the point of view of brotherliness, warfare is objectionable not because its conduct depends upon an adherence to purely technical conditions of possibility – an enemy which poses a merely physical threat to the political community – but because the individual is expected to face *death* in the community's interests. Because the community of warfare is a community unto death, death in battle differs from an everyday death, which would be significant only because it was unavoidable. In war, and only in war, 'the individual can *believe* that he knows that he is dying "for" something'.[104] This answer to 'for what?' overcomes the specific senselessness of death. Thus, 'the very extraordinary quality of brotherliness in war, and of death in war . . . raises the competition between the brotherliness of religion and of the warrior community to its height'. The challenge of political activity to brotherliness is that it has cultural as well as objective significance.

One of the most significant attempts to assert the primacy of the political through the sublimation of an existential need is contained in the Weimar writings of Carl Schmitt. In view of the increased interest in Schmitt in recent years, and the alleged continuity between his and Weber's politics, a comparison between the way he and Weber establish the non-ethical nature of the political is in order.

It was only by restricting the concept of the political to that of the state[105] in a manner which may strike us as hopelessly out of date that Weber was able to analyse the tension between religion and politics. This makes perfect sense in the light of his account of the independence of 'provinces of culture'. Schmitt's position is that one sphere – the political – founds an anthropology, and is able to 'dominate' the others. The analyses of the incommensurability of religion and politics offered by Schmitt and Weber are only superficially the same. The first point here is that neither is analysing conflicting value spheres *per se*, but rather a series of tensions from one point of view – in Weber's case salvation religion, in Schmitt's politics. But they do not approach the relation between religion and politics 'from opposite ends' and reach the 'same' conclusion. While the conclusion of Weber's analysis of the compromises to which a universalistic ethic is subject is that 'religion' is or has become one form of association amongst others, Schmitt, having secured the analytical autonomy of the political, transforms it into a concept of the all-embracing 'total state'.

Weber argues that, in contrast to primitive heroism, modern

state systems appeal to some version of ethical right in order to justify the pursuit of wholly power-political interests. He then writes:

> To any consistent religious rationalisation, this must seem only an aping of ethics. Moreover, to draw the Lord's name into such violent political conflict must be viewed as a taking of His name in vain. In the face of this, the cleaner and only honest way may appear to be *the complete elimination of ethics from political reasoning*.[106]

In *The Religion of China* Weber suggests that the possibility of such elimination is dependent upon an (albeit forgotten) heroic tradition, and that its absence in China led to what for Weber appeared to be an undignified 'justification' of warfare, the conflation of *existential* imperatives which had the capacity to become universally binding, and *ethical* imperatives.[107] But its undignified character is a reflection not only of the 'intrusion' of ethics into politics and consequent devaluation of the political, but also of the degradation of an ethical principle to the status of a political means. The potential degradation of the ethical is nowhere greater than in warfare.[108] From the point of view of religious ethics, 'the inner-worldly consecration of death in war must appear as a glorification of fratricide',[109] an ethical embellishment presenting itself as an ethical foundation.

Weber's sensitivity here contrasts markedly with Schmitt's attempt to eliminate the ethical from the political. Schmitt will argue that the distinction between the political and the non-political is inadmissible in the face of democratisation and its main consequence – the potentially political nature of everything. As long as in the eighteenth century the state did not recognise society as an antithetical principle, and in the nineteenth the state stood 'above' society, then religion, economy, art, etc. were accorded a politically neutral status. But in the twentieth century: 'As a polemical concept against such neutralisations and depoliticisations of important domains appears the total state, which potentially embraces every domain.'[110] Schmitt grounds the identity of each domain, not in the neo-Kantian manner, by means of ultimate values, but through a value opposition: morality is grounded in the opposition between good and evil, aesthetics in that between beautiful and ugly, economics in that between profitable and unprofitable. He concludes that the irreducibility of politics has to be secured through an equivalent distinction, the friend/enemy relation. Formulating domains of culture on the basis of a value opposition was a clever and necessary move. Had he done so on the basis of an ultimate value alone, Schmitt may have been led to the neo-Aristotelian conclusion that the excellence peculiar to politics was to be friendship as a parallel to goodness, beauty, or truth. But even so, the point of the whole construction is to secure the exceptional status of the political and the idea of the total state, and requires a category mistake. The friend/enemy opposition is not a value opposition at all, but rather defines an existential situation. Schmitt drives the concept of enmity to its logical limit: 'The friend, enemy and combat concepts receive their real meaning precisely because they refer to the real possibility of physical killing.'[111] Schmitt admits that 'has no normative meaning, but an existential meaning only'.[112] War can be 'justified' only politically, and that means instrumentally or tactically. If a war be justified by the claim that it is the war to end all wars, that it is the last war of humanity, after which the Idea of humanity would finally be actualised, this 'degrades the enemy into moral and other categories'.[113] Of all modern political philosophies, liberalism represents the starkest negation of the political, shifting truly political conflict into the spheres of the ethical (in its 'individualism'), the economic (in its doctrine of market competition) and the intellectual (in its emphasis on the 'discussion' of privately held opinions).[114] Instead of generating and maintaining a *public* friend/enemy distinction which is the essence of the political, the state becomes a mere 'ventilating system'[115] for *private* conflict. Liberalism 'recognises with self-evident logic the autonomy of different human realms but drives them towards specialisation and even towards complete isolation'.[116]

The reference to neo-Kantianism is obvious, but in Weber's case the complete isolation of value spheres is not a major thesis. The concept of vocation is ultimately what grounds his account of the need to measure up to the workaday world of political relationships. But his resolution of the tension between religion and politics is achieved in a manner wholly divergent from that recommended by Schmitt, which latter depends upon the claim that everything is potentially political. At an institutional level, Weber *does* accept that the political community *may* be capable of subsuming 'non-political' spheres, of 'arrogating to itself all the possible contents towards which associational conduct might be directed'.[117] Indeed, 'Germany . . . has been made into a unified economic territory . . . in a purely political manner'.[118] But theoretically, the contents of the *Zg*, through the very fact that it considers tensions from the point of view of universalist religious ethics, cannot be arrogated to political theory. For Weber, the dignity of a 'non-ethical' politics is a dignity which cannot undermine ethics.

In view of the fact that Weber's analysis of modernity culminates in an account of a plurality of universal validity claims, Schmitt's political theory, and the theory of culture which underpins it, must be seen as an example of one such claim. The few published comparisons between the two, which are restricted to the relationship between their accounts of the state or of political leadership or of parliamentarianism, all miss the point that these accounts are dependent upon different theories of culture and personality.[119] It might be argued that Weber was a liberal with a liberal concept of culture in which the political is simply one form of association among others. Leo Strauss suggests that this view would in turn be criticised by Schmitt on the grounds that 'culture' is always the cultivation of nature, that human culture presupposes human nature, a natural mode of human connection, and that the political is such a mode. On this account, the political would be foundational for, rather than a dimension of, culture. Weber's account of the logic of the cultural sciences is too anti-naturalistic to allow for this possibility. The claim that 'we *are* cultural *beings*' contains no state of nature argument. We are cultural beings because we are not natural beings. Chapter 6 will show that Weber's account of the political does imply that it threatens to fall outside the logic of 'culture', that its doing so seems to be the product of the type of category mistake required by Schmitt. But the difference is that the political becomes the most fruitful site for an examination of what Weber means, in the end, by 'culture'. He makes no foundational claim for it.

The difference between Weber's and Schmitt's concepts of culture is one between levels of abstraction. Schmitt describes his theory of the 'state of exception' as the *philosophical–metaphysical* basis of sovereignty, not as a juristic or even cultural scientific problem. The exception, and with it the entire conceptual apparatus with which Schmitt constructs his political theory, is tied to 'a philosophy of concrete life'[120] in which life 'breaks through the crust of a mechanism that has become torpid by repetition'.[121] We have seen how far Weber was from such vitalism, a *scientific* 'distancing' which enabled him time and again to co-ordinate points of view without reconciling them through pluralism or through the subordination of many viewpoints under one.

## The aesthetic and erotic spheres

Weber's analysis of the non-rational or anti-rational 'life forces' of the aesthetic and erotic follows the same course as that of economics and politics.

With respect to the aesthetic sphere, he distinguishes between 'the sublimation of the religious ethic and the quest for salvation' and 'the development of the autonomous logic of art'. He then describes this relationship as a tension between the *binding* quality of *meaning* and the *contingency* of artistic *form*. But once again, he drives the inherent logic of art to its limits in order to show how:

art constitutes itself as a cosmos of ever more consciously grasped and independent values. However it might be interpreted, it assumes the function of a thisworldly *salvation* from everyday life and, above all, from the increasing pressure of theoretical and practical rationalism.[122]

The link between the redemptory function of art and 'modernity' consists in the fact that a shift from ethical to aesthetic evaluation is 'a common characteristic of intellectualist epochs'.[123] In the conclusion to *The Religion of China* he had expressed this link in more general terms: 'for every stratum of genteel intellectuals the concept of 'sin' tends to have been felt to be embarrassing or worthless, and to be replaced through conventional or feudal or aesthetically formulated variants ("indecent" or "tasteless")'.[124] Our discussion of the intellectual sphere will tease out this link, and those between intellectualism and all other 'psychological substitutes' for salvation religion, in more detail.

With respect to the erotic sphere, Weber contrasts the rationalism of a universalist ethics of brotherliness with the inner, purely naturalistic and 'irrational' logic of sexual love. Then, formulating the development from the 'naive naturalism of sex' to eroticism in a somewhat superficial manner, he once again pushes this naturalistic logic to its limits.

The total content of human existence has now gone beyond the organic cycle of peasant life; life has been increasingly enriched in cultural content. . . . All this has worked, through the distancing of life content from that which is merely naturally given, toward a further enhancement of the special position of eroticism. *Eroticism was raised into the sphere of conscious enjoyment* . . . Despite, or perhaps because of this, it appeared to be a gateway to the most irrational *and thereby real* kernel of life.[125]

Eroticism for Weber represents a challenge to salvation religion in so far as it represents a consciously cultivated *return* to or rediscovery of a set of fundamental forces which not only govern sexual relationships but ground culture. Eroticism is sublimated naturalism.

## CONCLUSION

The *Wissenschaftslehre*, an account of the logic of cultural science, contains many hints that Weber's version of neo-Kantian value philosophy was one which enabled him to develop a theory of culture which was tragic rather than pluralistic or relativistic, which could not and would not develop a systematic account of the relationship between value spheres. The $Zg$ is the site on which this theory seems to be worked out most explicitly. But to understand this more fully, to see what is really at stake in this essay, we need to be clear that there is a qualitative difference between Weber's discussion of the tensions between the religious sphere and those of economics, politics, art and the erotic, and that of that between religion and the intellectual sphere. For just as the religious sphere can take on an exceptional status by becoming the 'tincture' given to all others, so it is, in the end, through a rationalist, secular rhetoric that the other spheres are able to assume that same status. The challenge which the intellectual sphere offers to religion does not amount merely to a direct clash between science and religion, but is also expressed through those already discussed.

More importantly, Weber had to find a way, in the midst of his historical inquiry, of expressing the fact that here, it was the grounds of his own intellectual curiosity, of his own vocation, which might be held to be the grounds of all others. As a scientist, he wanted both to express this possibility and reject it. In the face of modern scientism, of self-empowerment, he wanted to preach scientific modesty, self-assertion, an understanding of the limits of intellectual curiosity. The next chapter discusses the difficulties he faced in doing so.

# Chapter 5

# The *Zwischenbetrachtung* II
## A dual theory of tragedy

Generally speaking, a broadening of consumption corresponds to the specialisation of production. Even the most intellectually and occupationally specialised people today read the newspaper and thereby indulge in a more extensive mental consumption than was possible a hundred years ago, for even the most versatile and widely interested person.

(Georg Simmel)

Before going about their daily business, modern human beings have become accustomed to sampling a ragout, to being forced into a kind of chase through all spheres of cultural life, from politics to the theatre to everything else imaginable.

(Max Weber)

'One must value it if there's a man still left nowadays who is striving to be something integral,' Walter said.
'There's no longer any such thing,' Ulrich countered. 'You only have to look into a newspaper. You'll find it's filled with immeasurable opacity. So many things come under discussion that it would surpass the intellectual capacity of a Leibniz. But one doesn't even notice it. One has become indifferent. There is no longer a whole man confronting a whole world, but a human something floating about in a universal culture-medium.'

(Robert Musil)

## INTRODUCTION

Though the sections in the *Zwischenbetrachtung* on economics, politics, aesthetics and the erotic were already set down in *Economy and Society* in 1913, the sections on the intellectual sphere and 'stages of religious world-rejection' first appeared in the first version of the *Zg* in the *Archiv für Sozialwissenschaft und Sozialpolitik* in 1915. The final, 1920 version of the essay contains additions to the section on the erotic, and the famous reference to the concept of the 'intellectual sacrifice'. Schluchter speaks of three versions of the essay.[1] But the sections on the intellectual sphere and stages of world rejection are not 'additions', but transform, for the first time, the material from *Economy and Society* into the essay known as the *Zwischenbetrachtung*. The centrality of the 'intellectual sphere' to that essay will now be elaborated.

## THE INTELLECTUAL SPHERE

### Truth as a cultural value

Weber includes both empirical science and philosophy in the intellectual sphere. A religious account of the meaning of the world, of the source of the unity of culture, is opposed both to the scientific transformation of the world into a causal mechanism[2] and to a speculative, metaphysical account of the world's meaning. Weber expresses this in strictly neo-Kantian terms: 'A salvation religion offers an ultimate position towards the world by virtue of a direct grasp of its 'meaning' [*Sinn*], not ultimate intellectual knowledge of the *existent* or the normatively *valid*.'[3] The tension between religion and empirical research is a tension between a transcendental anchorage for the meaningfulness of the world and an intrinsic logic governing a mode of activity – the investigation of the world's 'immanent' characteristics and causal connections. Weber suggests that a reconciliation between religion and the intellect is possible as long as intellectual activity is governed by the intrinsic logic of the life order of the scientific community. Empirical science cannot 'challenge' religion as long as it endeavours simply to 'say what is'. He argues that the practical rationalism of ascetic Protestantism effects just such a reconciliation. But once again, he suggests that it is precisely this practical rationalism of world mastery which pushes the intrinsic logic of the intellectual sphere to its limit. Not only can the intellect offer the individual the objective task of investigating the world's empirical constituents. It can go further, contribute to the development of his/her personality in such a way that it promises an alternative account of the world's meaning, the sublimation of conflicts between value spheres. 'In all the attempts of philosophy to make demonstrable that ultimate meaning and the practical position which follows from grasping it, it [salvation religion] sees nothing other than the intellect's endeavour to escape its own logic.'[4] Despite the fact that the intellect cannot make demonstrable the presuppositions upon which it has created a 'cosmos of natural causality', that 'in reality' it is one value sphere among others, 'science, in the name of "intellectual integrity", has come forward with the claim to represent the only reasoned view of the world'.[5]

## A universalist rhetoric

From the sublimation of intrinsic logics into cultural values there emerged a series of universal validity claims which challenge those embodied in salvation religions. Within the realm of 'social philosophy', this produced a series of the 'only' perspectives from which the world might be justified. But the significance of the 'intellectual sphere' for Weber lay not merely in the emergence of a self-sufficient science as the source of an alternative account of the genesis and structure of the physical world, of another total world view, but in its provision of a universalist, rationalist rhetoric by means of which the transformation from partial to total world view in *any* sphere might be effected. This is why he states that the lawful autonomy of individual spheres has been made conscious through 'the development of the possession of inner and outerworldly goods towards rationality [in economics and politics] and conscious endeavour [aesthetics and eroticism] sublimated through *knowledge*'.[6] The challenge a partial world view presents to universalist religious ethics is buttressed both by its provision of psychological substitutes for salvation, and by its claim to be the only *reasoned* view of reality, by its being an anchorage for the self and a foundation for the world.

Between 1900 and 1920 Heidelberg and Munich were home to numerous 'movements' which exemplified this elevation of the partial to the total, and every line of the *Zg* bears the marks of their influence.[7] The most obvious was the (vulgar) Marxist thesis that the world is only intelligible as an economic phenomenon. Marxism does not see itself as a *Weltanschauung* forced to assert itself in the face of others, but, as science, provides an account of the meaning of the world and of history. That meaning is contained in the politics of socialism.[8] Other examples were: the claim that the world is only intelligible as a political phenomenon, witnessed by the elevation of the state into a realm 'increasingly shrouded in mystical darkness'; the claim that the world is only intelligible as a sexual phenomenon, witnessed by the 'sexual health' movement of which Weber took the Freudian Otto Gross to be a representative; and the claim that the world is only intelligible as an aesthetic phenomenon, witnessed by followers of Nietzsche, especially the circle around Stefan George.[9]

Although the latter two appear to be examples of 'irrationalism', Weber was quick to spot the point at which the craving for 'irrational' experiences, when it becomes the object of conscious endeavour, is transformed into rationalism:

> the spheres of the irrational, the only spheres that intellectualism has not yet touched, are now raised into consciousness and placed under its lens. For in practice this is where the modern intellectualist form of romantic rationalism leads. This method of emancipation from intellectualism may well bring about the very opposite of what those who take to it conceive as its goal.[10]

The point had already been made by Rudolf Eucken.

> To the extent that those partial movements make a claim to power, limit and intersect one another, they must heighten the confusion against which they struggle; perhaps today nothing causes division as much as this striving for unity. Never was there so much talk of monism, and never was humanity so far from itself.[11]

These movements challenge religion in so far as they promise a form of *self-realisation* as a confirmation of the world's meaningfulness. Thus, Marxism promises self-realisation through labour, certain forms of Freudianism self-realisation through sexuality, the George circle self-realisation through art and certain features of the German revolution self-realisation through politics. Although Weber refused to operate with the perhaps banal concept of the 'sacred' in order to assert the equivalence of these movements and salvation religion, he did insist upon the ineliminability of the human desire that the world be a meaningful totality. While there is a tension in his thought between the belief that this desire is something we all possess and the belief that it is an intellectual's demand, Weber did reproach all such movements for failing to recognise their own intellectualism.

## Polytheism and social differentiation

I am not sure that this account of intellectualism has received the attention it deserves. An example of its neglect is Habermas's *Theory of Communicative Action*, in which, on the basis of Weber's remarks on polytheism, he derives a theory of social differentiation in which the substantial unity of reason is 'split apart' into 'value spheres' which increasingly and exclusively follow their own logics, a development which culminates in the resurrection of 'old gods' in a disenchanted form.[12] But what I have tried to show is that these gods were interesting to Weber not as indices of a pluralistic culture, but as a proliferation of 'totalising' standpoints. Habermas suggests that the concrete referent for the famous passages on gods and demons is the 'scientific enterprise', 'the modern state' or 'the artistic enterprise'.[13] But the passages on gods and demons have another and, to my mind, more interesting meaning. The difference between a demon and a god is that while a demon has an existence for itself alone, it only becomes a god when it gathers about itself a circle of followers, when there develops a regular relationship between the god and a human community. When Weber refers at the end of 'Science as a Vocation' to the need to discover the *demon* which holds the very fibres of one's life, he means a demon in the Socratic sense, but also in the sense of Schiller's remark on the gods having retreated into the human breast. When he refers to the old *gods* having ascended from their graves he refers to their (charismatic) power to generate forms of community based on the alleged universal validity of ultimate values, not simply to modern institutional differentiation. Habermas uses the term 'counter-culture' to refer to movements based on eroticism or aestheticism.[14] But in Weberian terms it refers to any denial of 'culture', any denial, in the face of one's own foundationalist claims, of the mutual irreducibility of the grounds of different practices. In short, to any belief in the *natural* grounds of human community.

Weber claimed that his accounts of the tensions between religious ethics and the orders and powers of the world depended upon his conferring on those orders and powers the most rational forms reality can assume. He added that this logical construction:

> could under certain circumstances be something more. For the rational, in the sense of the logical or teleological 'consistency' of an intellectual–theoretical or practical–ethical position has

and has had power over man, however limited and unstable this power was and is in the face of other powers of historical life.[15]

These circumstances are those prevailing in an 'intellectualist epoch', but also in one in which polytheism can only be understood in terms of the legacy of the monotheism which preceded it. There is no going back behind the Judaeo-Christian tradition. Or in Blumenberg's terms, for modern human beings its absolutist questions seem non-negotiable. This is the drama of the contemporary cultural position of science and philosophy – they are the source of the universalist rhetorics without which, today, the challenge of the old gods would amount to no more than a cultural drift into a benign pluralism. Modern polytheism has not

'reemerged' intact from beneath a tradition which suppressed it. A social movement grounded in the consistency of an intellectual–theoretical position demands of its adherents the attempt to make the whole of reality conform to the most rational form which reality *can* assume and which that position emodies. This rational form 'is not a taxi that can be stopped at will'.[16]

**Polytheism and forms of rationality**

The ideal type of the economic or political or erotic sphere is its most rational form. The difference between the empirical actor and the empirical scientist is that the latter can live with the irony defined by the gap between ideal and reality, essence and existence, value and the purposes into which they must be forged for determinate conduct to have a meaning.[17] The ethic of brotherliness and its modern functional equivalents are haunted by the fact that, as Simmel puts it, 'the limits of the empirical validity of a principle are established only by the attempt to apply it to all possible cases'.[18] But for Simmel this attempt founders not on 'empirical reality', or 'the workaday world', but on opposing principles of equal depth and profundity, on other powers of historical life. In *The Philosophy of Money* (1978 (1900)) he adds that while reality may be defined as the reciprocal limitation of mutually contradictory principles (such as 'brotherliness' and 'war') a higher maxim is conceivable which determines the conditions under which one or the other actually obtains. Or in Weber's language, a standpoint from which this contradiction could be held to be resolved in a higher synthesis.

But for Simmel that maxim is found 'in the forces and relations of the constituent elements of history',[19] at the level of the object. It is not sociology's task, or that of the cultural sciences, to discover the maxim in which tensions between principles are resolved, but to elaborate those principles. Constructing the most rational forms reality *can* assume is the exhibition of scientific reticence in the face of this tragedy. It pushes to its limits a principle or form in order to show what the world would have to look like if the form were valid without the limits constituted by the validity of other forms.[20] The modern identity of the 'old gods' is defined by this process of intellectual abstraction. In the eyes of their rationalist followers, this identity will always precede their differences from others.[21] There is no modern pantheon. In Simmel has it: '*each* of the great forms of our existence must be capable of expressing the *totality* of life through its language'.[22] In Simmel's case, however, this leads to a pluralistic conclusion: for were this in fact to happen, one of these forms would 'have to fear no disturbance from the other, because it furnishes to this other the same right to world formation. They could coincide as little as tone coincides with colour'.[23] It is the absence of this disturbance which defines the personality, too.

This highlights once again the difference between value philosophy and life philosophy. Nietzsche himself expressed this most forcefully in *The Will to Power*, in which a distinction between ideal and reality becomes a defamation of the real. Art, morality and knowledge are unconditionals which thought invents as a means of adjustment to the conditional. The opposition between unconditional and conditional is that between art, morality or cognition and the reality of 'life'. For Weber, by contrast, they have a transcendental status – ideals never run up against 'life', only against other ideals.

## A scientistic history of science?

The analysis contained in the three pages on the 'intellectual sphere' was expanded in 'Science as a Vocation', and supports the link made between science's universalist rhetoric and 'total world views'. Weber presents a very rudimentary history of the 'inner meaning' of science, of the modes of legitimation of theoretical and empirical curiosity. The source of that legitimation always lay beyond curiosity's limits, so that science was at various times 'the way to true being', 'the way to true art', 'the way to true nature', 'the way to true God', 'the way to true happiness'. Today, argues Weber, it is the way to none of these, and he agrees with Tolstoy that 'science is meaningless because it gives us no answer to the question: "what shall we do and how shall we live?" '.[24]

When science, set free from its bondage to previous masters, derives its sense of its own worth from within, becomes the source of its own legitimation, achieves self-sufficiency, it is free to 'come forward as the only reasoned view of the world'. But it is also free to serve a series of new masters or ideologies. So while the history of the inner meaning of science is the history of a support for a world view, in which science's descriptive statements are derivable from the prescriptive ones of a prevailing *Weltanschauung*, under modern conditions this relationship is reversed. While the idea of science as 'the way to true X' meant that the pursuit of empirical fact was legitimated by a coherent and dominant world view, the idea of scientific self-sufficiency means that a particular world view or evaluative standpoint can be legitimated through the pursuit of empirical fact – if you know the facts of economic life, for example, you will know that the fundamental forces governing economic life govern, in the last instance, those of political, erotic or aesthetic life, and hence, what to do and how to live. The consequence of the democratisation of a universalist rhetoric is that the tension between opposing world views comes to be treated by their proponents as one between knowledge and ignorance, truth and error, rather than a tragic one between different, equally valid evaluative standpoints. It becomes a tension between rival claims to have access to the scientific means by which the tension might be overcome. So if the grandiose moral pathos of Christian ethics has for a thousand years blinded the Occident to tragedy, the rhetoric of the very science by which that ethics has been superseded allows it to blind itself once more. For Weber, as for Nietzsche, that is the meaning of the misinterpretation of the 'ascetic ideal' of truth. If the view that one mode of human activity is the natural ground of all the others calls upon science for its legitimation, this is because its desired self-image is of a world view which is a product of the pursuit of truth, which 'says what is' and thereby prescribes a way of acting in the world. Weber summed up his objection to the prescriptive derivations of psychoanalysis and Marxism with the complaint that the only question they were prepared to put to scientific knowledge was: 'can one eat it?' [25]

But if this is what Weber is saying, what of his own commitment to 'science', of his own last words, 'the true is the truth?' [26] Weber always insisted that 'intellectual integrity' was his 'inner need'. He wanted to show that his science has a cultural, not merely objective significance, that it is a calling, that, despite the absence of an external limit and legitimation, it and he can be saved from being set culturally adrift. The drama of Weber's science is that he wants to show that the most it can do is to point out the struggles which the modern claims of the intellect make possible, not take part in them on the assumption of their possible elimination. He wants to renounce the universalist rhetoric of which his science seems to be the most likely source. And when he writes that science has come forward 'in the name of' intellectual integrity as the only reasoned view of the world, he believed that science was taking the name of intellectual integrity in vain.[27]

But a problem remains. Even if Weber's culturalism commits him to the limited character of science, does this not mean that it functions as an implicit refutation of the universalist religious ethics whose experience of 'running up against the world' the *Zg* describes? Does not a *cultural* science 'teach a philosophy of its own' in the very act of describing the 'perspective' of a universalist religion? The *Zg* contains the outline of an answer in the section in 'Stages of Religious World Rejection'.[28] For in that section Weber introduces a link between 'culture' and 'guilt', suggesting that from the point of view of a universalist ethics, all 'culture' is guilt-ridden. Did he believe his own cultural science to be guilt-ridden, too?

## STAGES OF WORLD REJECTION

In a somewhat crude fashion Weber distinguishes between three stages of religious world rejection, three modes of discrepancy between the demand that the world evince a 'meaning' and the world's 'internal' characteristics. He presents the development as an increase in this discrepancy. Here at least, he gives us not so much world history as a history of the concept of the world.

## Suffering

Weber argues that the origin of all claims about the meaning-fulness of the world is the need for a compensation for the unequal distribution of the goods of 'this world' – health, wealth and long life, for the 'specific senselessness' of social stratification. But the fact that such compensation does not occur, that suffering remains as a brute fact, demands an explanation.

## Sin

This (priestly or prophetic) explanation is the idea that suffering is a punishment for, and a means of discipline in response to, sin. And, argues Weber, 'a world created for the committing of sin must appear still less ethically perfect than a world condemned to suffering'.[29] This is lifted straight from Nietzsche, who expressed the point thus.

> 'Sin' . . . has been the greatest event so far in the history of the sick soul: we possess in it the most dangerous and fateful artifice of religious interpretation. Man, suffering from himself in some way or other . . . uncertain why or wherefore, thirsting for reasons . . . receives a hint, he receives from his sorcerer, his ascetic priest, the *first* hint as to the 'cause' of his suffering: he must seek it in *himself*, in some *guilt*, in a piece of the past, he must understand his suffering as a *punishment*.[30]

For Nietzsche, any attempt to 'explain' suffering is an exhibition of baseness, since it is premised upon a belief in the possibility of suffering's elimination, and will explain suffering as the result of merit rather than destiny. Once one accepts that suffering is ineliminable, the perplexity it arouses, and the belief that the fortunate can somehow be held responsible for their fortune, and by implication that the sufferers can be held responsible for their own suffering, will evaporate. The centrality of *amor fati* is Nietzsche's exhibition of this acceptance

> My formula for greatness in a human being is *amor fati*: that one wants nothing to be different, not forward, not backward, not in all eternity. Not merely bear what is necessary, still less conceal it – all idealism is mendaciousness in the face of what is necessary – but *love* it.[31]

Formally, Weber's claim that struggle, power, domination is endemic to cultural life appears identical to Nietzsche's view of suffering. But once again, the difference between them lies in Weber's use of the term 'cultural'. Because the concept of culture is tied to that of value, because to be a cultural being is to be capable of taking a position grounded in values, of distinguishing between existence and the validity of those values, Weber could never, as Nietzsche did, describe idealism as mendaciousness. On the contrary, to be a cultural being is to know that the world could be otherwise. In the introduction to the economic ethics of the world religions, the nature of the demand that the world be a meaningful totality remains independent of the senselessness which occasions it.

The difference between suffering and sin is that while a theodicy of suffering is a response to '*something in* the actual world which is experienced as specifically senseless', sin is a *characteristic of* the world which is held to be specifically senseless.[32] The discrepancy between ethical postulate and the world increases with the abstractness attributed to the concept of a world, with the move from the world as the site of suffering to the world as the site of sin.

**Culture**

But once the ideas of an eternal God and an eternal world order have emerged, the fact that death and ruin overtake good as well as evil deeds in the world can 'appear to be a depreciation of precisely the supreme goods of this world'.[33] Weber then adds that 'in the face of this, values – and precisely the most highly cherished values – have been hallowed as being timelessly valid'.[34] From the point of view of a universalist ethic of salvation, the fact that there exists a *plurality* of timelessly valid values suffices for their ethical condemnation. The specific senselessness to which a religious ethical postulate responds is no longer that of something in the world – suffering – nor that of a characteristic of the world – sinfulness – but that of the world itself as 'culture'.

To the extent that the pursuit of cultural values appears to 'presuppose modes of existence which run counter to the demand for brotherliness', 'culture' is guilt-ridden.[35] The life orders of the artistic community, political community, economic enterprise, erotic relationship or scientific community are each aristocratic, by virtue less of their circumscribed internal logics than of the fact that they are grounded in 'cultural values' which can be held to be timelessly valid. The illegitimate attempt to extend the range of their applicability merely confirms their finitude. While 'the religious disposition of man . . . allows all possible regions . . . to be illuminated in a religious way',[36] advocates of the timeless, unconditional validity of cultural values are faced with the possibility either that those values are poor substitutes for religious conviction, or that they are the means towards a process of perfection which is potentially infinite, the mere accumulation of 'culture'. In the latter case, death appears as an arbitrary intervention in a process which knows no rational conclusion, and hence is senseless. Thus 'under the very conditions of "culture", senseless death seemed only to put the decisive stamp on the senselessness of life itself'.[37]

Since neo-Kantianism was prepared to accord the 'value sphere' of religion an exceptional status, it is perhaps no surprise that the *Zg*, having begun with a series of clashes between a universalist ethic of brotherliness and individual value spheres, should work towards this opposition between religion and culture as such. It was a standard opposition employed by German Protestantism. On its basis two positions were possible, the first of which resulted in the idea of cultural *critique*, the second in that of cultural *crisis*. In the first case it is possible for Christians to speak of 'true culture', to acknowledge the *'Eigengesetzlichkeit'* of cultural values while treating them as relative values. Here, religion is to culture for modern human beings as grace was to nature for the middle ages. There is a path from culture to religion, as there was from nature to grace. In the second, belief as such entails an ineradicable distinction between culture and religion and, by implication, a permanent cultural crisis whose basis is simply the fact that culture is the work of human beings.[38]

Weber had already employed the religion–culture opposition in 1907 in a much-quoted letter to Robert Michels.

There are *two* possibilities: either (1) 'my kingdom is not of this world' (Tolstoy, *or* syndicalism *thought to its conclusion*, which is *nothing more* than the proposition 'the goal means nothing to me, the *movement* everything' translated into a revolutionary-ethical, personal statement, but one that you have not thought through to its conclusion. I shall probably write something about *that* sometime) or (2) *affirmation* of culture (that is, objective culture, expressing itself in *technical* and other 'achievements') through *adaptation* to the conditions of all technique, whether it be economic, political, or whatever else. . . . Whoever wants to live as a 'modern man', if only in the sense that he has his newspaper, railroads, trams, etc. every day, *renounces* all those ideals which hover darkly around you as soon as he completely abandons the revolutionary standpoint *for its own sake, without* any goal, indeed without the *conceivability* of a goal.[39]

Weber, too, ties the affirmation of culture to living as a modern human being. He doesn't write of the affirmation or negation of 'modern culture' as an alternative between two ideological positions. Rather, culture itself seems to consist in nothing more than the conditions under which the conduct of modern individuals is possible, as that which is affirmed, implicitly, by that conduct. Modern human conduct *per se* is the display of a commitment to the world those conditions constitute, the abandonment of a universal ethical ideal and of an absolute conception of reality. Culture itself is not a goal, but the presupposition of its pursuit, not inwardness, subjectivity, personality, but outward form, externality, technique, 'civilisation'. 'Modern culture' becomes a tautology, because and to the extent that to live one's life as a modern human being is to be a cultural being. The modern personality is no longer defined in terms of an inward relationship to God, but in terms of the worldly activity or achievement of which it is capable, an achievement which cannot be interpreted as proof of that relationship.

Unfortunately, the rhetorical force of the final section of the *Zg* and the extreme nature of the oppositions and tensions Weber establishes here and in the Michels' letter have led those seeking a 'normative' or 'diagnostic' reading of the essay to identify Weber's own 'position' with either extreme. It has been asserted that 'for Weber, modern culture was guilt-ridden', *and* that intellectual integrity was his inner need,[40] that this section contains Weber's final judgement of, his last word on, 'modernity',[41] that this judgement is shot through with nostalgia,[42] or that it is resolutely 'modern' in its refusal to appeal to an ethic which is 'out of date'.[43]

The difficulty here is that Weber is:

1   establishing an opposition between the religious and the cultural being (*Kulturmensch*);

2  seemingly arguing that that opposition reaches its height when
   the latter type is represented by the individual whose ultimate
   value is 'intellectual integrity';
3  claiming that his 'own' 'ultimate value' is intellectual integrity;
4  displaying an 'empathic' understanding of the religious
   individual's '*Stellungnahme*' in accordance with the very 'cultural
   science' whose internal condition is intellectual integrity,
   thereby including both the *Kulturmensch* and the religious
   individual in the same 'culturalist' universe of discourse.

Weber's culturalism, even as a value-neutral methodological
device, appears to misdescribe the universalist ethic of brotherliness as the product of a human 'commitment' in the very act of
'empathising' with it. The religious individual becomes a
'*Kulturmensch*'. And the modern *Kulturmensch* Weber constructs in
opposition to the religious individual seems to possess the formal
characteristics of the 'cultural *beings*' the essay on Objectivity
claims that 'we *are*'.

Weber's use of the term *Kulturmensch* in the *Zg* recalls the
ambiguity discussed in Chapter 2. Religion is opposed to culture
as to a *Lebensführung* which is always *ständisch* and runs counter to
the (universalist) demands for brotherliness. On the one hand it
is an opposition between two accounts of the whole human being,
the one whose identity is anchored in an ethical imperative which
subordinates and penetrates all other, non-ethical spheres, the
other whose identity consists in a co-ordination between those
spheres, the goal of a cultivated individual in the Humboldtian or
Simmelian sense. But on the other, the opposition appears to be
between two accounts of how a personality anchors itself – in an
ethical imperative or in one ultimate value. The first version of this
anchorage issues in the universal validity of an ethic of
brotherliness, the other in a tragic relationship between particular
ultimate values. As we saw, it is through the idea of an anchorage
for the self that Weber could construct an opposition between
religion and culture at all. Analytically at least, a science which
treats religion as a historical force, as a 'life-order', is bound to
reduce ethical imperatives to cultural values even while warning
against doing so. But values become interesting to that science
precisely when it is claimed that they are 'something more'.

Weber's actual arguments here are pretty thin. His distance
from the tradition of *Sollensphilosophie* is expressed in the whole

manner in which he sets up the *Zg*, and even in the attempt to respect that tradition's integrity, in which he states that ethical imperatives and cultural values belong to different 'value spheres'.[44] The relativisation of ethics *vis-à-vis* other components of culture brings with it a relativisation of imperatives themselves, which become convictions. And while the identity of an ethical imperative – *Sollen* – is *maintained* outside its difference from other imperatives, the identity of a conviction – *Gesinnung* – is, for Weber, *developed* through tragic conflict with other convictions. 'Struggle cannot be eliminated from cultural life. One can alter its means, its object, even its basic direction and its bearers, but struggle itself cannot be eliminated.'[45] Within this metaphysics of struggle, convictions are not unconditional ideals but 'matters of will and conscience', not an authority but a standard which is 'developed in the struggle against resistances offered to them by life'.[46] *Weltanschauungen* are 'formed' in the struggle with others 'for all time'.[47]

Kalberg has suggested that the implication of Weber's remark that the substantive rationalisation of world religions stems from an experience of something in the world as specifically senseless, is that any world religion grounds its substantive postulates [note!] by rendering specifically senseless the postulates [note!] of *other world religions*.[48] But this fails to account for the imperativist's claim to have rendered them generally senseless, and his/her undoubted objection to the entire framework of the *Zg*, whose assumption is that rationality is a relational concept.

More than one commentator has complained that Weber's entire 'cultural science' is theoretical elaboration of a Protestantism,[49] and Kalberg is being disingenuous when he remarks that:

> Weber's fourfold typology of action – affectual, traditional, value–rational, and means–ends–rational action – refers to universal capacities of *Homo sapiens*. Instead of depending for their existence on societal, cultural, or historical constellations, these types of social action stand 'outside of history' as anthropological traits of man.[50]

Weber may in all honesty have meant it this way, but it also led Werner Stark to conclude that he 'had obviously never read a Catholic book',[51] an impression which is strengthened by Weber's remark that the only context in which imperatives and convictions seem to be reconcilable is the structure of the sect.

Only positive religions – more precisely: dogmatically bound *sects* – are able to confer upon the content of *cultural values* the status of unconditionally valid *ethical* commands. Outside these sects, cultural ideals which the individual *wants* to realise and ethical duties which he *should* fulfil possess, in principle, a different status.[52]

Every other assertion about the practical efficacy of an ethical imperative entails an ethical compromise. 'From scholasticism to Marxist theory the idea of something "objectively" valid, i.e. which *ought* to be, is amalgamated with an abstraction drawn from the empirical course of price formation.'[53] Weber himself was not unaware of the charge that his driest formulations were, if not scientistic, then the expression of a secularised Protestantism. It is hardly a defence when he writes that from the devout Catholic reading a cultural scientific church history, he expects:

no less – but *no more* – than the recognition that, *if* the course of events . . . could be explained without those supernatural interventions which an empirical explanation must eliminate as causal factors, it would have to be explained as science attempts to do so. But he can do that without being untrue to his belief.[54]

Two pages later Weber is telling us of the ineliminability of struggle in cultural life, of the universal tragedy of culture.[55] It seems that, just as the sectarian confers upon the content of cultural values the status of unconditionally valid ethical commands, so Weber confers upon the mode of ethical reasoning which this conferral embodies the status of an unconditionally valid methodological command, an illusion which grounds his scientific agency.

But, we might still ask, are Weber's statements about the ineliminability of struggle themselves an unconditionally valid ethical command? Is what he tells us about tragedy a series of exhortations, a demand that we become aware of that of which we do not want to become aware? I think a comparison with Simmel once again provides an answer.

## CULTURE AS TRAGEDY

### The difference between Simmel and Weber's concepts of tragedy

Superficially, the tripartite distinction between self, value and reality grounds Weber and Simmel's 'culturalism' in the same way. Both construct critiques of the idea of immediate experience through a distinction between an activity's cultural value and its intrinsic logic, and both operate with a 'developmentalist' account of personality, arguing that subjectivity depends upon the reassimilation of objective spiritual products. Both hold to a strong thesis about the incommensurability of value spheres, and the divergent directions in which their logics develop. But Simmel's formulation of 'the concept and the tragedy of culture' shows that their accounts of tragedy are very different. He writes:

> A work of art is supposed to be perfect in terms of artistic norms. . . . Religion exhausts its meaning with the salvation which it brings to the soul. The economic product wishes to be economically perfect. . . . All these sequences operate within the confines of purely internal laws.[56]

Art, economics, *and* religion are cultural value spheres. The significance of the fact that they all operate according to internal laws which are incommensurable, is that, although they might contribute to the development of the personality, they do so in a onesided and therefore *incomplete* fashion. As we saw, personality (and freedom) were always made to depend upon the (postulated) existence of a central core.

> Both concepts of freedom and personality contain, in an equal measure, emphasis upon an ultimate and fundamental point in our being which stands opposed to all that is tangible, external and sensual, both within and outside our own nature.[57]

But the *character* of the total personality, his or her uniqueness, consists in the relationship between the manner in which different cultural activities are performed.

> Only the combination and fusion of several traits in one focal point forms a personality which then in its turn imparts to each individual trait a personal–subjective quality. It is not that it is this *or* that trait that makes a unique personality of man, but

that he is this *and* that trait. The enigmatic unity of the soul cannot be grasped by the cognitive process directly, but only when it is broken down into a multitude of strands, the resynthesis of which signifies the unique personality.[58]

An individual will be more unique the greater the variety of his or her cultural practices.

The perspective from which Simmel constructs his account of the tragedy of culture is that of the individual whose identity consists in an achieved balance between different characteristics associated with different cultural values, their integration depending upon the existence of a single centre of gravity. On this account, the salvation of the soul is simply one cultural value among others. Were the individual to construct the meaning of his existence around the salvation of the soul alone, in such a way that other activities only made any sense in so far as they did or did not contribute to that salvation, this would amount to a distorted, onesided form of personal development. Striving for the salvation of the soul, or for scientific truth, or for profit, are not mutually exclusive activities for Simmel. They do depend upon different internal laws, but because Simmel defines the personality in terms of a pre-social core, his individual is free to develop in different directions without undermining his identity.

Simmel accepts that the freedom which is the starting point for his account of culture is also the product of a particular historical circumstance, the development of a money economy, the expansion of the collectivity upon whom the individual is dependent for his or her daily needs, the depersonalisation of relations of economic subordination and above all, the emergence of the modern city.[59] All these developments carry with them adequate forms of individuality which culminate in Simmel's concept of freedom. The preponderance of impersonal over personal relations of dependence, of reason over emotion in the metropolis, paradoxically leaves the individual free to develop increasingly sophisticated notions of privacy, intimacy and personal refinement. Much of *The Philosophy of Money* (Simmel 1978 (1900)) is devoted to a defence of this claim. Weber himself made the point through the example of Stefan George.

> I believe that a poetry such as that of Stefan George, such a degree of reflection on the ultimate grounds of purely artistic forms, could not have been achieved . . . without the poet

having allowed himself to be penetrated thoroughly by those impressions of the modern metropolis which wish to entangle him and tear apart and parcel out his soul.[60]

But just as the money economy acts as 'the gatekeeper of the most intimate sphere',[61] so the division of labour threatens it. If, for Simmel, the uniqueness of the 'total personality' consists in the manner in which a pre-social self integrates a variety of traits, the division of labour restricts severely the number of traits to be integrated. 'Commitment' to one activity rather than another appears as an arbitrary onesidedness. The individual is unable to turn his freedom to good account. A proliferation of forms of objective culture constantly escapes him, and he is left with a choice between a retreat into the untapped potential of 'privacy', and an extension outwards in one direction alone.

But this lack of balance is not tragedy. For Simmel, tragedy consists solely in the discrepancy between subjective and objective culture, between 'personality' and the immanent logics of particular cultural activities. The fact that the division of labour might force the indivdual to choose this *or* that, rather than this *and* that activity, amounts for Simmel not to tragedy, but simply distortion or lack of balance. For Weber, the source of this compulsion is not simply the division of labour, but the legacy of the Puritan idea of the calling, so that choosing one rather than the other *is* a tragic choice. We can represent Simmel's tragedy as formally as 'tragedy$_1$', and this second as 'tragedy$_2$'.

**Tragedy and alienation**

Both Simmel's account of cultural pluralism and Weber's of conflicting value spheres refer implicitly and repeatedly to Marx's theory of alienation. Indeed, the subject of communism in the celebrated passage in *The German Ideology* bears a formal equivalence to Simmel's ideal personality, in which one dimension of personal development does not rule out another.[62] And the essay on the tragedy of culture gives metaphorical status to and hence makes more widely applicable the theory of estranged labour. In the course of this widening the theory is transformed. The implication of Simmel's account of 'intrinsic logics' is that the distinction between subject and object within the sphere of the production and reproduction of material relations reappears in other spheres too, as the distinction between the personality and objective spiritual 'products'. But unlike Marx, Simmel does not argue that this reappearance is itself the 'product' of the primacy of sensuous activity. For Simmel, tragedy, or alienation, has to be examined each time afresh, since the forms it takes are mutually irreducible. For Marx, the condition of possibility of his and Simmel's personality, who can hunt in the morning, fish in the afternoon, rear cattle in the evening and be a critical critic after dinner[63] is the overcoming of alienation in the sphere of material production. Setting the subject free in one sphere sets him/her free in all others.

Weber accepts the 'critique' of Marx implied by Simmel's metaphorisation of 'production', arguing at numerous points that even if the separation of the worker from the means of production could be overcome, this would not imply the overcoming of the separation between the official and the means of administration, between the soldier and the means of warfare, between the researcher and the means of research.[64] But he goes further than Simmel, and concludes that the 'cultivated man' with the capacity to develop in a number of directions is an impossibility. 'The segment which the individual and passive recipient or the active co-builder can comprise in the course of a finite life becomes the more trifling the more differentiated and multiplied the cultural values and goals for self-perfection become.'[65] Personality must consist in passionate devotion to a single activity or realm of activity. The concept of vocation is significant for Weber because it allows him to develop this critque of Marx.[66] The difference between them can be formulated thus: for Marx, overcoming tragedy$_2$ depends upon the overcoming of tragedy$_1$ in the economic sphere. For Weber, even if an overcoming of tragedy$_1$ were possible in a single sphere – and it is not – this would merely heighten tragedy$_2$, bring home more clearly the tragedy entailed by conscious choice of a mode of living one's life.

Weber differs from both Marx and Simmel because his is a *dual* theory of tragedy. There is no tragedy in Marx, whose philosophy of history postulates a non-alienated world the bringing about of which is dependent upon a scientific knowledge of the route to it, and Simmel believes in the ineliminability of the discrepancy between objective and subjective culture but not in that of the conflict between different value spheres.[67]

But the deeper significance of the relationship between Marx,

Weber and Simmel is that Marx sets up the problem of alienation naturalistically. One *mode* of human activity is identified with human activity as such: 'the whole of human servitude is involved in the relation of the worker to production';[68] 'communism, as fully developed naturalism, equals humanism, and as fully developed humanism, equals naturalism'.[69] For Weber, Marx's non-alienated man is one example, the most historically significant, of a secularised functional equivalent of the 'man of religion', the man whose return to himself is at the same time the return of humanity to itself.[70] The 'so-called materialist conception of history', the thesis that humans individuate themselves in the sphere of production, was interesting to Weber as a form of onesidedness which misdescribed itself as something more.

And yet, if Weber and Simmel's accounts of tragedy are an 'advance' on Marx's theory of alienation, this cannot be due to the *ideals* of personality these accounts presuppose. If Weber really believed that all he had to teach was that one should become who one is, that the legacy of ascetic Protestantism was that one had to *be* a personality, he would not deserve the stature he had. If Simmel took himself to be presenting an ideal of allsided harmony, he would not be especially interesting to us. These accounts of the human condition deserve our attention because their analyses of tragedy account at the same time for the ethical compensation open to those for whom that tragedy is unbearable, a compensation for which Marx's reconciliatory philosophy of history found a place only in history's end, and which contemporary Marxist accounts of culture still find difficulty taking wholly seriously. In each case, the compensation makes sense of and illuminates the account of culture.

It is often assumed that Weber had a negative view of the unreflecting bureaucrat allowing his life to run on as an event in nature, as had Simmel of the blasé inhabitant of the modern metropolis who has lost all sensitivity to value differences and retreated into the intimate sphere. Their approach to the modern version of the problem of the relationship between unity and differentiation, between *Bildung* and *Brauchbarkeit*, can be understood in terms of the manner in which they set up the 'valuing subject'. Despite the refinement of his theoretical formulations, Simmel was as realistic as anyone about the possibility of Humboldtian allsided *Bildung* on a mass scale. The only contemporary, democratised version of it seemed to lie in the variety of information a newspaper demands that we absorb. Today, the modern tension between *Bildung* and *Brauchbarkeit* would be embodied in the commuter who reads the whole newspaper in silence on the way to his/her specialised work, and exhibits his/her general knowledge by finishing the crossword, again in silence, on the way home.

In the light of Simmel's frequent concessions to organicist accounts of the unity of culture, the blasé attitude, as a form of psychologism, is a logical response to fragmentation. The rationalisation of the logic of specific cultural practices brings with it the re-assertion of the pre-cultural sense of self whose integrity is to be defended. If the problem for modern individuals is the division of labour, lack of 'balance', the threat to an organic unity, then an appeal to a pre-social, pre-synthetic unity is an obvious ethical compensation. Simmel even suggested that because the modern factory demanded less from the worker's person it left him freer *as* a person, a view which also lay behind Lenin's oddly sympathetic view of Taylorism. It is not surprising that Cassirer remarked of Simmel that while claiming to speak the language of the sceptic by reminding us of the impossibility of a Kantian autonomy and stressing the dependence of personality upon determinate conduct, he speaks in fact that of the mystic, for whom 'all multiplicity is an illusion, regardless of whether it is that of things or of images and signs'.[71]

For Weber, too, there is an ethical compensation, but one which, in accordance with his concept of tragedy, moves in the opposite direction. Because the 'pre-conditional' self which confronts the world is always already a self constituted through a value relation, a retreat into a pre-synthetic unity devoid of a value relation is less an ethical compensation than a denial of one's capacity for becoming a cultural being at all. For Weber, allsidedness is ruled out from the start by value choice. The question is, can one accept the inevitablity of onesidedness, what for Simmel amounts to distortion, and live with the duality of tragedy, with the equal and possible universal validity of the values which ground another's choice and the discrepancy between cultural and objective significance of one's chosen vocation? While, as we will see, one way of not bearing it is to assert dogmatically the purity of one's ultimate values, another is to capitulate to the intrinsic logic of one's activity, to allow one's specialised activity to run on as an event in nature, not to reflect on its ultimate meaning. In an age in which it has become incumbent upon us to derive from *within* us the very values with which we establish a relationship in order to become a personality, being able to submit to the intrinsic logic of an activity, not having to think about tragedy, is a compensation the necessity of which Weber knew he had to acknowledge. 'We do not want to become aware' of the struggle which is culture. And, asks Weber implicitly, why should we?

In *The Will to Power* Nietzsche writes: 'Man, locked in an iron cage of errors, become a caricature of man, ill . . . the sinner: how will we nevertheless be able to *justify* this creature?'[72] It is Nietzsche, not Weber, who actually uses Bunyan's iron-cage metaphor,[73] but Weber's concern is the same: how can the modern individual, for whom the relationship between ideal and reality seems no longer to involve the forging of material according to a law of form but the attaching of a value to a reality which could well continue without it, who has nevertheless no choice but to be a personality anchored in a value choice, be justified?

By the concept of *culture*: the *'affirmation* of culture' which he tried to recommend to Michels is not what it turned out to be for critical theory, not a reconciliation with the social order, but the affirmation of a humanity struggling to be more than the product of its activity, to take a stand in the face of the world, even to say a secular, modern version of 'my kingdom is not of this world', but remaining blameless in its failure. With the concept of 'culture' Weber wanted to understand both what it means to announce the transvaluation of values and to 'go quietly about one's daily work'. Weber's *Fachmensch*, the bureaucrat, the specialist, *is* a *Kulturmensch* too, not because he/she is mired in the conditions of all techniques, but because he/she is *capable* of taking a position, which is precisely what lends pathos to the fact that he/she allows conduct to run on as an event in nature. This is nowhere better expressed than in the paradox of *Beruf* – as 'calling', the ascetic hardness towards oneself Weber admired, and as mere profession, the intrinsic logic of an activity which absolves us from the personal responsibility a calling confers. As Nietzsche puts it: 'a vocation makes one thoughtless; therein lies its saving grace. For it is a bulwark behind which one can retreat when doubts and worries of a general nature arise'.[74]

The blasé attitude and bureaucratic action are two escapes

from tragedy, and it is no accident that MacIntyre, for instance, should have argued that the modern world which *lacks* a sense of tragedy can best be described as 'bureaucratic individualism'. I think we lose a sense of this if we continue to read Weber as a thinker for whom the integrity of the personality had to be protected from the enchroachments of an impersonal bureaucracy, or as one who conceived of value spheres pluralistically. Both of these views can be found in descriptions of Weber himself. For Jaspers: 'he was a whole man, who derived a vast vision of the world from the depths of his being, which, *indivisibly one*, represents what a man can be, a seeker after truth.'[75] For Löwith:

> On no occasion did Weber present himself as a totality, but merely as belonging to one or another sphere in this or that role. . . . It is precisely in this separation of various spheres of life, the theoretical expression of which is value-freedom, that Weber's individuality revealed itself in its unique wholeness.[76]

Weber may, as Jaspers says, have been a seeker after truth, but he knew it to be a choice which implied the divisibility of his being, the differentiation of his personality, which Löwith recognises but then reduces to role-playing. Both seem to lack a sensitivity to the precariousness of Weber's science, of a search after truth which both purports to instruct us in how to share a tragic vision, and refuses to condemn those of us unable to do so.

## THE PRACTICAL STATUS OF CULTURALISM

### Intellectual integrity

Weber's concept of culture is to enable him to empathize with the view that 'culture becomes ever more senseless as a locus of imperfection, of injustice, of suffering, of sin, of futility', *and* exonerate the modern *Kulturmensch*, both the *Kulturmensch* who 'takes a position' and he/she who does not. But this is to be achieved by a *science* which says what is, whose ultimate value is truth, whose rallying cry is 'intellectual integrity'.

In the section on the 'intellectual sphere' Weber writes:

> There is absolutely no unbroken religion working as a power of life which is not compelled at some point to demand the *credo non quod, sed quia absurdum* – the 'sacrifice of the intellect.'[77]

The implication of this seems to be that all historically effective religions are intellectually dishonest. A necessary condition for meeting the 'demands of the day' would seem to be the eschewal of a 'religious conception of reality'.[78]

Recently Turner and Factor have argued that science's demand for intellectual integrity *can* be met by any universalistic religious ethic prepared to acknowledge that contract with the world entails an intellectual sacrifice.[79] But this attempt to save Weber from his own alleged scientism ignores the fact that even if Weber understands 'intellectual integrity' as a human quality which is something more than an excellence peculiar to science,[80] he treats religion's demand for an intellectual sacrifice not as an admission of intellectual defeat, but as a positive attempt to expose the intellect's limitations.

The difficulty is that a cultural science which says what is says that the unity of culture is a postulate but never an actuality;[81] that a cultural science which says what is takes as its starting point a 'world' which for a salvation religion is derivative of other-worldliness. How can intellectual integrity be exhibited by both? At best, the answer seems to be that for salvation religion that integrity consists in the recognition of the *existence* of an 'immanentist', worldly cultural science, one of whose central claims is that the orders and powers of the world follow their own immanent logics. It cannot consist in a religion's recognition of its own vulnerability. But this is precisely that in which Weber's own intellectual integrity does consist. A science able to *demand* it of religion is not a Weberian science. In the essay on the meaning of value freedom, Weber writes: 'an "ethical" conviction which would allow itself to be superseded through the psychological "understanding" of other values would be about as *valuable* as religious beliefs which are destroyed by scientific knowledge.'[82] This destruction, of course, 'occurs frequently'. Weber does not elaborate the circumstances in which it does so, but it is most likely precisely when religion adopts the criteria of intellectual integrity peculiar to science. Its own integrity depends upon the sacrifice of the intellect.[83] The young Schelling once demanded 'monotheism of reason and heart, polytheism of imagination and art'.[84] The monotheism of Weber's reason lay in a will to truth whose product was a science which displayed and attempted to teach a polytheism of imagination, nothing more. If what it asks is what few can achieve, it is, from the point of view of a universalist ethics, guilt-ridden. But Weber's view is that it is bound up with tragedy. It is absurd to suggest that Weber took culture to be tragic *and* guilt-ridden.[85] The only way in which he could have done so would have been through Hegel's argument that what interests us in (ancient) tragedy is that the destruction of figures with equally valid ethical claims occurs through their both acquiring 'guilt through their opposition to an ethical idea . . . which, purified and in triumph over this onesidedness, is thereby reconciled in us'.[86] Weber's intellectual integrity gave him no access to such an idea, to the only (universalist) point of view from which guilt could have a meaning. At times it led him to adopt standpoints which exceeded even Nietzsche's secularism. While Nietzsche could argue that 'only Christian *practice* . . . is Christian' and that 'genuine, primitive Christianity will be possible at all times',[87] by 1920 Weber had concluded that 'under the technical and social conditions of rational culture, the life of Buddha, Jesus, or St Francis seems condemned to failure for purely external reasons',[88] i.e. because of the state of the modern conditions of all technique.

But at the same time, in 'Politics as a Vocation', Weber treated such a life as an impossible without the striving after which the possible would never be achieved. In the last two chapters we have seen some of the moves which might have led Weber to this conclusion, and in the next I will try to show why it is in *PV* that that conclusion is reached, in what sense the political personality was, for him, the true personality. For if there is a sphere on which Weber himself confers an exceptional status, it is the political sphere.

# Chapter 6

# Dogmatism, vanity and vocation
# The political personality

The fact that the dialectical drive toward knowledge and scientific optimism has succeeded in turning tragedy from its course suggests that there may be an eternal struggle between the theoretical and the tragic world view, in which case tragedy could be reborn only when science had at last been pushed to its limits and, faced with those limits, been forced to renounce its claim to universal validity.

(Friedrich Nietzsche)

## INTRODUCTION

'Politics as a Vocation' is Weber's most sustained attempt to develop a 'non-ethical' interpretation of politics. It culminates in an account of what it is to be a political personality, of political maturity. It locates the ideal political personality, one who has a vocation for politics, within a conceptual space at whose limits lie what I will call 'dogmatism' and 'vanity'. The key to understanding this account is the concept of 'distance'. But this account of the pragmatics of political action will turn out to be much more, an account of 'the activities and conditions of human willing as such',[1] of the tragedy of culture and the fate of the cultural beings which we are. It will conclude, not that it is in the political sphere that human beings construct and reveal their identities, but that the ordeal to which the politician subjects herself is an exemplary ordeal.

## THE PROBLEM

### The primacy of the political

We have seen that 'culture' in its neo-Kantian sense is tied to the concept of value, in two ways. Firstly, in the sense that modern human beings have to derive their relationship to ultimate values from within their own breasts. Secondly, in the sense that culture consists, analytically, in a series of value spheres, a mosaic of domains of normativity. The relationship between spheres of culture could not be expressed systematically, there was no Archimedian point from which they might be co-ordinated. Rather, the struggles and tensions between the grounds of those spheres of culture had to be examined each time afresh. For Weber, the only general account of their relationship seemed to require a metaphysics of struggle, summed up in his use of the term 'polytheism', and in the fact that this modern polytheism was distinguished by the absence of a pantheon, by its being haunted by the inescapable logic of the monotheism it had superseded. The idea of an ultimate value entailed that the grounds of one sphere of culture be understood in terms of a possible claim that they were the grounds of all others.

But it seemed, too, that neo-Kantians such as Rickert and Windelband wanted to avoid the nihilistic implications of this account of culture by granting to the 'religious sphere' an exceptional status, partly as a support for the possibility of an ethical grounding for culture as such. And in his attempt to do justice to the integrity of an ethical imperative Weber himself seemed prepared to make this move. But in the end, while Simmel was unwilling, Weber was unable to do so. For the Simmelian personality whose ground was a pre-cultural *core*, religion was one value sphere among others, as it was for the Weberian personality whose ground was an evaluative *anchorage*. In addition, because for Weber 'personality' was defined through, rather than in the face of, specialised achievement, the only question which modern individuals could put to the division of labour was not: how can it be overcome or escaped, but: is my unavoidably specialised activity culturally or objectively significant?

Recent interpretations have attempted to show that for Weber, 'the political' has precisely the exceptional status the possibility of which the *Zwischenbetrachtung* seems to be prepared to grant to religion alone. There are two types of argument to this effect. The first, which ties Weber to a tradition of classical political philosophy, extrapolates from Weber's remarks on the type of human being fit for *politics* to an ideal of 'personality' appropriate to the 'total ethical economy of human life', and concludes that for Weber, to be a political actor is to be a 'genuine man',[2] or even that 'he lived in the continuum of political freedom that began with the Greeks'.[3] On this account, the neo-Kantian theory of value spheres is subordinated to the neo-Aristotelian point that, in the face of the rise of 'the social' in the nineteenth century, Weber had rediscovered a tradition for which the political life is the natural, truly human life, the good life towards which human conduct tends, that it is in political life that humans construct and reveal their identities.[4] The second is analytically neo-Kantian, but claims that the collapse of religion as a force for cultural unity meant that 'politics would inevitably play a greater role in mediating value conflicts than it had in the past', and more strongly, that 'value choices in a secular society are inevitably political'.[5]

Weber's work does contain evidence for both. Hennis made much of Weber's use of the concept of *Lebensführung* in order to bring it into line with his view, expressed in 1963, that just this was the object of an Aristotelian practical science.[6] And indeed, when in his Freiburg inaugural address Weber writes of the 'one *political standard of value* which is supreme for us economic nationalists', he adds that: 'In truth, the ideals we introduce into the substance of our science are not peculiar to it, nor have we worked them out independently: they are *old-established human ideals of a general type*.'[7] And in the essay on objectivity, Weber refers to 'the most important constitutive element of every cultural life: the state, and . . . the most important form of its normative regulation, law'.[8]

But the neo-Aristotelian view cannot be reconciled with Weber's culturalism, with his implied account of the relationship between nature and culture. 'Nature' in Weber can have only two meanings, either a causal mechanism, a set of law-like regularities through which an infinite reality is mastered and ordered; or a set of internal drives, a *status naturalis*, the overcoming of which is the establishment of a relationship to ultimate values as a prerequisite for 'personality'. The plausibility of the Jaspers–Hennis position would have to depend upon a demonstration that 'nature' for

Weber is *physis*, not *natura*. As for the second view, the definition of the national state as 'the temporal power-organisation of the nation'[9] rules out its role in the 'mediation' of value conflicts.

Weber's inaugural address, and most of his other substantive political writings, represent the self-assertion of the political (not its self-empowerment) in the face of a threat from other 'methods of approach' which claim to derive ideals from the material under investigation. The threat here lies in the universalistic ethical consequences which are held to follow from the scientificity of these methods. The suspicious character of each of these hermeneutics consists in the implicit claim to be able to explain other hermeneutics while they cannot explain it. To locate the sources of Weber's 'world view' in his interpretation of politics is to mistake what was merely the self-assertion of the autonomy of the political for the self-empowerment of its primacy. If Weber is not part of Jaspers' continuum – and he is not – it is not just because the context in which Greek political theory makes sense has been lost,[10] but because Weber's culturalism allows room for doubt about the enduring quality of political action. If politics is merely one cultural sphere, rather than the *telos* of human conduct, the very concept of the political is threatened by the universalist claims of other spheres. Like science, it is subject to cultural drift, in need of an anchorage. Perhaps it is this vulnerability which helps explain why Weber never developed a 'political philosophy' of his own.[11]

And yet, despite the polytheistic symmetry of the *Zg*, Weber does grant the political an exceptional status. For while religion, sexuality, art, science and even the economic sphere can be defined in terms of an excellence peculiar to them, the political is the one sphere which he does not define in the terms set down by neo-Kantian value philosophy. We saw in Chapter 4 that Carl Schmitt's concept of the total state depended upon a category mistake, upon a distinction between the existential friend/enemy opposition and the evaluative oppositions peculiar to other domains. In Weber's work, a similar process occurs, only here, Weber's account steps outside the logic of neo-Kantianism, not in order that the political might dominate other domains, but that through the exceptional status of the political his account of culture and personality might be vindicated. Politics becomes the arena in which the fate of the *Kulturmensch* is revealed most directly. Weber writes:

> It is not possible to define a political association – not even a 'state' – through an account of the *purposes* of its action . . . there has been no purpose which political associations have *not* on some occasion pursued, none which *all* political associations have pursued. Thus one can define the 'political' character of an association *only* through the *means* – which, though not peculiar to it, is at all events indispensable for its nature: violence [*Gewaltsamkeit*]. Under certain circumstances, this means is elevated to an end-in-itself.[12]

Compare this with the opening of Aristotle's *Politics*:

> Observation shows us, first, that every polis (or state) is a species of association, and, secondly, that all associations are instituted for the purpose of attaining some good . . . We may therefore hold that all associations aim at some good; and we may also hold that the particular association which is the most sovereign of all, and includes all the rest, will pursue this aim most, and will thus be directed to the most sovereign of all goods. This most sovereign and inclusive association is the polis . . . or the political association.[13]

For Weber, 'politics as a vocation' entails a *commitment* to politics, which means: to a mode of human action which can only be defined in terms of its means, in terms of an existential logic, not a valid value which might confer upon it its own purpose, such as the good life for human beings. In the vacuum which defines it, 'ultimate values clash'. Politics is always already the possible degeneration of means into ends, and the object of a science of politics is the fate of the human being who makes this commitment, and what becomes of him/her on being made aware of that fate. And in being made aware of what becomes of him we learn what it is to be a cultural being. The idea of the 'calling' is central to what it means to be a cultural being. Politics, despite the exemplary nature of the ordeal of personality to which its participants submit, remains a specialised activity, and only makes sense in relation to the inescapability of the division of labour. We have already seen how this ruled out the subject of communism in *The German Ideology* and Simmel's ideal personality. Just as only certain individuals are artistically or economically or religiously 'musical', so only those with a 'calling' for politics are fit for political activity. Few are called, and fewer chosen.

## The status of intermediate groups

This has to be stressed here because according to those who believe that he thought politics had the function of 'mediating' value conflicts, Weber believed that this was to be achieved via an 'organic' account of the relationship between value spheres.[14] Nothing could have been further from Weber's intentions, and his references to organic theories of the state or the use of organic metaphors in the human sciences, of which there was no shortage during his lifetime, range from the belief that they are at best a preliminary means of orientation[15] to outright hostility.[16]

Just as German thought from Schiller and Humboldt to Simmel had sought a personal compensation for the division of labour in a harmony between provinces of the soul, so corporatism from Adam Müller and Hegel to Gierke and Durkheim sought its political compensation in a corporate articulation of the state.[17] But according to Weber, just as the impossibility of the harmony of the soul would find its ultimate compensation in the soul's pre-synthetic unity, so the impossibility of the state's corporate articulation would find its ultimate compensation in the state's mystical unity. We have already established the difference between his and Simmel's accounts of personality. But his insistence that the national state 'is not, as some people believe, an indeterminate entity raised higher and higher into the clouds in proportion as one clothes its nature in mystical darkness, but the temporal power-organisation of the nation',[18] is also directed against the political–theoretical consequences of organicist thinking, against the fall-back position which this thinking will inevitably have to adopt.

But more importantly, the presupposition of all corporatist theories was a degenerate intepretation of *Brauchbarkeit*. Here, *Beruf* is not calling, but profession. One only needs to compare Weber with Durkheim here to see this. For Durkheim, the source of morality is to be the state, not, as for Weber, the human breast;[19] for Durkheim's political theory what matters is an activity's objective, for Weber its cultural significance; for Durkheim, the state has a purpose and is a *universitas*, for Weber it has none and is a *societas*;[20] Durkheim proposes a second chamber with representation by collegial bodies, for Weber the only acceptable form of representation is parliamentarianism;[21] for Durkheim the key intermediate group between the family and the state is the professional group, the corporation or the *Genossenschaft*, and has a necessarily political function, for Weber it is the voluntary association, the sect or the business club, and does not.

Because vocation is a calling rooted in human commitment or conviction, there is no obvious link between vocation and citizenship. The state, having no purpose, is a framework of legality, and its citizen is a *Staatsbürger*, a member of the state in a direct sense, not by virtue of his/her membership of an intermediate body. Weber rejected every proposal for a '*berufsständische Verfassung*', a constitution based on the vocational group.[22] The state has no purpose, but, as we saw in Chapter 3, the freedom of the personality is the freedom of purposive activity. And it is precisely because the state has no purpose that the intermediate group for Weber is the group formed for collective purposive endeavour, and not itself a branch, member or organ of the state. This relationship between the state and the intermediate group is expressed in the only two types of freedom to which Weber refers explicitly: freedom of movement and freedom of conscience.[23] The Hobbesian idea of freedom of movement expresses a direct relationship of protection and obedience between the individual and the state. But Hobbes saw corporations and by implication all intermediate bodies as 'worms in the entrayles [*sic*] of a natural man',[24] and the only freedom of conscience for which he made provision was one which would find no outward expression.[25] The centrality of the voluntary purposive association for Weber lay in the fact that its ideal type was the Puritan sect, for him, *the* guarantor of freedom of conscience, 'the oldest human right there is'.[26] It is in determinate purposive association that freedom of movement is turned to good account. It is no accident that Weber refers in *PV* to Dostoyevsky's Grand Inquisitor, in which the opposition between the structural principles of a church and of a sect is unfolded. The justification for the Grand Inquisitor's view that what human beings seek is a 'harmonious and incontestable anthill', a form of external ecclesiastical regulation, is that 'there is nothing more alluring to man than his freedom of conscience, but . . . nothing more tormenting either'.[27]

It was de Tocqueville who had said that in democratic societies the isolation of the citizens of the state meant that they 'are weak and feeble' and 'become powerless if they do not learn voluntarily to help one another'.[28] In a society such as America, the need to form associations for the most 'trivial' purposes was deeply felt. The product of Weber's own visit to America in 1904 was the essay 'The Protestant Sects and the Spirit of Capitalism', which focused exclusively non-political *voluntary* associations – American business clubs – as the secularised functional equivalents of Puritan sects. Weber announces to the first meeting of the German Sociological Association that America is 'the land of the association par excellence', and goes so far as to say that 'the man of today is among other things an associational being [*Vereinsmensch*] to a degree hardly before imagined'.[29] If the theory of culture is vindicated by the fate of the politician in the modern state, it culminates in the freedom of determinate, purposive conduct in civil society.

Weber's account of the relationship between the state and the intermediate group is thus a vindication of the romanticist claim that the state is more than 'a heap of isolated private people',[30] but one which rejects decisively its organicist conclusions. The whole is greater than the sum of its parts, but not by virtue of its being a larger version of one of them, a 'personality'.[31] This is especially important to an understanding of Weber's account of bureaucratisation. He saw no way back behind an age of mass democracy and the *Staatsbürger*. But an organicist functionalism based on the degenerate interpretation of *Beruf* would amount to a plea for a romantic restoration whose effect would be its opposite. For the degenerate interpretation of *Beruf*, embodied in the trained specialist whose conviction is at best alleged rather than real, was precisely that which accorded with a rational–bureaucratic structure of domination. While Luther's concept of *Beruf* had been traditional to the extent that it didn't threaten the basic structure of the *Ständesstaat*, the Gierkean or Durkheimian theory of the corporation was traditional to the extent that it had no room for the individual *capable* of refusing to allow his/her conduct to run on as an event in nature. It believed it could comprehend the modern phenomenon of functional specialisation through a medieval idea of functional specification.[32]

### Self, value, reality

We saw in Chapters 2 and 3 that Simmel, Rickert and Weber all distinguished sharply between self, value and reality, in order to establish the mediate character of cultural experience, but also that the product of that experience was a cultural reality which emancipated itself from the process which produced it, objective culture. The task of modern culture seemed to be to confer value upon a world whose recalcitrance, whose character as hard boards, consists in its being a product which has not merely emancipated itself, but which was the ground of that activity in the first place. For while 'culture' is equated with 'the world', in contrast to the demands made upon it by salvation religion, to be a (modern) cultural being is to have to suffer the fate of being capable of *taking a position towards* that world. If secularisation has a significance for Weber, it consists in the idea that the world itself might contain the demand that it be transcended, but that it is the only source of the means of fulfilling that demand. Weber never really found an adequate expression of the idea that every (modern) claim made on the world is a sublimation of worldly properties. Kant warned against mixing the intelligible and the sensible and offering the mixture to the sick as if it were a medicine, a warning which goes unheeded among those today who find such distinctions 'problematic' dualisms. If Weber's account of culture does amount to this mixture, the peculiar pathos which accompanies it makes it, at best, hard to swallow.[33]

We saw that for Weber:

> the 'freer' . . . an action is, that is, the *less* it bears within itself the character of a natural event, the more there comes into force that concept of 'personality' which finds its essence in the stability of its inner relationship to certain ultimate 'values' and 'meanings' of life, which are forged into purposes and translated into rational–teleological action.[34]

Here, personality is defined in terms of a stable *relationship* to values, but also in terms of the manner in which the relationship between the valuing subject and reality is effected, by the translation of values into purposes. It is the nature of this translation which will determine whether an individual is fit for politics. And Weber will argue that that individual is one prepared to take the risk of purposive–rational action, but one who can do so without that action sliding into an exclusive orientation to means. The pejorative use of the term 'instrumental rationality' as a translation of *Zweckrationalität* has sometimes obscured this point, and led to many fruitless debates over the question of Weber's individualism versus his *Realpolitik*.[35] It is not true that anything which is not value-rational action must therefore be instrumentally rational action. Or at least, the distinction's legitimacy is restricted to neo-Aristotelian arguments for which there is only *praxis* or *poiesis*, action for its own sake and action for the sake of something outside it, but for which, equally, Weber is no more of a sinner than any other 'modern' thinker.[36] If by instrumentally rational action we mean strategic action, action conceptualised in terms of the successful achievement of a non-universalisable purpose, then, as we will see, Weber's value-rational actor is no less an instrumentalist than his purposive–rational actor[37] and non-instrumentality would have to be sought in the two other categories of action, affectual or traditional action.[38] Here, I will take purposive–rational action to be the richest concept in Weber's armoury. It accounts for both his contribution to the 'methodology of the social sciences' and his vision of humanity.

### Value, purpose, means, consequence

But values and purposes are only two components of action for Weber. The third is means. Indeed, 'Every thoughtful reflection on the ultimate elements of meaningful human action is immediately tied to the categories of means and purposes.'[39] The fourth is consequences. And just as the capacity to be a personality depends upon the acceptance of the need to translate values into purposes, so the capacity to be a political personality will depend upon the manner in which the relationship between values, purposes, means and consequences is understood.

But if this is so, we see Weber's account of personality pulling immediately in two directions. On the one hand, personality depends upon a *stable* relationship to ultimate values, on the other, upon the undermining of that stability through the introduction of more action components, perhaps even to the extent that the idea of 'ultimate' values no longer makes any sense. Indeed, turning 'values' into one component of action among others seems to strike at the heart of the value philosophy upon which so much of Weber's account depends. But it is Weber's view that it is precisely from the risk of their being compromised that ultimate values derive their strength.

The fate of a cultural epoch which has eaten from the tree of knowledge is to have to know . . . that '*Weltanschauungen*' can never be the product of increasing empirical knowledge, and thus that, and for all time, the highest ideals, which move us most forcefully, become effective only in the struggle with other ideals, which are just as sacred to others as ours are to us.[40]

It is not simply that the purity of ultimate values may be undermined through their translation into purposes, but that through this translation those values themselves are developed. But how can one accept the tragedy this conception defines and remain a personality, if personality depends upon a stable relationship to values? Doesn't the latter view entail that the identity of ultimate values is prior to their difference from other ultimate values, while the the tragic view implies that their identity is preceded by that difference? *PV* is Weber's confrontation with this problem, and the aporias into which it leads him. Here, the *development* of ultimate values is consistent with the *stability* of the relationship to ultimate values which defines personality in the first place. How is this consistency maintained?

## THE SOLUTION

### Three qualities

Weber begins that section of *PV* devoted to the internal conditions of political action by distinguishing three components of the psychological make up of the 'kind of human being' permitted to 'put his hand in the spokes of the wheel of history'.[41] 'One can say that three pre-eminent qualities are decisive for the politician: passion, a feeling of responsibility, and a sense of proportion'.[42] In the next sentence Weber forestalls a naturalistic interpretation of this passage. 'Passion' means *'matter of factness'*,[43] it is already an ascetic concept, and has nothing to do with irrationality, or with an animal passion to be kept in check by other, 'objective' qualities. When he described the passion of the scientist as a 'strange intoxication',[44] he meant that that strangeness lay in passion's being 'the firm taming of the soul'. As Weber's statement on the relationship between freedom, value and purpose in the 1906 Knies essay shows, when he gave the lecture in 1919 Weber had long since settled his accounts with life philosophy. The personality is initially he or she who has already resolved the problem of the irrational. It is the act of choice of a cause – *eine Sache* – to which one is passionately devoted which is irrational, since such a cause could be considered irrational from another point of view. It has nothing to do with the idea that the object of the choice cannot be understood by others. This is the significance of Simmel's remark that reference to a subject is actually not very essential for an understanding of value. When Weber writes that ultimate values have retreated into the human breast, he means that the manner in which we construct a *relationship* to those values has done so. Devotion to a cause remains devotion to something greater than oneself, to an ultimate value through which one makes one's way in the world. It is not true, as Schluchter has suggested, that 'the civil servant accepts a publicly recognised purpose, the politician tries to turn his own into a social cause'.[45] The difference turns rather on whether one's conviction is real or alleged.

> The honour of the civil servant is vested in his ability to execute conscientiously the order of the superior authorities, exactly *as if* they agreed with his own conviction. . . . Without this moral discipline and self- denial . . . the whole apparatus would fall to pieces.[46]

The difference between the politician and the bureaucrat is a difference between devotion to '*die Sache*' and mere *Sachlichkeit*, between two types of self-denial. Like that between cultural and natural science, it is less a difference between spheres of activity than one between modes of human sense-making.

But on the other hand, and by implication, while value is vital to the constitution of subjectivity, it is not the whole of it. The significance of value lies far more in the fact that, as that to which the action of every subject is referrable, it is that to which every action of this or that subject is referrable, it is held to provide for a continuity between practices. It was ascetic Protestantism's alleged capacity to do this, through 'the attempt to take the self by the forelock and pull it out of the mud, forming it into a "personality" ',[47] and the apparent absence of such a referent in other religions, which lay at the heart of Weber's sociology of religion.

And yet, a belief in the immutablity of ultimate values to which an individual is devoted can, Weber believes, lead to a belief that the self is immutable, too. It promotes that crippling connection between guilt and responsibility which was the object of so much of Nietzsche's venom and which has since been taken up by those followers of Foucault who talk of a 'politics of the subject'.

> The 'total personality', as we would say today, and not some individual action, is provided with a value accent of eternity. The nonreligious version of this religious valuation of belief, resting on a determinism applied to this world, is that specific kind of shame and, so to speak, godless feeling of sin appropriate to modern man by virtue of an ethical systematisation of conduct into a *Gesinnungsethik*, irrespective of its metaphysical foundations. Not that he has done something, but that, without his own doing, and through his unalterable disposition, he 'is' such that he *could* do it, is the secret anguish which he bears, and which others express in their deterministically applied 'pharisaism'.[48]

### Value rationality and purpose rationality

Whatever Weber's admiration for the Puritan sects and for this ethic of conviction (*Gesinnungsethik*), the distinction between value and self is the initial means by which he guards against the possibility of either a sense of self reduced to ultimate values, or a sense for ultimate values being lost in the escape from pharisaism into 'the modern chase after experience'. 'It is not true – as has been claimed – that the "personality" is and should be a "unity" in the sense that it is, so to speak, injured if it is not visible on every occasion.'[49] If the individual is to develop, to become who she or he is, if the values in relation to which she defines herself are to be made effective in the struggle and conflict with other values, she must be capable of purposive–rational action. Why should this be so? Given the lamentary tones in which *Zweckrational* action gets equated with 'instrumentalism',[50] Weber's definition is worth quoting in full:

> Like every action, social action can be determined: (1) *purpose-rationally*: through expectations about the behaviour of objects in the environment and of other human beings, and through the use of these expectations as 'conditions' or as 'means' for the rational success of those *purposes* for which one strives and calculates; (2) *value-rationally*: through conscious belief in the

ethical, aesthetic, religious – or however interpreted – unconditional *intrinsic* value of a determinate mode of behaviour
purely as such and independent of success. . . . The individual
acts purpose-rationally who orients his conduct to purpose,
means and consequences and thereby rationally *weighs* the
means against the purposes, as much as the purposes against
the consequences or the purposes against each other. . . . The
decision between competing or colliding purposes or consequences can in turn be oriented value-rationally. In this case,
conduct is purpose-rational only in its means. . . . From the
standpoint of purpose-rationality value-rationality is always
*irrational*, the more so the more it elevates the value to which
conduct is oriented to the status of an absolute value, and
therewith reflects less on the consequences of conduct, and is
devoted exclusively to this value (pure conviction, beauty,
absolute good, absolute duty). But absolute purpose-rationality
of conduct is really a constructed limiting case.[51]

From this regrettably not untypical passage we can draw two
conclusions. Firstly, the fact that the purposive–rational actor's
reflections include only means, purposes and consequences does
not entail that ultimate values are less constitutive of his subjectivity than that of the value-rational actor. They simply remain
*outside* any process of deliberation. There is nothing to suggest
that the purposive–rational actor is less capable of human commitment than the value-rational actor. Nor does this imply that
the purposive–rational actor is incapable of a recreative understanding of the content of those values opposed to his own. Secondly,
and more importantly, a version of this distinction appears in *PV*,
namely in the distinction between ethic of conviction
(*Gesinnungsethik*) and ethic of responsibility (*Verantwortungsethik*).[52]
The precise relationship between these two distinctions has given
rise to a good deal of unnecessary head-scratching and tortuous
scholasticism in the literature, but it is in fact fairly straight-
forward. The latter distinction is one between different accounts
of what constitutes ethical reasoning. The *Gesinnungsethiker*
believes that human purposes never, or should never, emancipate
themselves from human values, that nothing gets lost in the
translation from the latter to the former. Purposes are simply
moments in the development of the concept of value, emanating
uninterruptedly from an ultimate source, with the result that an

act can be described as having an intrinsic value, intrinsic by virtue of that value's being conferred upon it directly. The *Gesinnungs-ethiker's* ideal self-description is the value-rational actor, the ideal description of his concrete purposes nothing more than an account of the content of those values.

To this Weber opposes the *Verantwortungsethiker* who agrees with Nietzsche that the idea of the intrinsic value of an act is absurd,[53] and believes that without a consideration of conse-quences the idea of determinate conduct, of a substantive self, in the sense that the formation of purposes is partially dependent upon external, worldly conditions, makes no sense. And this is so regardless of whether an individual's ultimate value is a formal ethical imperative or substantive idea of the good society. It has been suggested that because *Gesinnungsethik* and *Verantwortungsethik* depend upon prior decisions about what constitutes ethical reasoning, both are examples of value rationality.[54] But this is an attempt to complicate matters unnecessarily. When 'value-rational' refers to anything other than *action*, it concerns the basis of belief in the legitimacy of a social order. In any case, if the *Verantwortungsethiker* believes that the dignity of human beings consists in their being able to put their ultimate values to the test against 'the resistances offered to them by life', and the *Gesinnungsethiker* believes that it does not, and these positions are mutually exclusive, there is no more reason to suppose that irreconcilability to be based upon competing value rationalities than to assume that those holding those positions do so for fear of the consequences of not doing so, on the basis of purpose rationality.

The acknowledgement of the ordeal of personality is the foundation of the second quality of the politician, a sense of responsibility. The concept of *Verantwortung* is actually employed by Weber in two senses. Firstly, and more familiarly, besides passion the ideal political personality requires a sense of responsi-bility to the cause to which he/she is devoted. Responsibility here entails refusing to treat the world's failure to conform to an ideal as a result of the world's own guilt-ridden character. The conse-quences of such 'moralistic complaints'[55] would be injury to those ultimate values which defined the meaning of political activity in the first place.

The second meaning involves responsibility to future generations, and addresses the quality of life of a political community itself. Political action is lifted out of its particularity by virtue of its connection with the fate of that community. This conception of 'consequences' first appears in the Freiburg rectoral address.

> Even our highest, our ultimate, terrestrial ideals, are mutable and transitory. We cannot presume to impose them on the future. But we can hope that the future recognises in our nature the nature of its own ancestors. We wish to make ourselves the forefathers of the race of the future with our labour and our mode of existence.[56]

This is not a philosophy of history, an ideology of progress, but the expression of a relationship of historical dependence, of the ideals of the future on those of the present, and of those of the present on those of the past. Weber himself believed that the idea of human rights no longer made any sense, but equally that without it nobody, not even the most conservative, could live the life that he/she leads today.[57]

These two senses of responsibility recall the duality of culture, and Weber's political writings oscillate between responsibility understood in relation to autonomy – '*no matter* what the outcome – *this war is great and wonderful*'[58] – and as a concomitant of human solidarity, between the rationalism of ultimate values and the rationality of practice, between the reduction of politics to ethics and the claim that ethical life culminates in the life of the political community. But once again, the question remains, how can I acknowledge the historical mutability of my ideals while grounding my political action in their apparent unassailability? What theoretical provision does Weber make for the overcoming of this tension? Does he make any at all?

### Distance

The type of individual able to combine passion and responsibility possesses, above all, the third quality, a sense of proportion (*Augenmass*). The politician's decisive quality is:

> his ability to let realities work on him with inner concentration and calmness. Hence his *distance* to things and men. 'Lack of distance' *per se* is one of the deadly sins of every politician. It is one of those qualities the breeding of which will condemn the progeny of our intellectuals to political incapacity.

> . . . daily and hourly, the politician inwardly has to overcome a
> quite trivial and all-too human enemy: a quite vulgar vanity,
> the deadly enemy of all matter-of-fact devotion to a cause, and
> of all distance, in this case, of distance towards one's self.[59]

This threefold typology of distance, towards things, other human
beings, and one's self recalls that distinction between reality, value
and self. The equation this implies between 'other human beings'
and 'values' might appear a little forced, but the publicly
understandable nature of 'values' does, I think, justify it.

Weber's entire account of personality culminates in the
relationship he establishes between these *three* types of distance. If
we restrict ourselves to what Weber says about distance towards
others, we will miss this point. 'Distance' is not reducible to a
Humboldtian 'reserve', to the defence of privacy, or, as Hennis
would have us believe, to 'ethical personalism'.[60] Distance is not to
be achieved:

> exclusively on the 'cothurnus' of snobbishly setting oneself off
> from the 'far too many', as is maintained by the various miscon-
> ceived 'prophecies' which go back to Nietzsche. On the
> contrary, when today it is in need of this inner support, distance
> is always spurious.[61]

Formally, an understanding of the relationship between self and
reality is effected through distance towards values, of the
relationship between value and reality by a distance towards the
self, and of the relationship between self and value by a distance
towards reality. Although the only worthwhile achievement is a
specialised one, within the restrictions that imposes, personality
consists nevertheless in an achieved balance or harmony between
these forms of distance. The upsetting of this balance is the end of
the personality. But in what precisely does this balance consist,
what is the relationship between self-distance and value distance
for the purposive–rational actor?

Clearly, allowing external realities to work upon one – to affect
one's choice of purpose – entails the mutability of the self. But
does it entail that of those values of which one's purposes are the
imperfect translation? Are ultimate values to be treated as criteria
of significance with which one makes sense of the world before
mastering it, or as the imperfect tools of such mastery? If the
development of the political personality is a process of

self-overcoming, if 'fundamental doubt is the father of all knowledge',[62] including self-knowledge, what is overcome, upon what is doubt cast?

The most important recent attempt to answer this question is the evolutionary solution of Schluchter. In an analysis of the ethic of responsibility which owes much to Elias, Schluchter argues that Weber associates an ethic of responsibility with a later stage in cultural development than that represented by an ethic of conviction. For Elias, the capacity to consider consequences, of foresight and hindsight, is part of the historical transformation of 'warriors into courtiers', of the development of ever-more sophisticated modes of self-control.[63] On this basis, Schluchter constructs the following account of the fully *zweck-rational* act in order to 'strengthen Weber's position'[64] against Habermas's charge that Weber's teleological theory of action is 'monologic'. Distinguishing between the four action components I outlined above, Schluchter argues that the fully rational act has four 'aspects':

1  selection of ends on the basis of value analysis;
2  rational consideration of alternative means to the end;
3  rational consideration of the relation of ends to secondary consequences;
4  rational consideration of the importance of different ends.

Armed with these weapons Schluchter establishes a hierarchy within Weber's fourfold typology of action at the beginning of *Economy and Society*. Traditional action includes (2) alone, affectual action (2) and (4), value-rational action (1), (2) and (4), and purpose–rational action all four. He then adds that 'in moving from means to ends, the means are freed for selection; in the transition from concrete ends to abstract value, the ends are freed, and from value to consequence the values themselves become subject to rational choice'. Because he finds Weber's account of action 'systematically unsatisfactory',[65] Schluchter ignores the version of value philosophy which bulked so large in his work, and transforms Weber into a consequentialist. In rescuing Weber from an existentialist decisionism,[66] he arrogates him to critical rationalism, for whose leading exponent 'there are no convictions which are epistemologically uninteresting'.[67] Not only does this ignore the psychology of *Weltanschauungen*, but forgets that at a very minimum, the dignity of human beings for Weber always lay

precisely in the existence of convictions which *were* epistemologically uninteresting, which lay beyond the limits of science,
limits of which Weber was as conscious as Nietzsche, and from
which he was to draw the same tragic conclusions. The grounds of
human *commitment* cannot be a knowledge of how the social and
political world actually is, however much one's reasons for
adopting a particular course of *action* may be dependent upon
such knowledge. Put another way, for Weber, intellectual and
personal dogmatism were not the same thing. *PV* is an
appreciation, but rejection, of the former and a condemnation of
the latter. The difference between them is expressed in that
between what I call dogmatism and vanity, and in the idea that the
mutability of selfhood which the latter denies does not have to be
achieved at the cost of the mutability of the ultimate values to
which the former is in thrall. To make this clearer, we need to
understand the difference between the types of lack of distance
which define dogmatism and vanity.

For the *Weltanschauung*'s politicians Weber describes towards
the end of the essay, 'the world is base, not I'. Weber wonders
about the degree of inner poise lying behind this *Gesinnungsethik*,
and concludes 'that in nine cases out of ten I deal with windbags
who do not *genuinely feel* what they take upon themselves, but
intoxicate themselves with romantic sensations'.[68] These
individuals have reduced their sense of self to the content of an
ultimate value, and in thus collapsing the distance between self
and value, have infintely extended that between this purely
evaluative self and the world. This is the mutual annulment of
person and condition whose avoidance Schiller described as the
task of culture. For if there is no distance towards value, there is
no possibility of understanding the relationship between self and
world. Hence the reference to lack of inner poise or balance. A
lack of sense of proportion is expressed in the disproportion
between modes of distance. The *Weltanschauung*'s politician
believes that the will contains its realisation within itself, and
strictly speaking forms no purposes. Put another way, the
sequence of purposes generated by the attempt to actualise values
collapses to a single point, at which each instance of political
activity is describable in the same terms.[69] She can compensate
herself for the world's failing to conform by retreating into
another world. Unlike the genuine utopian, who knows that her
ideal has no reality and that therefore both the overcoming of the

world's resistance and the overcoming of herself require commitment and effort, and who Weber respected, the *Weltanschauung's* politician already has an alternative – romantic – reality.[70] As the bureaucrat leaves the world as it is by going about her daily work and escaping tragedy, so the dogmatist leaves the world as it is by remaining blindly committed and denying tragedy.

But this objection to dogmatism is by implication an objection to vanity, too, to 'the need personally to stand in the foreground as clearly as possible'.[71] For the lack of balance displayed by those for whom ultimate values are the only source for the stability of personal identity is also that displayed by those for whom those values are no source at all. Since the vain individual craves immediate experience, he becomes a sop to public opinion. As Nietzsche puts it: 'The vain person is delighted by every good opinion he hears of himself . . . just as every bad opinion pains him: for he submits to both, he feels subjected to them in accordance with that instinct of submission which breaks out in him'.[72] Here, sensitivity to ultimate values is collapsed into self-intoxication, and once again lack of distance between value and self engenders an infinite distance between self and world, the mutual annulment of person and condition.

In the first case, the individual takes solace from the thought that 'the world is base, not I', in the second, he/she experiences the 'sudden inner collapse of typical representatives of this mentality'[73] as a result of this self-same thought. In the first case, the politician's self-distance is so great that the self becomes nothing more than a vehicle for the expression of a *Weltan-schauung*, devotion to a cause becomes submission to a cause; in the second, the self is so close to itself, and value distance so great, that the substantive content of values becomes tangential to political action, devotion to public opinion becomes submission to public opinion. The only relationship to values which this individual is able to secure is the desire to have already established values attributed to him.[74]

The self-distance which defines the political actor with a vocation for politics lies between the two. For neither dogmatism nor vanity promote the testing of criteria without which self-overcoming, political experience, are impossible. Rather, the dogmatic belief in the intrinsic value of an act merely confirms a world view, while the vain belief in the intrinsic personal significance of an act merely confirms a (positive or negative) sense of self. Both deny a conflict between formal and substantive rationality which Weber thought unavoidable, dogmatism by confronting the formal rationality of given procedure with the substantive rationality of ultimate values, vanity by subordinating the substantive content of ultimate values to the formal rationality of a purely personal striving for power.

It is clear that Weber regarded vanity as by far the greater of these evils. The centre of gravity at which the politician with a calling achieves a balance between modes of distance is not at some mid-point between them. Vanity 'is the product of a shoddy and superficially blasé attitude towards the meaning of human conduct'.[75] The dogmatist's personality does at least depend upon a relationship, albeit subordinate, to ultimate values, and a potential sensitivity to value differences. But 'the blasé person . . . has completely lost the feeling for value differences',[76] is incapable of taking a position. Furthermore, having ridiculed the *Gesinnungsethiker* on the penultimate page of *PV* Weber then suggests that *Gesinnungsethik* and *Verantwortungsethik* 'are not absolute contrasts but rather supplements, which only in unison constitute a genuine man – a man who can have the calling for politics'.[77]

### The unbearable nature of tragedy

But why does Weber make this move? Why does he compromise himself? After all, the *Verantwortungsethiker*'s purpose-rationality is not chosen at the expense of those ultimate values without which political experience could not begin. It is no *Realpolitik*. Why does Weber make this concession to a *Gesinnungsethik* which he allegedly found wanting? The answer is, I think, that, in the course of his account of the conditions of possibility of political experience, Weber finds himself in aporias from which his tragic view of history cannot free him. His account of purpose-rationality can be formulated thus: 'Values without purposes are empty, purposes without values are blind'. It is only through the acknowledgement of the dependency of purpose on means and consequences that the individual is capable of a determinate political experience at all. But if values, too, are subjected to rational choice, that determinacy, in which freedom consists, becomes the heteronomy of the *Realpolitiker*. While Weber formulated his own commitment to science as the 'intellectual integrity' of one who 'says what is', the politician's intellectual integrity consists in extending the sequence of one's purposes in an acknowledgement of the fact that the actualisation of one's values is infinitely deferred, and that the reason for this is that the resistances offered by life are themselves a product of this acknowledgement on the part of those with incommensurable ultimate values. Yet no matter how much the politician makes himself aware of this and other ethical paradoxes, and no matter how much he is made aware by the scientist of 'what may become of him under the impact of these paradoxes', the *Verantwortung-sethiker* 'somewhere reaches the point where he says: "Here I stand, I can do no other".'[78] The fruit of the tree of practical political knowledge from which the politician has eaten is not a new set of values, or a modification of old values in the light of the infinity of the sequence of purposes, but the reassertion of the *same values*, with the *same content* as before, coupled with a greater awareness of that in which the difficulty of actualising them consists.

The historical scientist can offer the politician two types of knowledge: of those 'inconvenient facts' to which the politician has a cognitive responsibility to attend in the formation of her purposes; but also of tragedy – that the ultimate inconvenient fact is that the ideals of others are as sacred to them as ours are to us. But as we saw in Chapter 5, as soon as a historical science as capable of self-reflection as Weber's invokes tragedy, it has to recognise its own, the limit beyond which it is in no position to define the cognitive responsibilities of historical agents. It is not true, as some have claimed, that Weber's work implies that 'convictions can be examined for their feasibility',[79] that 'conscience itself should be subjected to critical self-examination in order to eliminate all the blindly and compulsively operating factors',[80] or that 'politics must face up to scientific considerations without being fully determined by them'. It is not surprising that Schluchter, who holds the latter view, talks of a Weberian 'model' of the science/politics relationship without considering what the source of this imperative might be, whether the relationship between science and politics is scientific or political. The task of science, in its 'narrow circle of activity', may be political education, but the political personality is less its product than he/she who is prepared to *be* politically educated. Science cannot engender an ethic of responsibility.

In *PV* Weber is making the more important point that the historical agent will reject a knowledge of tragedy because a life led in its permanent shadow is unbearable. The mutability of ultimate values is, for Weber, world-historical, not personal. A compensation for the discrepancy between ideal and reality was the possibility of the valuing subject's being able to fall back on the belief that she sets her own purposes, to step out of tragedy's shadow. Maturity then, is opposed to the heroism so often attributed to Weber. As Hegel has it:

> The *heroic* self-consciousness (as in the tragedies of the ancients . . .) has still not advanced out of its native state to reflection on the difference between act and action, external event and intention and knowledge of circumstances, to the subdivision of the consequences, but accepts responsibility for the whole compass of the act.[81]

The mature politician knows that there are consequences for which he/she cannot accept responsibility. This is the real meaning of the last sentence of the extract from *Economy and Society*: 'absolute purposive–rationality of conduct is really a constructed limiting case'.

Some have described this as a relativist position, and have attempted to rescue Weber from it. But relativism is pertinent only in the case of *Weltanschauungen* which are held to dogmatically from the start. For the *Gesinnungsethiker*, the dogmatist, the point at which he says 'Here I stand I can do no other' has always already arrived. It always means 'the world is base, not I'. The individual with a vocation for politics is a personality, not by virtue of that which is to be protected from being swallowed up and forgotten in the sequence of his purposes, not by virtue of the objective practicality of an imperative, but by virtue of the fact that, and unpredictability of the point at which, he will retire from that sequence and reassert the integrity of those values from which all purposes are, temporarily, held to flow. This reassertion, the *Verantwortungsethiker*'s 'Here I stand I can do no other' is thus no expression of helplessness. Nor is it an expression of the belief that the world, or culture, is guilt-ridden. It is the dogmatist who is trapped by this belief, just as it is the vain person who is trapped by the thought that the guilt is all his. It is, to be sure, a failure of value distance, but the discrepancy between person and world is a utopian, not a romantic or dogmatic one. In turn, this sequence of points at which the personality returns to itself to feed on experience's dogmatic residue, is itself infinite. Even if the perfectability of humanity has a goal, the maturity of human beings knows none. It is hard to read this account of the balance between self-distance and value-distance without recalling Hegel's discussion of conscience and the good in the *Philosophy of Right*, the last part of the section on morality before the transition to ethical life.[82] Like Hegel, Weber wants to deny the radicality of an opposition between the particularity of the self and the universality claimed for values, but without sublimating it in the substantiality of *Sittlichkeit*. A balance between self-distance and value-distance cannot be allowed to overcome a distance towards the world, the ineradicability of which is the meaning of culture.

Those values whose unassailability is, 'in spite of all', asserted, or re-asserted, clash in that evaluative and teleological vacuum abhored by those for whom political life is the natural form of human connection. And so, to have a vocation for politics is to commit oneself to an activity defined not in terms of the validity of a value, but in terms of an understanding of the tragic relationship between values and the resistances life offers to their actualisation. The 'ultimate value' of politics is a relationship between self, value and world, between validity and existence. And have we not seen that the separation between validity and existence was what defined the field of a cultural science whose object is the fate of the *Kulturmensch*? And does not Weber refer in *Politics as a Vocation* to 'the tragedy with which *all* action . . . is truly interwoven'? In fact, while the political sphere can only be defined in terms of the means peculiar to it, Weber's discussion of this very fact is the means by which he reveals what he takes to be the fate of the cultural being. The *Gesinnungsethiker*'s failure to be a political personality is far more. It is a failure to understand what makes us cultural beings, the ordeal of determinate, purposive conduct. The political personality has undergone an experience with the world, understood its tragedy, and, in the light of tragedy's unbearability, retained a twofold faith, in a personal 'demon' and in the integrity of the diabolic forces of politics. Political experience, or for that matter, political education, is not a process in which the individual accumulates a growing body of cultural products and ceaselessly reinterprets them as having flowed from his own activity. Nor is self-development or maturation an increasing understanding of the historical appropriateness of, and therewith willingness to renounce, one's own values. The mature politician is neither so flexible that she capitulates to the intrinsic logic of an activity – she is no *Realpolitiker* – nor so rigid that she collapses that distance between self and value without which value would not provide for the mediate character of human experience – she is neither vain nor dogmatic. This does not mean that to be a politician is to lead the truly human life, but that one leads a truly human life, in whatever sphere of activity, when one leads that life politically.

# Conclusion

It is hard to take on the study of Weber without being overcome by the desire to avoid having to live, interpretively, from hand to mouth, to establish a continuity between writings which might otherwise drift apart on the tides of intellectual fashion, to be picked up by some factory ship producing anthologies on bureaucracy, authority or power in modern society. Like any branch of intellectual history, Weber research has its hermeneuticists and structuralists, those for whom the coherence of his *oeuvre* lies in its meaning, in a single theme on which, if one twists it sufficiently, one can hang everything else, and those for whom that coherence resides in the teleology of the texts themselves, in a systematic goal obscured only by his chaotic mode of composition. It may strike us as paradoxical that a thinker who took such pains to avoid essentialism and who detested the gratuitous theoreticism of the system should provoke both among his leading commentators. But once the decision is made to treat Weber as a topic rather than a resource, these moves, which appear completely to misunderstand him, are almost inevitable. They are our way of coping with what would otherwise appear a meaningless infinity. In the first chapter of *ES* Weber remarks that the use of functional concepts is only the beginning of sociological work, that the interpretive disciplines are able to achieve something more – the understanding of the conduct of participating individuals. An apparently innocent, even banal statement of the mutual irreducibility of meaning and function. But it is just the fact that Weber was as capable of the hardest-nosed of structural-functional analysis as he was sensitive to the subtlest nuance of feeling and mood, that will always defeat our attempts to appreciate that combination intellectually. How many of those who are genuinely passionate about his achievements have not ended up lost and confused in his conceptual labyrinth, and how many of those who took the labyrinth for a maze have reached the centre and still had the energy to say what lies there?

Weber took part of the meaning of his science to be the transience of its truths, and a substantial part of his greatness lies in the fact that he was always a man to be reckoned with, never to be followed, that he could not have founded a school. Of subsequent thinkers he is closest here to Wittgenstein and Foucault. All exerted an endless fascination, all responded to expressions of it with 'don't ask me who I am'. Instead of saying what they meant, they showed it. But while Wittgenstein and Foucault got the followings they didn't want, Weber remained curiously aloof even from his most ardent admirers, offering them little more than the advice, 'be yourself'.

The interest in the 'biography of the work' which has grown in the last twenty years shouldn't be seen as a mere substitute for an adequate biography of the man. That, if and when it is written, may enrich our anecdotal knowledge, but won't contribute a great deal more to our understanding of his work. We only believe that it will if we believe that the source of that understanding lies outside, behind or above the texts, a secret waiting to be disclosed. In this short essay I have tried to avoid both the search for that secret and the construction of a series of tables and matrices into which, in principle, everything Weber wrote can be fitted. The one is as frustrating as the other is sterile. But nor have I tried to be fair to Weber, a worthy enterprise but one which rarely produces interesting results. Instead, I hope to have shown the manner in which certain features of his work can be made to hang together. In particular, how we can appreciate the importance, the centrality even, of politics, without grounding it in the belief that the goal of politics is the good life, and without having to downplay the significance of neo-Kantianism. In fact, if we understand what the account of value spheres amount to for Weber, it might be just this which fosters that appreciation.

And if it also fosters an appreciation of the fact that 'modernity' cannot be the proper object of a cultural science practised on neo-Kantian assumptions, that 'modernity' is not an historical individual, we have a second type of disjunction between modernity and politics. It is not that modernity implies the usurpation of a properly political understanding of human association. Rather, a scepticism towards the concept of an epoch and with it towards the concept of modernity, and the exceptional status of politics, are both explicable in terms of a single concern – the fate of the cultural being, the ordeal of personality.

If the theory of tragedy through which this ordeal is expressed is at the same time modernity's theoretical self-consciousness, the proof lies less in explicit statements by Weber that, 'today', something is the case, than in the manner in which the analytical distinctions between church and sect, compulsory and voluntary organisation, ethical imperatives and cultural values, nature and culture, life and value, entail a preference for the second term.

It is in *PV* that the language of culturalism, value philosophy and tragedy bears its richest fruit but at the same time casts the spores of these suspicions to the winds. It is here, too, that we see Weber struggling to hold together two apparently antinomic accounts of the political personality: a passionate but stable relationship to ultimate values; and personal development. We saw that this attempt, to maintain a dialectical view of the self within what seemed to be a dogmatic framework, could not be severed from decisionism – whether one should be politically educated is not a question for political educators, whether one should think dialectically is not a question for dialecticians.

The lesson of political life is that the task for the ideal personality faced with tragedy is, like that of the philosopher faced with the hermeneutic circle, not how to escape it, but how to enter it in the right way. But Weber's greatness lies in the fact that the same analysis which leads him to tragedy provides for the desire, for the need, to escape it, to become blasé, to become a harmonious whole, to submit to the logic of one's own specialism, to get lost in the mists of dogma, or finally, to return to the grounds of one's own commitment. This is more than just intellectual generosity. It is the exoneration of humanity.

# Notes

## INTRODUCTION

1 See D. Beetham, *Max Weber and The Theory of Modern Politics*, Cambridge, Polity, 1985.

2 See L. Strauss, *Thoughts on Machiavelli*, Seattle, University of Washington Press, 1958; *Political Philosophy*, New York, Pegasus, 1975; E. Voegelin, *The New Science of Politics*, Chicago, Phoenix, 1966.

3 See especially C. Schmitt, *Der Leviathan in der Staatslehre des Thomas Hobbes*, Hamburg, Hanseatische Verlagsanstalt, 1938; *The Concept of the Political*, New Brunswick NJ, Rutgers University Press, 1976; *Political Theology*, Cambridge, MIT Press, 1985a.

4 See H. Arendt, *The Human Condition*, Chicago, Chicago University Press, 1958, Ch. 2; *On Revolution*, London, Penguin, 1963, Ch. 2.

5 See especially M. Foucault, *Language, Counter-Memory, Practice*, Ithaca, Cornell University Press, 1977; E. Laclau and C. Mouffe, *Hegemony and Socialist Strategy*, London, Verso, 1985.

6 C. Schmitt, *Politische Romantik* 2. Auflage, München, Duncker & Humblot, 1925, p. 11.

7 H. Dubiel, *Was ist Neokonservatismus?*, Frankfurt, Suhrkamp, 1985, p. 14.

8 P. Ricouer, *Hermeneutics and the Human Sciences*, Cambridge, CUP, 1981.

9 J.B. Elshtain, *Public Man, Private Woman*, Oxford, Martin Robinson, 1981, p. 27.

10 E. Durkheim, *Professional Ethics and Civic Morals*, London, Routledge & Kegan Paul, 1957, p. 82.

11 See K. Jaspers, *Leonardo, Descartes, Max Weber*, London, Routledge & Kegan Paul, 1965; W. Hennis, *Max Weber: Essays in In Reconstruction*, London, Allen & Unwin, 1988; P. Lassman and I. Velody, *Max Weber's Science as a Vocation*, London, Allen & Unwin, 1988; and R. Eden, *Political Leadership and Nihilism*, Tampa, University of Florida Press, 1983.

12 I am not sure that an acceptance of the view that Weber was a neo-Kantian is as hermeneutically restrictive as Hennis and Scaff seem to believe. It is true that the Rickert connection has produced

texts almost exclusively concerned with problems of methodology and objectivity, but this is not inevitable. To show that there is more to the *Wissenschaftslehre* than a methodological treatise by distancing it from neo-Kantianism is to assume that there is little more to neo-Kantianism than problems of concept formation. Should a broadening of the field of Weber research demand the very type of restriction which allegedly occasioned it?

13  Tenbruck, and more recently, Scaff and Arnason have pointed to the centrality of *Zg*. See F. Tenbruck, 'The Problem of Thematic Unity in the Work of Max Weber', *British Journal of Sociology*, vol. 31, no. 3, 1980, pp. 316–51; L. Scaff, *Fleeing the Iron Cage*, Berkley, University of California Press, 1989; J.P. Arnason, *Praxis und Interpretation*, Frankfurt, Suhrkamp, 1988.

14  See the characterisation of Geoffrey Hartman in R. Tallis, *Not Saussure*, London, Macmillan, 1988, pp. 22–25.

## 1  THE COHERENCE OF THE CONCEPT OF MODERNITY

1  See M. Riedel (ed.) *Rehabilitation der praktischen Philosophie*, Frankfurt, Suhrkamp, 1975; H.–G. Gadamer, *Philosophical Hermeneutics*, Berkeley, University of California, 1976.

2  See Habermas's contribution to O. Stammer, *Max Weber and Sociology Today*, Oxford, Blackwell, 1971; and H. Marcuse, 'Industrialisation and Capitalism', *New Left Review*, no. 30, 1965, pp. 3–17.

3  See W. Hennis, *Politik und Praktische Philosophie*, Frankfurt, Suhr-kamp, 1963; and E. Voegelin, *The New Science of Politics*, Chicago, Phoenix Books, 1966.

4  See J. Habermas, 'Modernity: An Incomplete Project' in H. Foster (ed.), *Postmodern Culture*, London, Pluto Press, 1983; and *The Theory of Communicative Action*, vol. 1, Cambridge, Polity, 1984a.

5  See in particular the essays 'Verantwortung heute' and 'Der post-kantianische Universalismus in der Ethik im Lichte seiner aktuellen Misverständnisse' in K.–O. Apel, *Diskurs und Verantwortung*, Frankfurt, Suhrkamp, 1988.

6  W. Hennis, *Max Weber: Essays in Reconstruction*, London, Allen & Unwin, 1988.

7  Ibid. p. 22.

8  O. Marquard, 'Temporale Positionalität', in R. Herzog and R. Koselleck, *Poetik und Hermeneutik XII: Epochenschwelle und Epochen-bewusstsein*, München, Fink, 1987.

9  Ibid. p. 349.

10  W. Mommsen, 'Max Weber's Political Sociology and His Philosophy of World History', *International Social Science Journal*, vol. 17, 1965, pp. 9–22.

11  J.-F. Lyotard and P. Thebaud, *Just Gaming*, Manchester, Manchester University Press, 1985, p. 82.

12  *MSS*, p. 155.

13  The two dominant approaches here are the attempts by Jaspers and

Hennis to grasp what Max Weber really meant, and by Habermas and Schluchter to say what Max Weber ought to have meant.

14 I formulate the problem in this manner in order to highlight the often bureaucratic character of 'radical' theorising about an object whose defining characteristic is taken to be legitimation through legal–rational means. On this account the radical lament would be that legal–rational legitimation was less 'efficient' than religion.

15 I discuss this at greater length in Chapters 4 and 5.

16 See H. Blumenberg, *The Legitimacy of the Modern Age*, Cambridge, MIT Press, 1985; K. Löwith, *Meaning in History*, Chicago, Chicago University Press, 1949.

17 Löwith, 1949, p. 37.

18 M. Foucault, *The Order of Things*, London, Tavistock, 1970, p. 320.

19 Voegelin had used the term gnosticism to refer to any form of thought which treats the world as foreign, outside of which, in an order of Being, human beings must find their new home. Hegel's alienated spirit and Heidegger's 'thrownness' are the most notable expressions of this sense of homelessness, but Voegelin's point is that modern society as a whole has been thoroughly penetrated by this idea, which denies the virtue of intellectual curiosity and can be summed up as *'Das Verbot der Fragestellung'* – the ban on the putting of questions. 'It is a case of opinions whose representatives know that and why they cannot tolerate a critical analysis, and who therefore turn the ban on the testing of premises into the content of a dogma'. See E. Voegelin, *Politik, Wissenschaft und Gnosis*, München, Kosel, 1959, p. 31. Voegelin's influence on Hennis is evident in the original title of the latter's book on Weber, *Max Weber's Fragestellung*.

20 Blumenberg, 1985.

21 For the theory of the two modes of evaluation see Nietzsche, *Beyond Good and Evil*, New York, Vintage Books, 1966, part 6; *The Genealogy of Morals*, New York, Vintage Books, 1967a, Essay III. For Weber's implicit critique of it, a critique which needs to be taken into account in any discussion of Weber's Nietzscheanism, see *FMW*, p. 271.

22 The idea that it is not, that reason's very need to answer theological questions is a sign of the incapacity of modern philosophy to generate a mode of intellectual curiosity which is self-justifying, is the thrust of the somewhat neglected work of Stanley Rosen. See his *The Ancients and the Moderns*, New Haven, Yale University Press, 1989.

23 I. Kant, *Groundwork of the Metaphysics of Morals*, New York, Harper & Row, 1964, p. 54.

24 Ibid. p. 55.

25 Nietzsche, *Twilight of the Idols*, London, Penguin, 1968, p. 116.

26 Kant 1964, p. 59, emphasis added.

27 M. Foucault, 'What is Enlightenment?', *in The Foucault Reader*, New York, Pantheon, 1985.

28 K. Popper, *The Open Society and Its Enemies*, London, Routledge & Kegan Paul, 1966, pp. 119–20.

29 Nietzsche, *The Gay Science*, New York, Vintage Books, 1974, sect. 377.

30 Ibid. sect. 276.

31  J.F. Lyotard, *The Postmodern Condition*, Manchester, Manchester University Press, 1984, p. xxiii.

32  See O. Marquard, *Schwierigkeiten mit der Geschichtsphilosophie*, Frankfurt, Suhrkamp, 1973.

33  Adorno and Horkheimer write: 'Man imagines himself free when there is no longer anything unknown. That determines the course of demythologisation. . . . Enlightenment is mythic fear turned radical. The pure immanence of positivism is its ultimate product.' See T.W. Adorno and M. Horkheimer, *Dialectic of Enlightenment*, London, Allen Lane, 1973, p. 16. The relationship between myth and enlightenment set down here would bear fruitful comparison with that between magic and disenchantment. For Adorno and Horkheimer the development of *theoretical* rationality from myth to enlightenment entails an increase in the ratio of the known to the unknown. For Weber, the development of *practical* rationality from magic to disenchantment entails an increase in the ratio of the calculable to the incalculable. Weber was as prepared as critical theory to accept the irrational roots of rationalism. It was only 'in principle' that there were no longer any incalculable forces in the world. We might even say that for Weber disenchantment is magical fear turned radical and that the world mastery of ascetic Protestantism is its ultimate product. Not only does Protestantism push disenchantment to its limit, but it finds its expression in Weber's very concern with the development of practical rationality and its investigation through the magic/disenchantment dualism.

34  On this see M. Jay, 'Review of Blumenberg's *The Legitimacy of the Modern Age*', *History and Theory*, vol. 24, no. 2, 1985, pp. 185–96.

35  M. Heidegger, *The Question Concerning Technology*, New York, Harper & Row, 1977.

36  See the afterword to J.–F. Lyotard, 1984.

37  L. Strauss, 'The Three Waves of Modernity', in *Political Philosophy*, New York, Pegasus, 1975.

38  Machiavelli, *The Prince*, London, Penguin, 1981, p. 133.

39  Strauss, 1975, p. 46.

40  Ibid.

41  L. Strauss, *Thoughts on Machiavelli*, Seattle, University of Washington Press, 1958, p. 14.

42  K. Löwith and L. Strauss, 'Correspondence Concerning Modernity', *Independent Journal of Philosophy*, vol. 4, 1983, p. 107.

43  L. Strauss, *Studies in Platonic Political Philosophy*, Chicago, Chicago University Press, 1983, p. 211.

44  Strauss, 1975, p. 43.

45  See A. MacIntyre, *After Virtue*, London, Duckworth, 1981. Many of MacIntyre's points are made in Horkheimer's *The Eclipse of Reason*, New York, OUP, 1947.

46  E. Durkheim, *Suicide*, London, Routledge & Kegan Paul, 1981, p. 256. The idea of the past as a series of hastily experienced stages is Kierkegaard's definition of aesthetic experience, an experience opposed to that of the ethicist, between whose actions there exists a

continuity grounded in individual choice. See S. Kierkegaard, *Either/Or*, Princeton, Princeton University Press, 1987.

47  MacIntyre, 1981.
48  Ibid. p. 27.
49  Ibid. p. 33.
50  H. Arendt, *The Human Condition*, Chicago, Chicago University Press, 1958.
51  For this discussion see *ES*, p. 55.
52  This use of classicism should be distinguished from that of Lyotard, for whom classicism refers to any belief in fixed criteria, and modernity to the absence of such belief: 'anytime that we lack criteria, we are in modernity, wherever that may be, whether it be at the time of Augustine, Aristotle or Pascal. The date does not matter.' Lyotard and Thebaud, 1985, p. 15.
53  MacIntyre, 1981, pp. 134–5.
54  Ibid. p. 103.
55  Arendt, 1958, p. 277.
56  J. Habermas, *The Philosophical Discourse of Modernity*, Cambridge, Polity, 1987a, p. 7.
57  See G.W.F. Hegel, *The Phenomenology of Spirit*, Oxford, OUP, 1967.
58  Compare Weber's remark about the 'charismatic glorification of "Reason"' in *ES*, p. 1209.
59  Habermas, 1987a, p. 40.
60  Ibid. p. 40.
61  This marks a break with Habermas's less optimistic ruminations on the relation between theory and practice, in which the difficulty was 'to distinguish groups at which active work of enlightenment can be directed from the opponents held captive by ideology'. See J. Habermas, *Theory and Practice*, London, Heinemann, 1974, p. 31.
62  Habermas, 1987a, p. 59.
63  R. Rorty, 'Habermas and Lyotard on Postmodernity', *Praxis International*, vol. 4, no. 1., 1985, p. 7.
64  *ES*, p. 17.
65  A. Schmidt, *History and Structure*, Cambridge, MIT, 1984. p. 53.
66  K. Marx, *Grundrisse*, London, Penguin, 1973, p. 106.
67  I. Kant, *Critique of Practical Reason*, New York, Bobbs Merrill, 1956, p. 166.
68  See G.W.F. Hegel, *Philosophy of Right*, Oxford, OUP, 1952, sect. 124.
69  Apel, 1988, p. 98.
70  Quoted in W. Schluchter, *The Rise of Western Rationalism*, Berkley, University of California, 1981, p. 21.
71  MSS, p. 55.
72  See K. Jaspers, *Leonardo, Descartes, Max Weber*, London, Routledge & Kegan Paul, 1965, p. 257.

## 2    THE THEORY OF CULTURE

1  See J. Niedermann, *Kultur: Werden und Wandlungen des Begriffs und*

*seiner Ersatzbegriffe von Cicero bis Herder*, Firenze, Libreria Editrice, 1941; W. Perpeet, ' "Kulturphilosophie" ', *Archiv für Begriffsgeschichte*, Jg. 20, 1976, pp. 42–99; F. Rauhut, 'die Herkunft der Worte und Begriffe *"Kultur"*, "Civilisation", und *"Bildung"* ', Germanisch–Romanische Monatshefte, 1953, pp. 81–91; H.–P. Thurn, 'Kultursoziologie – zur Begriffsgeschichte der Disziplin', *Kölner Zeitschrift für Soziologie und Sozialpsychologie*, vol. 31, 1971, pp. 422–9.

2  See R.V. v. Bruch, F. Graf und G. Hübinger, *Kultur und Kulturwissenschaften um 1900*, Stuttgart, Steiner, 1989; W.H. Bruford, *The German Tradition of Self-Cultivation*, Oxford, OUP, 1975; N. Elias, *The Civilising Process, Part 1*, Oxford, Blackwell, 1978.

3  Most famously, O. Spengler, *Der Untergang des Abendlandes*, München, Beck, 1920.

4  See R. Eucken, *Geistige Strömungen der Gegenwart* 4. Auflage, Leipzig, Veit, 1909; H. Rickert, 'Lebenswerte und Kulturwerte', *Logos*, Jg. 1, 1911, pp. 131–66; H. Schnädelbach, *German Philosophy 1831–1933*, Cambridge, CUP, 1984a; F.–Z. Schwab, 'Beruf und Jugend', *Die Weissen Blätter*, 4. Jg., 1917, pp. 97–113.

5  See F. Graf, 'Kulturprotestantismus', *Archiv für Begriffsgeschichte*, vol. 28, 1984; H. Liebersohn, *Religion and Industrial Society*, Philadelphia, American Philosophical Society, 1986; M. Scheler, 'Kultur und Religion', *Gesammelte Werke vol. 1*, München, Francke, 1971.

6  For the best account of Weber's relationship to this ideal of personality, see now H. Goldman, *Max Weber and Thomas Mann*, Berkeley, University of California Press, 1989.

7  See the article 'Bildung' in W. Conze u.a., *Geschichtliche Grundbegriffe*, Stuttgart, Klett-Cotta, 1972–89.

8  Elias, 1978, p. 19.

9  Ibid. p. 27.

10  Bruford, 1975, remains the most useful introduction.

11  F. Schiller, *Letters on the Aesthetic Education of Man*, Oxford, OUP, 1967, Letter VI, 7.

12  F. Hölderlin, *Hyperion*, Stuttgart, Reclam, 1961, pp. 171–2.

13  J. W. Goethe, *Wilhelm Meisters Lehrjahre*, Stuttgart, Reclam, 1982, p. 301.

14  M. Mendelssohn, 'über die Frage: Was heisst aufklären?', in E. Bahr (Hsg), *Was ist Aufklärung?*, Stuttgart, Reclam, 1974, p. 5.

15  Ibid. p. 7.

16  I. Kant, *Political Writings*, Cambridge, CUP, 1970, p. 48.

17  Ibid. p. 51.

18  See F.M. Barnard, *Herder on Social and Political Culture*, Cambridge, CUP, 1974.

19  W. v. Humboldt, *On Language*, Cambridge, CUP, 1988.

20  W. v. Humboldt, 'Ideen zu einem Versuch, die Grenzen der Wirksamkeit des Staats zu bestimmen', in *Gesammelte Schriften* Bd. 1, Berlin, Behr, 1903, p. 106.

21  See F. Meinecke, *Weltbürgertum und Nationalstaat*, Oldenburg, 1907. This tendency reaches its extreme in versions of romanticist political philosophy which resolve themselves into mystical accounts of the

personality of the state. On this see P. Kluckhohn, *Persönlichkeit und Gemeinschaft*, Halle, Niemeyer, 1925; H.S. Reiss, *The Political Thought of the German Romantics*, Oxford, OUP, 1955; and Carl Schmitt's idiosyncratic interpretation, *Politische Romantik* 2. Auflage, München, Duncker & Humblot, 1925.

22  Sombart, 'Politik und Bildung', *Morgen: Wochenschrift für Deutsche Kultur*, vol. 1, 1907, p. 40.

23  F. Nietzsche, *The Twilight of the Idols*, London, Penguin, 1968, pp. 51–2. See also *The Will to Power*, New York, Vintage Books, 1967b, sects 121, 462.

24  Lepenies and Hennis in particular have referred to this connection. See W. Lepenies, *Between Literature and Science: the Rise of Sociology*, Cambridge, CUP, 1988; W. Hennis, *Max Weber: Essays in Reconstruction*, London, Allen & Unwin, 1988. The most sustained treatment is Goldman's. See Goldman, 1989.

25  T. Mann, *Reflections of a Non-political Man*, New York, Frederick Ungar, p. 14.

26  Ibid. p. 21.

27  G. Lukács, 'Die alte und die neue Kultur', in *Taktik und Ethik*, Darmstadt, Luchterhand, p. 131.

28  Ibid. p. 141.

29  Ibid. p. 142.

30  Ibid. p. 146.

31  H. Marcuse, 'Bemerkungen zu einer Neubestimmung der Kultur', in *Schriften* Bd. 8, Frankfurt, Suhrkamp, 1975, p. 115.

32  Ibid. p. 122

33  For a recent standardised Frankfurt-style account of the relationship between culture and civil society see H. Brunkhorst, 'Kultur und bürgerliche Gesellschaft', in A. Honneth u.a., *Zwischenbetrachtung*, Frankfurt, Suhrkamp, 1990. The analytical separation of the two is combined with the idea that it is in civil society, and here alone, that human individuation occurs. For Weber and Simmel, a theory of culture is already a theory of modes of that individuation, a theory of civil society.

34  In English, the 'Intermediate Reflections' essay in *FMW*, 1948.

35  *GARS*, pp. 408–9; *WuG*, pp. 145, 155, 578, 639–40, 650–2, 677.

36  *GARS*, p. 408; *WuG*, 1972, pp. 145, 677.

37  *GARS*, p. 408.

38  Ibid. p. 408.

39  Ibid. pp. 408–9.

40  *WuG*, p. 578.

41  Ibid. p. 578.

42  *RC*, pp. 226–49; *RI*, p. 342.

43  See the discussion of this in Chapter 3.

44  The paradox of Hennis's position is that his stress on *Lebensführung* is justified at precisely the point in which he professes to have little interest, the problem of the constitution of the object domain of cultural science. It is weakest when it claims to aid our understanding of Weber's 'world-view', for that is expressed in the retreat of

ultimate values into the human breast, a 'modern' phenomenon to which traditional political philosophy as Hennis conceives it cannot, I think, do justice.

45  Lukács' 'new culture' would in fact be the return of Weber's old *Kulturmenschentum*. For the romantic revolutionary, Weber's *Kulturmenschentum*, premissed upon an insuperable discrepancy between 'ideology and *Lebensführung*', trapped between the old which will never return and the new which will never arrive, is unbearable.

46  I. Kant, *Critique of Practical Reason*, New York, Bobbs Merrill, 1956, p. 71.

47  Schiller, 1967, XI, 6.

48  Ibid. XIII, 2.

49  Ibid. XX, 4.

50  Ibid. XXIII, 6.

51  J.G. Fichte, *Beitrag zur Berichtigung des Publikums über die Französische Revolution*, Hamburg, Meiner, pp. 51–2.

52  Ibid. p. 55.

53  Ibid. p. 108.

54  Kant, 1956, p. 166.

55  *RK*, p. 88.

56  In the fifties, Reinhart Koselleck, under the influence of his teacher Schmitt, had characterised the history of enlightenment as the history of the development, within an absolutist political structure, of 'conscience', from a chink in Hobbes' otherwise closed system, from a private sphere of personal opinion which could be left to itself as long as it did not undermine the workings of the state, to an expanded realm of 'morality', to the site from which the workings of the state could be assessed and criticised. The idea of (moral) critique which enlightenment makes possible implies a crisis in the concept of the political itself. This crisis reached perhaps its highest point in Fichte's account of the French Revolution, in which the right of the people to alter the constitution is grounded in the all-embracing conscience. The concept of the political as the concept of that which prevents civil war and ensures the orderliness of human association, and in relation to which morality is this or that private opinion, is usurped by an idea of universal morality with which this or that political order or state is to be judged. See R. Koselleck, *Critique and Crisis*, Oxford, Berg, 1988; and C. Schmitt, *Der Leviathan in der Staatslehre des Thomas Hobbes*, Hamburg, Hanseatische Verlagsanstalt, 1938.

For Weber the legacy of this development is the need, today, to find *something* in which the personality is rooted, some foothold or anchorage. We can, with Marianne Weber, call this anchorage a *Sollen*, but if we do we should be clear from the start that Weber's freedom of conscience is as likely to amount to private opinion. And when Weber does use 'freedom' normatively, he speaks, to be sure, of freedom of conscience, but as often of freedom of movement, a resolutely Hobbesian formulation. His political theory exists within a tension between these two types of freedom. See Chapter 6, this volume.

57 See O. Marquard, 'Hegel und das Sollen', in *Schwierigkeiten mit der Geschichtsphilosophie*, Frankfurt, Suhrkamp, 1973, p. 45.

58 M. Scheler, 1971, p. 350.

59 *WL*, p. 148.

60 In fact, Simmel sets up the essay 'The Metropolis and Mental Life' as an account of what happens, 'empirically', when Schiller's *Stoff-* and *Formtrieb* begin to do each other's work, when the receptive faculty becomes too active – metropolitan life 'agitates the nerves to their strongest reactivity for such a long time that they finally cease to react at all' – and reason too passive – in the attitude of reserve, when 'culture' fails to keep them apart. The real story of the metropolis and mental life is perhaps less that of the triumph of objective over subjective culture, than that of the defeat of culture itself. See Simmel, 'The Metropolis and Mental Life', in K. Wolff (ed.), *The Sociology of Georg Simmel*, Glencoe, Illinois, Free Press, 1950.

61 G. Simmel, 'Vom Wesen der Kultur', in *Brücke und Tür*, Stuttgart, Köhler, 1957, p. 87

62 Ibid. p. 87.

63 Ibid. p. 88.

64 Ibid. p. 89.

65 Ibid. p. 90.

66 G. Simmel, 'On The Concept and Tragedy of Culture', in *The Conflict of Modern Culture and Other Essays*, New York, Teachers University Press, 1968, p. 225.

67 G. Simmel, *The Philosophy of Money*, London, Routledge & Kegan Paul, 1978, pp. 452–3. Translation altered.

68 W. Humboldt, *Gesammelte Schriften* Bd. 1, pp. 106, 118.

69 Simmel, 1957, p. 92.

70 G. Simmel, 1968, p. 224.

71 Ibid. p. 227.

72 Sombart, 1907, p. 3.

73 Simmel, 1978, p. 296.

74 Simmel, 1968, p. 235.

75 Ibid. p. 232.

76 G. Simmel, *Gesammelte Schriften zur Religionssoziologie*, Berlin, Duncker & Humblot, 1989, pp. 146–51.

## 3  THE ILLUSION OF THE EPOCH

1 H. Blumenberg, *The Legitimacy of the Modern Age*, Cambridge, MIT Press, 1985, Part 1.

2 See J. Habermas, *Towards a Rational Society*, London, Heinemann, 1971; K. Löwith, *Meaning in History*, Chicago, Chicago University Press, 1949.

3 See J. Habermas, *The Theory of Communicative Action* vol. 1, Cambridge, Polity, 1984a; *The Philosophical Discourse of Modernity*, Cambridge, Polity, 1987a.

4 See 'The Grand Inquisitor' in F. Dostoyevsky, *The Brothers Karamazov*, London, Penguin, 1953.
5 See the introduction to W. Connolly (ed.), *Legitimacy and the State*, Oxford, Blackwell, 1984.
6 *GARS*, p. 501; *FMW*, p. 281.
7 See E.B.F. Midgeley, *The Ideology of Max Weber*, Aldershot, Gower, 1983.
8 See T. Burger, *Max Weber's Theory of Concept Formation*, Durham NC, Duke University Press, 1987; T. Huff, *Max Weber and The Methodology of the Social Sciences*, New Brunswick, Transaction Books, 1984; and the introduction by Oakes to *RK*.
9 *RK*, p. 94.
10 A. Schopenhauer, *The World as Will and Representation* vol. 2, New York, Dover, 1966, p. 440.
11 Ibid. p. 440.
12 Ibid. p. 442.
13 F. Nietzsche, *Untimely Meditations*, Cambridge, CUP, 1983, p. 77.
14 Nietzsche, op. cit., 1983, p. 78.
15 Ibid. p. 79. On the distinction between the undisciplined curiosity of the 'historical sense' and what Nietzsche referred to later as 'measure', 'choosy curiosity' or in a phrase which Weber made his own, 'intellectual integrity', see F. Nietzsche, *Beyond Good and Evil*, New York, Free Press, 1966, sects 224, 227; *The Genealogy of Morals*, New York, Vintage, 1967a, Essay II, sect. 11; *The Twilight of the Idols and The Anti-Christ*, London, Penguin, 1968, pp. 122–3, 137.
16 Nietzsche, 1983, p. 162.
17 Ibid. p. 163.
18 Ibid. p. 163.
19 Ibid. p. 115.
20 Ibid. p. 84.
21 See Carl Schmitt's *Römischer Katholizismus und Politische Form*, Heilbronn, 1923, for an explicit critique of Comte's attempt to compare the scholar and the industrial merchant with the medieval 'representative' types, the priest and the knight. Modern *civil society* is incapable of representation, which only makes sense in the context of a *'ständisch'* articulation of society – Comte's two exemplary figures are 'either private people or exponents, not representatives' (p. 43) The modern concept of representation is mere *Vertretung*, the degeneration of *Representation*, a standing for rather than a standing before. Schiller makes a related point about the absence of representative figures as a characteristic of the modern age. And as we saw, MacIntyre judiciously uses the term 'characters'. See F. Schiller, *Letters on the Aesthetic Education of Man*, Oxford, Clarendon, 1967; A. MacIntyre, *After Virtue*, London, Duckworth, 1981.
22 Blumenberg, 1985, pp. 239–40.
23 Nietzsche, 1966, sect. 224.
24 Nietzsche, 1968, pp. 95, 119–21.
25 Nietzsche, 1967a, Essay II, sect. 12.
26 Ibid. Essay II, sect. 12.
27 Ibid. Essay III, sect. 24.

28  *RK* p. 223, n.54. The distinction between the logical – fatalistic – and psychological – activist – consequences of ideas is nowhere more acute. For further formulations see *PE*, pp. 89–90, 97–8, 187–8, 192, 232, 265; *MSS*, p. 96. For the opposite, 'liberal' view, see K. Popper, *The Open Society and Its Enemies*, London, Routledge & Kegan Paul, 1966; and I. Berlin, *Four Essays on Liberty*, Oxford, OUP, 1969. Berlin argues that to take literally the metaphors which constitute descriptions of historical inevitability 'is to commit oneself to the view that the notion of individual responsibility is in the end an illusion. The puppets may be conscious and identify themselves happily with the inevitable process in which they play their parts; but it remains inevitable, and they remain marionettes' (pp. 54–5). He goes on to claim that the eschewal of those categories with which we approach history in order to defend the idea of personal responsibility '*psychologically greatly restrains our capacity*' (p. 70). He identifies the only positive effect of deterministic theories with their capacity to limit our sense of human freedom when this might be expedient. Simmel too appears to subscribe to this view. In the preface to the second edition of *Problems of the Philosophy of History*, New York, Free Press, 1977, he writes: 'history as a brute fact, a reality, and a super-personal force threatens the integrity of the self quite as much as nature. . . . It is necessary to emancipate the self from historicism in the same way that Kant freed it from naturalism' (pp. viii–ix).

29  *MSS* p. 112. Compare Schiller on the difference between the '*spekulative Geist*' and the '*Geschäftsgeist*' and the effect of their separation: 'The one was bound to become a victim of empty sub-tilities, the other of narrow pedantry; for the one stood too high to discern the individual, the other too low to survey the whole' (Schiller, 1967, VI, 10).

30  C. Taylor, 'Interpretation and the Sciences of Man', *Review of Metaphysics*, vol. 25, 1971, pp. 3–51.

31  W. Dilthey, *Selected Writings*, Cambridge, CUP, 1976, p. 170, emphasis added.

32  Ibid. p. 194.

33  Ibid. p. 170.

34  For a defence, see R. Makreel, 'Dilthey and the neo-Kantians', *Journal of the History of Philosophy*, vol. 7, no. 4, 1969, pp. 423–40. As we will see, Rickert's critique of Dilthey at times rests on the attribution to his opponent of a mentalism which is not there. There is a difference between the primordiality of 'experience' and the primordiality of 'mental life'. 'Experience', even 'immediate experience', is always experience 'of' something.

35  Dilthey could never have written the first sentence of *Economy and Society*.

36  *RK*, p. 250, note 46.

37  A. Nehamas, 'Immanent and Transcendent Perspectivism', *Nietzsche Studien*, 12, 1983, pp. 473–90.

38  *WL*, pp. 175–6.

39  See Marianne Weber, *Max Weber*, New York, Wiley & Sons, 1975, pp. 67–8.

40  On this see H. Schnädelbach, *German Philosophy 1831–1933*, Cambridge, CUP, 1984. The removal of moral values from the top of a hierarchy of values, which clears the ground for neo-Kantian accounts of value spheres, is at least one area in which Nietzsche was not the decisive influence on Weber. This should be borne in mind by Weber scholars who, on encountering Nietzsche's remarks in *The Will to Power*, New York, Vintage Books, 1967b, sect. 583, and in 1968, pp. 81–2, are tempted to overestimate its significance. This is not to say that Nietzsche recapitulates Lotze's position. Indeed, the manner in which he undermines the primacy of moral values is entirely different. While Lotze effectively multiplies forms of uncondition- ality, Nietzsche insists first on the conditional status of moral values, and then deduces the dependence of all values upon 'life'. Indeed, we might say that Weber and Rickert felt a need to go 'back to Lotze' in the face of a challenge which Nietzsche expressed most forcefully in the statement that:

> one would have to have a position *outside* life, and on the other hand to know it as well as one, as many, as all who have lived it, to be allowed to touch on the problem of the *value* of life at all. . . . When we talk of values, we do so under the inspiration and from the perspective of life: life itself compels us to establish values, life itself evaluates through us *when* we establish values'.
>
> (Nietzsche, 1968. p. 45)

41  W. Windelband, *Introduction to Philosophy*, London, T. Fisher Unwin, 1921.
42  Ibid. p. 216.
43  Ibid. p. 216.
44  H. Rickert, *The Limits of Concept Formation in Natural Science*, Cambridge, CUP, 1986, pp. 216–7.
45  For the clearest expression of this position, see Windelband, 1921, pp. 176–82.
46  G. Rose, *Hegel Contra Sociology*, London, Athlone Press, 1981, p. 13.
47  Rickert, 1986, p. 146.
48  G. Simmel, *The Philosophy of Money*, London, Routledge & Kegan Paul, 1978, p. 63.
49  Rickert, 1986, pp. 116–29.
50  Ibid. p. 141.
51  H. Rickert, 'Lebenswerte und Kulturwerte', *Logos*, Bd. 1, 1911, p. 153.
52  Ibid. p. 154.
53  Ibid. p. 155.
54  Marianne Weber, 1975, p. 260.
55  *WL*, p. 132.
56  This term is taken from H. Rickert, *Science and History*, Princeton, D. Van Nostrand Company Inc., 1962, p. 34.
57  *GARS*, p. 14.
58  Schnädelbach, 1984a.
59  A notable misunderstanding of this point was Schutz's *The*

*Phenomenology of the Social World*, London, Heinemann, 1977. Although he is not attempting to provide an exposition of or even build on Weber's 'theory of action', it is significant that he (a) assumes that the main purpose of *ES* is contained in its first chapter; (b) accuses Weber of having failed to grasp what human action 'really is'; (c) does not use the term 'value' once, and instead argues that the meaningful construction of the social world is to be deduced from 'the most primitive and general characteristics of consciousness' (p. 12).

60  Simmel, 1978, pp. 138–43.
61  Ibid p. 68.
62  *MSS*, pp. 138–43.
63  Ibid. p. 76.
64  Ibid. p. 85.
65  *WL*, p. 175.
66  Ibid. p. 184–5, emphasis in original.
67  ibid. p. 180.
68  G.W.F. Hegel, *The Philosophy of Right*, Oxford, OUP, 1952, sect. 151.
69  E. Cassirer, *Zur Logik der Kulturwissenschaften*, Darmstadt, 1961, p. 63.
70  *WL*, p. 148.
71  *MSS*, p. 84.
72  Ibid. p. 143.
73  *GARS*, p. 203.
74  Rickert, 1986, p. 151.
75  *MSS*, p. 151.
76  *WL*, p. 531.
77  Ibid. p. 524.
78  Ibid. p. 263. For the same point see *MSS*, pp. 144–5, 148, 160.
79  Ibid. p. 247.
80  Rickert, 1986, p. 135.
81  Ibid. p. 137, note 2.
82  *RK* p. 175–6.
83  PE, p. 30.
84  *RK*, p. 267, note 77. Whether this entails a rejection of metaphysics as such depends upon whether Weber elevated the purposes of science (including the reduction of 'philosophy' to the study of *Weltanschauung*) to a rejection of philosophy. Scheler argues that Weber reduced the great metaphysicians to 'prophets'. The most charitable interpretation of this would be that Weber knew that in order to distinguish his science from metaphysics he had to remain ignorant of metaphysics. His lumping together of a disparate group of prophets, philosophers and theologians under 'the speculative view of life' is the self-conscious expression of this ignorance, and of the knowledge that, in order to understand metaphysics deeply enough to reject it, one must become a metaphysician. Midgeley's charge, that for Weber 'any philosophical debate, to the extent that it denies that it is ideological, is deemed to be not tenable', is misplaced. Heidegger's statement, that a philosophy of values is 'the greatest blasphemy imaginable against being' is more readily applicable

to Rickert – who did claim to be posing 'fundamental questions' – than to Weber – who did not. See M. Scheler, 'Max Weber's Exclusion of Philosophy', in P. Lassmann and I. Velody (eds), *Max Weber's Science as a Vocation*, London, Allen & Unwin, 1988, p. 90; Midgeley, 1983, p. 129; M. Heidegger, *Basic Writings*, London, Routledge & Kegan Paul, 1978, p. 228.

85   This gives the concept of culture the polemical character pointed out in Chapter 2.
86   *WL*, p. 494.
87   See W. Hennis, *Max Weber: Essays in Reconstruction*, London, Allen & Unwin, 1987, pp. 62–104.
88   *RK*, p. 204
89   Dilthey, 1976, p. 198.
90   *WL*, p. 97, note 3. The affinities between Weber's 'point of view' and Nietzsche's 'perspective' may be pursued by comparing Nietzsche, *The Gay Science*, New York, Vintage, 1974, sect. 143; 1967b, sect. 600; and most famously 1967a, Essay III, sect. 12.
91   *WL*, p. 122.
92   See the subtitle to Marshall Berman's *All that is Solid Melts into Air*, London, Verso, 1983, a work which exhibits many of the character- istics against which Weber's methodological strictures are directed. The opening sentence gives the game away: 'There is a mode of vital experience – experience of space and time, of the self and others, of life's possibilities and perils – that is shared by men and women all over the world today. I will call this body of experience "modernity" ' (p. 15).
93   *PE*, p. 11.
94   *PE*, pp. 76–8; *FMW*, p. 293.
95   *MSS*, p. 155.
96   Ibid. pp. 5–6; *FMW*, pp. 134–7.
97   Simmel, 1978, p. 256.

## 4   THE *ZWISCHENBETRACHTUNG* I: THEORY OF MODERNITY OR THEORY OF CULTURE?

1   The most notable interpretations here are those of Schluchter and Habermas, both of whom appear to be engaged in an attempt to correct what they perceive to be Weber's systematic shortcomings. On the other hand, more 'humanistic' interpreters such as Hennis or Scaff, and to a certain extent Mitzman, often feel it necessary to jettison much epistemological baggage in order to reveal Weber the human being. They all assume that the *Zg* can be read as a 'diagnosis of our time', but none takes seriously the question of the extent to which the diagnosis is undermined by its extension to the science which makes it.
2   The main texts with which the *Zg* should be compared are Simmel's 'On the Concept and Tragedy of Culture', in *The Conflict of Modern Culture and Other Essays*, New York, Teachers College Press, 1968;

W. Windelband, *Introduction to Philosophy*, London, T. Fisher Unwin, 1921; H. Rickert, *System der Philosophie*; C. Schmitt, *The Concept of the Political*, New Brunswick, NJ, Rutgers University Press, 1976; and E. Spranger, *Lebensformen*, Halle, Niemeyer, 1930 (especially section 2, 'Die idealen Grundtypen der Individualität').

3   Weber, *GARS*, p. 537.

4   Ibid. pp. 536–7. The translation by Gerth and Wright Mills contains one negative too many: 'They are not intended to show that there is no standpoint from which the conflicts could not be held to be resolved in a higher synthesis.' See *FMW*, p. 323.

5   Ibid. pp. 127, 152, 281, 324; *RC*, p. 235; *RK*, p. 192; *ES*, pp. 450–1, 499, 545.

6   Windelband, 1921, p. 328.

7   M. Scheler, 'Kultur und Religion: Eine Besprechung zu Rudolf Eucken's "Der Wahrheitsgehalt der Religion" ', in *Gesammelte Werke* vol. 1, München, Francke, 1971.

8   H. Rickert, 'Lebenswerte und Kulturwerte', *Logos*, Bd. 1, 1911, pp. 131–66.

9   G. Simmel, *Gesammelte Schriften zur Religionssoziologie*, Berlin, Duncker und Humblot, 1989, p. 110.

10   Ibid. p. 112.

11   Ibid. p. 114.

12   *GARS*, p. 536. Although in the essay Weber adheres fairly closely to this purpose, in other contexts these schemata serve him remarkably well in the articulation of his own '*Weltanschauung*'.

13   On the use of the term *Naturmensch* see M. Green, *Mountain of Truth*, Hanover NH, University Press of New England, 1986.

14   J. Habermas, *The Theory of Communicative Action* vol. 1, Cambridge, Polity, 1984a, p. 158. In the light of the discussion in Chapter 2, these distinctions are bound to appear forced. Certainly, the 'Author's Introduction' does not give the impression that art, architecture, music, science or religion are less worthy of the status of explananda. The 'fact' that Weber's work was oriented towards capitalism, the modern state and formal law was a product of his 'point of view'. It did not mean that art, religion or science were mere explanans, nor that they represent a 'premodern' 'stage' of rationalisation. If the development of modern capitalism is to be 'explained', the explanans might as easily be the rationalisation of law, politics, or indeed economic activity. If talk of stages is warranted here, it can refer only to logical stages of concept formation: (i) the selection of a culturally significant segment of an infinite reality; and (ii) the selection of a causally significant segment from the possible causal factors in the emergence of the segment under investigation. If Weber happens to investigate the causal significance of early modern religious doctrine for modern economic practice, this is a corrective to – and thereby rejection of – Marxism, not the construction of an 'alternative' stage model.

15   Ibid. p. 159.

16   *GARS*, p. 541.

17  Habermas, 1984a, p. 234.
18  Incidentally, the diagram on p. 235 of Habermas, 1985a, contains a category mistake. If, as the diagram suggests – and this classification is highly debatable – the goods germane to the practices of science, economics, politics and 'hedonistic countercultures' are knowledge, wealth, power and love(!), that appropriate to art cannot be 'art'. Weber refers explicitly to the danger of this mistake. See *MSS*, p. 150; *WL*, p. 252.
19  Habermas, 1984a, p. 237.
20  W. Schluchter, *The Rise of Western Rationalism*, Berkeley, University of California, 1981, p. 19.
21  Ibid. p. 19.
22  Ibid. p. 27.
23  Ibid. p. 28.
24  See note 2.
25  *FMW*, p. 328.
26  Ibid. pp. 147–8.
27  Ibid. p. 35.
28  Guy Oakes ignores the ambiguity at work in Weber's concept of culture:

> Weber locates the polytheism of values historically and socio-logically. It is not a characteristic of all cultures. On the contrary, it is the product of a specifically modern culture. Simmel, on the other hand, bases the multiplicity of forms on ontological considerations.
>
> (See, G. Simmel, *Essays on Interpretation in Social Science*, Manchester, Manchester University Press, 1980, p. 91)

29  *WL*, p. 605. Here, the epochal significance of 'modernity' seems to be secured through a rhetoric of recognition of the type discussed in Chapter 1. The splitting apart of a substantial cultural unity is revealed as the discovery that that unity never existed.
30  *MSS*, p. 17.
31  Ibid. p. 18.
32  *GARS*, p. 145. Erich Kahler argues that in the ancient world, at any given time or place there could never have been a struggle between different gods. Life was unambiguous, and the task of the wise man – in contrast to that of the modern cultural scientist – was to disclose that lack of ambiguity, not to 'force' upon the individual a choice between gods. It is one thing to argue that a choice must be made, but that once it is made the demands placed on an individual are unambiguous. It is another to argue, as Weber does, that one must choose when to follow one god and when another.
    Kahler's remark that the ancient gods were living beings rather than conceptual abstractions is also apposite. He attempts to criticise Weber with Weber's own resources, arguing that the binding quality of conceptual abstractions can never match that of a living being. But Weber did allow for this – the binding quality of value spheres develops precisely when the intrinsic logics of the conceptual

abstractions we call 'the market' or 'the state' are 'personified', are treated as actors rather than loci for action. See E. Kahler, 'The Vocation of Science', in P. Lassman and I. Velody, *Max Weber's Science as a Vocation*, London, Allen & Unwin, 1980.

33  *FMW*, pp. 278–9.
34  Ibid. p. 277.
35  H. Blumenberg, *The Legitimacy of the Modern Age*, Cambridge, MIT Press, 1985, p. 47.
36  K. Löwith, *Max Weber and Karl Marx*, London, Allen & Unwin, 1982, p. 40.
37  *GARS*, p. 252.
38  Ibid. p. 253.
39  See Nietzsche, 1967b, sect. 20.
40  *FMW*, p. 325.
41  *GARS*, p. 537.
42  *MSS*, p. 92.
43  G.W.F. Hegel, *Lectures on the The Philosophy of History*, New York, Dover, 1956, p. 131.
44  Ibid. p. 132.
45  *GARS*, p. 445.
46  Tenbruck's celebrated essay appears to presuppose that these are the only two viable alternatives, and chooses a version of the second. See F. Tenbruck, 'The Problem of Thematic Unity in the Works of Max Weber', *British Journal of Sociology*, vol. 31, no. 3, 1980.
47  *AJ*, p. 4.
48  *GARS*, p. 512.
49  Ibid. p. 267.
50  *ASAC*, p. 385.
51  *WL*, p. 257.
52  See Chapter 1, note 32.
53  *WL*, p. 612.
54  *FMW*, p. 329.
55  Ibid. p. 329.
56  *GARS*, p. 544.
57  *WL*, p. 584.
58  Ibid. p. 585.
59  Ibid. pp. 636–7.
60  G. Simmel, *The Philosophy of Money*, London, Routledge & Kegan Paul, 1978, p. 296. Compare Nietzsche, 1974, sect. 40. We have already seen that for Weber, the modernity of culture consisted precisely in the identification of *Persönlichkeit* and *Leistung*, in the idea that person ality was to be expressed through, rather than maintained in the face of, the impersonal character of worldly achievement. Or, if we accept the personality/achievement distinction, the dignity of human beings lies precisely in the individuality *of* achievement, and is indeed compromised by the constant striving to express an allegedly pre-existing individuality *in* achievement. Weber makes the point in a letter to Sombart, albeit in a tone which seems to undermine it:

The difference in our standpoints consists in the fact that: *You* want to write 'personal' books. *I* am convinced that personal uniqueness ... is expressed, and *only* expressed, when it is *not willed*, when it retreats behind the book and its objectivity, as all great masters have retreated behind their works. Where one *wants* to be 'personal', one disturbs the artistic value and almost always gets stuck in the orbit of the 'typical'. That which you want to exhibit before the public as 'I' has ... thoroughly typical and very few 'personal' characteristics, i.e.: precisely that feature of the personal which is *significant* disappears and everyone has the impression that they are dealing with one of the many representatives of the usual 'aestheticism' and the *typical* 'aristocracy' which corresponds to it.

Simmel had expressed this in the same way in his Kant lectures:

It is precisely Kant's work which is Kant's 'personality', since it is only here that he is wholly individual and incomparable, certainly not in circumstances of his so-called personal life, whose qualities he shares with numerous others, and which are actually the impersonal aspects of the human being.

(See *MWGA*, p. 605; G. Simmel, *Kant: Sechzehn Vorlesungen*, Leipzig, Duncker & Humblot, 1904, p. 5)

61  *WL*, p. 581.
62  *AJ*, p. 345.
63  *WL*, p. 587.
64  *FMW*, p. 331.
65  On this, as on many other features of Weber's discussion of the market, Marx remained an essential resource. See K. Marx, *The Poverty of Philosophy*, Moscow, Progress, 1975a, especially the section on 'the personification of society'.
66  Incidentally, it would be false to believe that the term 'religious ethic of brotherliness' could be held, by analogy, to be a description of Marxism, and that this is the manner in which Weber intended it to be read. Weber was highly critical of those such as Kautsky who would attempt to identify the early Christians with a proto-proletarian movement. In this critique Weber interprets the ethic of brotherliness as a virtuoso ethic, a set of demands few could meet. It resists the universalism attributed to it by Kautsky. The difference between Catholicism and Marxism for Weber would be that while Catholicism represented the institutionalisation of an ethic which in its purest form demanded a love few could exhibit, Marxism set its standards fairly low from the start, grounding its ethical appeal, and not just its institutionalisation, in average human qualities.
67  *ES*, p. 560.
68  *WL*, p. 560.
69  The tension between the ultimate value of brotherly love and the level of personal ethical accomplishments which can be realistically demanded of a member of a universalist religious institution is pushed to its limits in Dostoyevsky's 'The Grand Inquisitor'. Its

influence on the *Zg*, and indeed on much of the rest of Weber's work, is clear if not well documented. Only Honigsheim made anything of it. The Grand Inquisitor accuses Christ of demanding from others a capacity for love of which only a few are capable. His is a virtuoso ethic masquerading as a universalist ethic. The very worldly success of the Catholic Church lay in its preparedness to accept that the vast majority were incapable of exhibiting the brotherly love in whose name it acted, to deny its adherents the freedom of conscience on which that love was held to depend. See F. Dostoyevsky, *The Brothers Karamazov*, London, Penguin, 1953.

70  *FMW*, p. 332.
71  *PE*, p. 172.
72  Ibid. p. 109.
73  Ibid. p. 97.
74  Ibid. p. 147, emphasis added.
75  Ibid. pp. 181–2.
76  *RC*, p. 235.
77  Ibid. p. 235.
78  *RI*, p. 342.
79  *RC*, p. 235.
80  S. Kierkegaard, *Either/Or*, Princeton, Princeton University Press, 1987, p. 176.
81  Ibid. p. 211.
82  Ibid. p. 212.
83  Ibid. p. 270.
84  Ibid. p. 262.
85  *FMW*, p. 321, emphasis added.
86  *PE*, p. 222.
87  Ibid. p. 53. Beetham ignores this point in claiming that Weber wanted to show how profit making can be 'seen in an ethical light'. If this were so, it would make Weber a Marxist or a Nietzschean. See D. Beetham, *Max Weber and the Theory of Modern Politics*, Cambridge, Polity, p. 269.
88  *PE*, p. 58.
89  *FMW*, p. 309.
90  *PE*, p. 276.
91  Ibid. p. 262.
92  Schluchter, 1981, p. 171.
93  J. Habermas, *The Theory of Communicative Action* vol. 2, Cambridge, Polity, 1987b, p. 304.
94  Habermas, 1984a, p. 228.
95  *FMW*, p. 333.
96  Ibid. p. 333.
97  *WL*, p. 407.
98  Ibid. p. 413.
99  Ibid. p. 414.
100  *FMW*, p. 336.
101  Ibid. p. 334.
102  *GARS*, p. 547.

103  Ibid. p. 549.
104  Ibid. p. 548.
105  *WL*, p. 55.
106  *FMW*, p. 334.
107  *RC*, p. 113. Weber's adolescent preference for Homer over Virgil never left him. See Marianne Weber, *Max Weber*, New York, Wiley & Sons, 1975.
108  See, for instance, the article 'Zum Thema der "Kriegsschuld" ', in *GPS*.
109  *FMW*, p. 336.
110  C. Schmitt, 1976, p. 22.
111  Ibid., p. 33.
112  Ibid. p. 49.
113  Ibid. p. 36.
114  It should prove possible to show that Schmitt's work contains the resources for a critique of Habermas's theory of communicative action. which presupposes a context of argument between private individuals who, while constituting a public, are not themselves constituted through the act of communication. Although the ideal speech situation is tied to an evolutionary perspective which implies a process of moral development, Habermas claims that it is a presupposition which any competent speaker brings to any interaction. The communicating individual must be a linguistically complete subject on each occasion of his/her communicative activity.
115  Schmitt, 1976, p. 70.
116  Ibid. p. 72.
117  *ES*, p. 902.
118  Ibid. p. 913
119  For examples of work which assume a ready comparability between Weber and Schmitt, see W. Mommsen, *Max Weber and German Politics*, Chicago, Chicago University press, 1984; and W. Hennis, *Max Weber: Essays in Reconstruction*, London, Allen & Unwin, 1988.
120  C. Schmitt, *Political Theology*, Cambridge, MIT Press, 1985a, p. 15.
121  Ibid. p. 15. There is a formal connection here between Schmitt's state of exception and some of the gestures of post-modernism, most notably the thesis according to which an 'outside' is constitutive of an 'inside' which is conventionally taken to be foundational.
122  *GARS*, p. 555.
123  *FMW*, p. 342.
124  *GARS*, p. 515.
125  Ibid. p. 558.

## 5   THE *ZWISCHENBETRACHTUNG* II: A DUAL THEORY OF TRAGEDY

1  W. Schluchter, 'The Paradox of Rationalisation', in G. Roth and W. Schluchter (eds), *Max Weber's Vision of History*, Berkeley, University of California Press, 1979a, pp. 59–64.

2  Discussion of the relationship between 'meaning' and 'cause' in Weber's work still tends to be restricted to courses devoted to Weber's 'methodology', thereby reducing it to a problem in the philosophy of the social sciences.

3  *GARS*, p. 566. The translation is: 'It does not claim to offer intellectual knowledge concerning what is or what should be.'

4  Ibid. p. 566.

5  *FMW*, p. 355.

6  *GARS*, p. 542.

7  Weber's attitude to the modern passion for founding new sciences should be compared with Nietzsche's views on the modern proliferation of philosophies of life. See *MSS*, p. 69; F. Nietzsche, *Human, All Too Human*, Cambridge, CUP, 1986, pp. 24, 103, 116; *Beyond Good and Evil*, New York, Vintage, 1966, pp. 111, 146, 150–3. And see now L. Scaff, *Fleeing the Iron Cage*, Berkeley, University of California Press, 1989.

8  cf. G. Simmel, *Problems of the Philosophy of History*, New York, Free Press, 1977, pp. 185–202.

9  See Chapter 4, note 12.

10 *FMW*, p. 143

11 R. Eucken, *Geistige Strömungen der Gegenwart* 4. Auflage, Leipzig, Veit, 1909, p. 5.

12 A theme which runs throughout Habermas's works. See especially *The Philosophical Discourse of Modernity*, Cambridge, Polity, 1987a.

13 J. Habermas, *The Theory of Communicative Action*, vol. 1, Cambridge, Polity, 1984a, pp. 234–5.

14 Ibid. pp. 161, 166, 234, 235.

15 *GARS*, p. 537.

16 This image, borrowed from Schopenhauer (who presumably was) was used by Weber in *PV* to characterise revolution. It would be wrong for Marxists to treat this as a caricature. At roughly the same time as Weber was writing *PV* Rosa Luxemburg, who hardly shared Weber's world-view – he once said she belonged in a zoological garden – was writing:

> The 'golden mean' cannot be maintained in any revolution. The law of its nature demands a quick decision: either the locomotive drives forward full-steam ahead to the most extreme point of historical ascent, or it rolls back down again to the starting point at the bottom; and those who would keep it with their weak powers half way up the hill, it but drags down with it irredeemably into the abyss.
>
> (See R. Luxemburg, *The Russian Revolution*, Ann Arbor, University of Michigan Press, 1970, p. 38)

17 See S. Kierkegaard, *The Concept of Irony*, London, Collins, 1966.

18 Simmel, 1977, p. 122.

19 Ibid. p. 123.

20 This gives the lie to Habermas's claim that 'Weber himself made no attempt to order systematically and to analyze from formal points of view the value spheres that he gleaned inductively and treated in a

descriptive attitude'. See Habermas, 1984a, p. 186. For a sensitive treatment of this issue see F. Tenbruck, 'Formal Sociology', in L. Coser, *Georg Simmel*, Englewood Cliffs NJ, Prentice–Hall, 1959.

21  Rationalists can normally be distinguished from irrationalists on the basis of the priority accorded to identity or difference.

22  G. Simmel, *Gesammelte Schriften zur Religionssoziologie*, Berlin, Duncker & Humblot, 1989, p. 110.

23  Ibid. p. 111

24  *FMW*, p. 143. The impulse to construct the history of science in this way was provided, once again, by Nietzsche. See F. Nietzsche, *The Genealogy of Morals*, New York, Vintage, 1967, Essay III sects 23, 24; *The Gay Science*, New York, Vintage, 1974, sects 37, 123.

25  See Weber's letter to Else von Richtofen, recommending that the *Archiv für Sozialwissenschaft und Sozialpolitik* reject an article by 'Dr. X', in *ST*, p. 333–8.

26  Marianne Weber, *Max Weber*, New York, Wiley & Sons, 1975, p. 698.

27  *FMW*, pp. 151–6; *MSS*, pp. 18–19, 23, 24, 44, 52–4, 58, 110; *ES*, pp. 104, 112.

28  The English translation omits this subheading, thereby leading the reader to believe that the four and a half pages devoted to it are part of the section on the intellectual sphere.

29  *FMW*, p. 354.

30  Nietzsche, 1967a, Essay III sect. 20, II sects 6, 7, III sect. 14; and *The Will to Power*, New York, Vintage, 1967b, sect. 121.

31  Nietzsche, 1967b, p. 258. See also pp. 287, 324, 343; and 1974, sect. 276; 1967b, sects 450, 1041.

32  *FMW*, p. 281.

33  Ibid. p. 354.

34  Ibid. p. 354.

35  Ibid. p. 354.

36  Simmel, 1989, pp. 115–16.

37  *FMW*, pp. 140, 356.

38  A recognition of culture's *Eigengesetzlichkeit* was a feature of one of the two main strands of German *Kulturprotestantismus*, centred on the *Deutsche Protestantenverein*, established in 1863, whose aim was the reconciliation of religion and culture, to be achieved by the integration of cultural spheres in a *'nationaler Kulturstaat'*. For the group around *'Die Christliche Welt'* (such as Baumgarten, Martin Rade and Troeltsch) this amounted to a liberal accommodation to culture and an overoptimistic belief in progress. For both, incidentally, the allegedly German distinction between culture and civilisation collapses – as it does for Weber. See H. Liebersohn, *Religion and Industrial Society*, Philadelphia, American Philosophical Society, 1986; F. Graf, 'Kulturprotestantismus', *Archiv für Begriffsgeschichte*, vol. 28, 1984.

39  *MWGA*, p. 606.

40  See Scaff, 1989, for a statement of both these positions.

41  Schluchter, 1979, p. 63.

42  See Scaff, 1989, and W. Hennis, *Max Weber: Essays in Reconstruction*, London, Allen & Unwin, 1988, pp. 64–5, 78.

43  Schluchter and, by implication, Habermas, who wishes to identify
    what Weber refers to as a universalist ethic of brotherliness with
    'communicative ethics'. In doing so he wishes to recover an ethics
    which on his own account of Weber appears 'pre-modern'. If this
    periodisation means anything, the attempt to graft this rationalism
    on to an ethic of fraternisation, and refer to it as 'the project of
    modernity', will always be forced. From the point at which they meet,
    they appear to lead in opposite historical directions, fraternisation as
    far into the past as the overcoming of a dualism between in-group
    and out-group morality, reason as far into the future as Habermas is
    prepared to push it. The greater the purity demanded of either, the
    greater the tension between them.
44  *WL*, p. 504.
45  Ibid. p. 51.
46  Ibid. p. 152.
47  Ibid. p. 154.
48  S. Kalberg, 'Max Weber's Types of Rationality', *Sociology*, 1979,
    pp. 127–40.
49  See L. Strauss, *Studies in Platonic Political Philosophy*, Chicago, Chicago
    University Press, 1983; E.B.F. Midgeley, *The Ideology of Max Weber*,
    Aldershot, Gower, 1983.
50  S. Kalberg, 'Max Weber's Types of Rationality', *American Journal of
    Sociology*, vol. 65, no. 5, 1980, p. 1148.
51  W. Stark, 'Max Weber and the Heteronomy of Purpose', *Social
    Research*, vol. 34, 1967, pp. 249–64.
52  *WL*, p. 154. One suspects that the joy Weber expressed in the first
    footnote to the essay on the Protestant sects in response to Troeltsch's
    use of the Church/Sect distinction was more than merely method-
    ological. See *FMW*, p. 450; *ES* pp. 56, 131, 386, 456, 493, 582, 602,
    610, 1164, 1204–10; *PE*, pp. 145, 152, 254–5.
        Without commenting on its wider significance Kalberg has
    described 'value rationalisation' as the elevation of a practical
    rationality of *interest* to the status of the substantive rationality of an
    ethical *standard,* and refers to value postulates which 'take on an
    ethical *dimension'*. His account makes clear, perhaps unwittingly, that
    a sociology for which 'the vast majority of rationalisation processes
    are rooted in interests and fail to legitimate themselves adequately at
    the level of values' is anathema to Catholicism. See Kalberg, 1980,
    p. 1173. The authority – not the 'standard'! – of revelation consists
    precisely in the 'fact' that it cannot be rationalised, nor subjected to a
    causal explanation whose explanans includes the interest situation of
    the intellectual strata who are its 'bearers'. Weber's 'Protestant'
    account of action in the *WL* would be rather trivial were it not for his
    frequent assertion of the illegitimacy of imposing modern categories
    on pre-modern cultural forms.
53  *MSS*, p. 95.
54  *WL*, p. 603.
55  Ibid., p. 605.

56  G. Simmel, *The Conflict of Modern Culture and Other Essays*, New York, Teachers College Press, 1968, p. 36.

57  G. Simmel, *The Philosophy of Money*, London, Routledge & Kegan Paul, 1978, p. 302.

58  Ibid. p. 296.

59  See G. Simmel, *On Individuality and Social Forms*, Chicago, Chicago University Press, 1971, pp. 259–93, 324–39; 1978, Ch. 4.

60  Weber, 'Geschsftäbericht der Deutschen Gesellschaft für Soziologie (1910)' *Verhandlungen des ersten Deutschen Soziologentages*, Tübingen, J.C.B. Mohr (Paul Siebeck), pp. 98–9.

61  Simmel, 1978, p. 470.

62  K. Marx and F. Engels, *The German Ideology*, London, Lawrence & Wishart, 1977, p. 54. And, one might add, to the practical theorist of communicative action, whose distorted onesidedness is proportionate to the imbalance in the opportunity for the discursive redemption of validity claims.

63  This remains a somewhat impoverished description of the realm of freedom.

64  *FMW*, p. 131; *ES*, pp. 139, 218–19, 285, 980–3, 1261, 1394.

65  *FMW*, p. 356.

66  Ibid. p. 135.

67  K. Marx, *Early Writings*, London, Penguin, 1975, p. 333.

68  Ibid. p. 348.

69  Weber (and Simmel for that matter) did not need to have read the Paris Manuscripts in order to recognise this.

70  cf. *ES*, pp. 1001–2. Compare Weber's formulation of this choice between 'personality types' with that of that between bureaucracy and dilettantism in 'the field of administration' (pp. 223–4).

71  E. Cassirer, *Zur Logik der Kulturwissenschaften*, Darmstadt, Wissenschaftliche Buchgemeinschaft, 1961.

72  F. Nietzsche, *The Will to Power* (1967b), sect. 397.

73  J. Bunyan, *The Pilgrim's Progress*, London, Dent, 1954, pp. 36–7. Weber could have used the term '*eiserner Käfig*' ('iron cage'), but chose '*stahlhartes Gehäuse*', which is always translated as 'iron cage', but which would be more literally rendered as 'a casing as hard as steel'. Although Weber is not noted for his literary style, the idea that a light cloak could become an iron cage is Parsons'. What I think he is trying to convey is that that which was once a means by which one could make one's way in and thereby transform the world has become, at best, nothing more than an unwieldy means of defence against the world that transformation created. Perhaps he should have written that the light cloak had become a suit of armour.

74  F. Nietzsche, *Human, All Too Human*, Cambridge, CUP, 1986, sect. 537.

75  K. Jaspers, *Leonardo, Descartes, Max Weber*, London, Routledge & Kegan Paul, 1965, p. 195.

76  K. Löwith, *Max Weber and Karl Marx*, London, Allen & Unwin, 1982, p. 58.

77  *FMW*, p. 352.

78  Those who think Weber attached unambiguously positive personal

significance to meeting the 'demands of the day', and have done the phrase to death because of it, should consult now one of Weber's letters to Jellinek, in which he castigates his friend for suggesting that things were as bad for them both:

> If you had the faintest idea of the course of my existence, as it has developed in its leaden unity for nine years now [i.e. since his breakdown] and – with luck! – will develop further, you would not, even as a joke, insinuate that things are no different for me than for others. My existence rests on the *possibility* of not being *reminded* of how I live, and I have over the years developed a sure method, of neither thinking of the past, present or future, nor of brooding, but of living as the day demands and in accordance with what it offers. Please do not disturb this circle.
>
> (See *MWGA II*, pp. 427–8)

79  S. P. Turner and R. Factor, *Max Weber and the Dispute over Reason and Value*, London, Routledge & Kegan Paul, 1984, p. 51.
80  See *FMW*, pp. 151–2; *MSS*, p. 3.
81  On the 'cultural unity' of the middle ages, Weber writes:

> even during these periods of cooperation Occidental hierocracy lived in a state of tension with the political power. . . . In the Occident authority was set against authority, legitimacy against legitimacy, one office charisma against the other, yet in the minds of rulers and ruled the ideal remained the unification of both political and hierocratic power.
>
> (*ES*, p. 1193)

82  *WL*, p. 504.
83  Possible doubts about the extent to which Weber repudiated a scientistic critique of religion may be dispelled by comparing the *Zg* with another 'cultural diagnosis', Freud's 'Civilisation and its Discontents'. Compare especially the phrase 'sacrifice of the intellect' with the crudity of Freud's 'intimidation of the intelligence'. See *The Penguin Freud Library*, vol. 12, London, Penguin, 1985.
84  Quoted in M. Landmann, *Pluralität und Antinomie*, München, Beck, 1963, p. 124.
85  As, for example, Landmann has done, and as Scaff seems to want to do. See Landmann, 1963, p. 132; Scaff, 1989, p. 125.
86  G.W.F. Hegel, *Philosophy of Right*, Oxford, OUP, 1952.
87  Nietzsche, 1968, p. 151.
88  *FMW*, p. 357.

## 6  DOGMATISM, VANITY AND VOCATION: THE POLITICAL PERSONALITY

1  I. Kant, *Groundwork of the Metaphysics of Morals*, New York, Harper & Row, 1964, p. 58.
2  See R. Eden, *Political Leadership and Nihilism*, Tampa, University Press of Florida, 1983, Ch. 6.

3   K. Jaspers, *Leonardo, Descartes, Max Weber*, London, Routledge & Kegan Paul, 1965, p. 227.
4   It is this Arendtian view which informs Hennis's work.
5   M. Warren, 'Max Weber's Liberalism for a Nietzschean World', *American Political Science Review*, vol. 82, 1988, p. 36.
6   See W. Hennis, *Politik und Praktische Philosophie*, Frankfurt, Suhrkamp, 1963, pp. 38, 49.
7   *NS*, p. 440.
8   *WL*, p. 166. The translation obscures this. See *MSS*, p. 66.
9   *NS*, p. 438.
10  Jaspers, 1965, p. 227.
11  *SV* is a statement of science's vulnerability. Wolin gives a hint of this: 'Weber never set down a coherent political theory comparable to the great theories of the tradition of political theory. That inability may well be the meaning of social science.' See S. Wolin, 'Max Weber: Legitimation, Method and the Politics of Theory', in W. Connolly, *Legitimacy and the State*, Oxford, Blackwell, 1984, p. 67.
12  *ES*, p. 55.
13  Aristotle, *Politics*, Oxford, OUP, 1948, 1252a.
14  The theory of the incommensurability of cultural value spheres has led both Warren, and Turner and Factor to the conclusion that Weber's position implies an 'organic' theory of culture. In the essay on value freedom, he writes that 'every single important action and ultimately life as a whole, if it is not to be permitted to run on as an event in nature but is instead to be consciously guided, is a series of ultimate decisions through which the soul, as in Plato, *chooses* its fate – that is, the meaning of its doing and being'. See *WL*, pp. 507–8. He then notes that (a) representatives of this view have often been interpreted as 'relativists' and (b) that the link between the idea that the soul chooses its fate and relativism requires the support of 'a very special type of ("organic") metaphysics'. Neither Turner and Factor nor Warren acknowledge that this is a reference to the Hinduism and Buddhism essay. For the individual tied to the Hindu *karma* mechanism of rebirth, conduct in this life determines one's caste position in the next, which implies in turn that one is 'responsible' for having been born into one's caste position in this life, that one has chosen one's fate. This doctrine of individual compensation was combined with the ineliminable character of the caste order to produce 'an organic relativism of world-affirmation' in which 'the struggle of man with man in all its forms was as little a problem as his struggle with animals and gods ... Men were not ... in principle equal, but forever unequal'. There was no natural law with which to contrast positive law, and hence no development of anything resembling the modern western concepts of a 'public sphere' or 'human rights'. The possibility of fraternisation in the Occidental Christian sense, upon which a universalist ethics might be based, was absent. See Weber, *The Religion of India*, New York, Free Press, 1958, pp. 144, 192; Warren, 1988; S.P. Turner and R. Factor, *Max Weber and the Dispute over Reason and Value*, London, Routledge, 1984.

15  *WuG*, p. 7.
16  On the use of organic metaphors see *WL*, pp. 10, 11, 19, 21, 24, 33–5, 44, 66, 138, 141.
17  See here G.W.F. Hegel, *Philosophy of Right*, Oxford, OUP, 1952; O. Gierke, *Das Wesen des menschlichen Verbandes*, Darmstadt, Wissenschaftliche Buchgemeinschaft, 1902; E. Durkheim, *The Division of Labour in Society*, London, Macmillan, 1984, Preface to second edition; *Professional Ethics and Civic Morals*, London, Routledge & Kegan Paul, 1957; and A. Black, *Guilds and Civil Society*, London, Methuen, 1985.
18  *NS* p. 438.
19  Durkheim, 1957, p. 73.
20  On this distinction see O. Gierke, *Natural Law and the Theory of Society*, Cambridge, CUP, 1957; M. Oakeshott, 'On the Character of a Modern European State' in *On Human Conduct*, Oxford, Clarendon, 1975. At several points Weber describes the modern state as an 'enterprise', a defining feature of *universitas*. But as far as a 'normative' political theory can be extracted from Weber's work, what Oakeshott calls the character of the state must, for Weber, be *societas*. For the state as an enterprise, see *GPS*, pp. 321, 388, 390, 401; *WuG*, pp. 29–30.
21  On collegiality see *WuG*, pp. 161–75. Weber's objections to corporatism are more than a theoretical rejection of organicism. The basic presupposition of modern corporatism is that economic action can be ethically regulated. It was his suggestion that the impersonality of the capitalist–worker relationship ruled this out that caused so much fuss at the Protestant–Social Congress in 1894. See 'Referat des Generalsekretars Pastor Paul Göhre und Professor Max Weber uber die Deutschen Landarbeiter', *Bericht über die Verhandlungen des 5. Evangelisch-Sozialen Kongresses*, Berlin, Rehwitsch und Seeler, 1894. The further assumption of an identity of intra-professional interest was attacked in the section of the objectivity essay on 'the interests of agriculture'. See *MSS*, pp. 108–10. For the opposite view, that 'there are as many forms of morality as there are callings', see Durkheim, 1957, pp. 23–4. For Weber's more negative remarks on corporatism, see *GPS*, pp. 325–6, 333, 348, 350, 356, 366, 396; *WuG*, pp. 435–40, 531–40, 361.
22  On Weber's rejection of proposals for a *berufsständische Verfassung* and the concept of the *Staatsbürger* which supported that rejection, see *WuG*, pp. 161–75, 360, 378, 836; *GPS*, pp. 324, 400.
23  On freedom of movement see *GPS* p. 333; *WuG*, p. 515. On freedom of conscience, see *GPS*, p. 347.
24  T. Hobbes, *Leviathan*, London, Penguin, 1968, p. 375. The conclusion from Hobbes' view of corporations to his antagonism towards intermediate groups as such, by means of a facile analogy between the corporation and the modern trade union, was drawn by Carl Schmitt. See C. Schmitt, *Der Leviathan in der Staatslehre des Thomas Hobbes*, Hamburg, Hanseatische Verlagsanstalt, 1938. A serious account of the relationship between Schmitt's and Weber's political

theory cannot restrict itself to questions of 'charismatic leadership' or even Weber's influence on Schmitt's friend/enemy distinction. See the discussion in Chapter 4.

25  Hobbes, 1968, pp. 332, 366, 477–8, 500–1, 700.

26  For the absurd passage in which Weber suggests that the idea of freedom of conscience may be the oldest right of man, and the sect's capacity to protect it, see *WuG*, pp. 724–6.

27  F. Dostoyevsky, *The Brothers Karamazov*, London, Penguin, 1953, p. 299.

28  A. de Tocqueville, *Democracy in America* vol. 2, New York, Harper & Row, 1945, p. 115. On de Tocqueville and Weber, see D. Freund, 'Aktuelle Gedanken zur Demokratie bei Alexis de Tocqueville und Max Weber', *Schweizer Monatshefte für Politik, Wirtschaft und Kultur*, vol. 53.2, 1974, pp. 857–62.

29  Weber, 'Geschäftsbericht der Deutschen Gesellschaft für Soziologie (1910)', *Verhandlungen des ersten Deutschen Soziologentages*, Tübingen, J.C.B. Mohr (Paul Siebeck), 1911, p. 53.

30  On the provenance of this term, see P. Kluckhohn, *Persönlichkeit und Gemeinschaft*, Halle, Niemeyer, 1925; and P. Mayer-Tasch, *Korporativismus und Autoritärismus*, Frankfurt, Athanaeum, 1971; Hegel makes much of it in *Philosophy of Right*, Oxford, OUP, 1952, sect. 182; as does Weber in the Protestant Sects essay. See *FMW*, p. 310.

31  See the attack on Gierke, whose *Das Wesen des menschlichen Verbandes* of 1902 had 'once again broken a lance for the "organic" doctrine of the state', falsely concluding the real existence of a community from the ethical significance of a feeling for it. *WL*, pp. 35–6.

32  For this distinction see *WuG*, p. 80.

33  See Kant, 1964, p. 91. The relationship between Kantian and Weberian ethics, for all the emphasis on Weber's neo-Kantianism, remains largely unresearched. In view of the difficulty which I think lies at the centre of Weber's understanding of culture, it would be too easy to pretend to resolve it with the claim that for him there are only hypothetical, never categorical imperatives. A remark in a birthday message to Marianne in 1908 gives a hint of it: 'I know that *in* every critique I seek the warming sun which is higher than all critique'. *MWGA*, p. 535.

34  *WL*, p. 132.

35  On this see W.J. Mommsen, *Max Weber and German Politics 1890–1920*, Chicago, Chicago University Press; and D. Beetham, *Max Weber and the Theory of Modern Politics*, Cambridge, Polity, 1985.

36  Schöllgen goes so far as to suggest that after Hegel the idea that freedom of action can consist in anything other than purpose–rational action 'disappears'. See G. Schöllgen, *Handlungsfreiheit und Zweckrationalität*, Tübingen, J.C.B. Mohr (Paul Siebeck), 1984.

37  Perhaps just a less successful one.

38  On the basis of Weber's typology of action, comfort for the neo-Aristotelian view that human flourishing consists in a set of practices whose goods are internal to them must be sought in

traditional action. Weber's *Wertrationalität* – action performed for its own sake – may recall Aristotle's *praxis*, as Schnädelbach for instance believes, but there is no way that the 'ultimate values' which define subjective individual commitment could be made to accord with an idea of the good life for human beings. And value-rational action for Weber is as consistent with the aim of undermining a political community as with that of maintaining it. See H. Schnädelbach, 'What is Neo-Aristotelianism?', *Praxis International*, vol. 7, no. 3/4, 1988.

39   *WL*, p. 149.
40   Ibid. p. 154.
41   The sense of dangerousness the ambiguity of this metaphor conveys is lost in the English translation, which gives the impression that Weber is employing the Platonic metaphor of the leader as maritime navigator.
42   *GPS*, p. 545. A much earlier formulation of these 'qualities' occurs in 'Russlands Ubergang zur Scheindemokratie', in ibid. p. 202.
43   Ibid. p. 546.
44   *WL*, p. 591.
45   W. Schluchter, 'Value-neutrality and the Ethic of Responsibility', in Roth, G. and Schluchter, W., *Max Weber's Vision of History*, Berkeley, University of California, 1979, p. 100.
46   *FMW*, p. 95.
47   *RI*, p. 342.
48   *WuG*, p. 348.
49   *WL*, p. 494.
50   Value-rational action may be action performed for its own sake, and it may be that the formation of the purposive–rational actor's purposes is partially dependent upon a consideration of available means. But the English 'instrumentally rational action' can only mean either: strategic action without regard for the objective quality of life of the community in which it takes place, of which the value-rational actor is certainly an example, or: action whose ultimate purpose has been forsaken for an exclusive orientation to its means.
51   *WuG*, pp. 12–13.
52   *GPS*, pp. 550–6; *FMW*, pp. 119–24.
53   Nietzsche, 1967b, sects 164–6.
54   Schluchter, 1979b.
55   See 'Parliament and Government in a Reconstructed Germany', supplement to *ES*.
56   *GPS*, p. 13.
57   Ibid. p. 333.
58   Marianne Weber, *Max Weber*, New York, Wiley & Sons, pp. 521–2.
59   *GPS*, p. 546: *FMW*, pp. 116–17.
60   Hennis writes: 'Simmel characterised the core of Nietzsche's moral philosophy as "ethical personalism". I know of no better term for the heart of Weber's sociology.' See Hennis, 1988, p. 150. But in a part of that sociology to which Hennis does not refer, Weber himself writes: 'The religious duty of the pious Chinese . . . enjoined him to

Notes 203

develop himself within organically given, personal relations. . . . The personalist barrier to matter of factness, as a barrier to objectifying rationalisation, was of major significance for the economic mentality.' See *GARS*, p. 523. 'Matter of factness': I know of no better term for the heart of Weber's theory of personality.

61  *FMW*, p. 393.
62  *GARS*, p. 496; *MSS*, p. 7.
63  W. Schluchter, *The Rise of Western Rationalism*, Berkeley, University of California Press, 1981, pp. 39–66. The relationship between Weber's account of 'rationalisation' and Elias's theory of 'civilisation' cannot be discussed here. I would only point out that the attempt to assimilate them in some Foucault-inspired account of 'discipline' is most likely to founder on Elias's reliance on a version of Freudian drive theory. Elias assumes, implicitly, the existence of a constant substance which is the real object of increasing self-discipline. In this respect at least Weber was too much of an idealist to do the same. Foucault's work implies that the idea of a drive is as modern as that of that which ought to suppress it.
64  Schluchter, ibid., pp. 138–40.
65  Schluchter, 1979b, p. 53, note 150.
66  Note here that Weber's 'decisionism', as part of an account of the pragmatics of political action, bears no relation to Schmitt's, which implies, as part of a theory of sovereignty, that the source of the legitimacy of the state is a decision which has always already been made. This radical anti-positivism can have a wholly positivistic effect, in which it is distinguished from positivism only by the fact that it finds a source for the normative power of the factual in a decision which precedes all norms.
67  H. Albert, *Treatise on Critical Reason*, Princeton, Princeton University Press, 1984.
68  *GPS*, p. 559. For an earlier use of this characterisation, see K. Marx, *The 18th Brumaire of Louis Bonaparte*, Moscow, Progress, 1954. Marx himself took the phrase from Proudhon.
69  G. Simmel, *The Philosophy of Money*, London, Routledge & Kegan Paul, 1978, Ch. 3.
70  For an explicit formulation see C. Schmitt, *Politische Romantik* 2. Auflage, München, Duncker & Humblot, 1925, p. 256.
71  *FMW*, p. 116.
72  Nietzsche, 1966, p. 261.
73  *GPS*, p. 547; *FMW*, p. 116.
74  On this see G. Deleuze, *Nietzsche and Philosophy*, London, Athlone Press, 1983.
75  *GPS*, p. 547; *FMW*, p. 117.
76  Simmel, 1978, p. 256.
77  *FMW*, p. 125.
78  *GPS*, p. 559.
79  Schluchter, 1979b, p. 109.
80  K. Mannheim, *Ideology and Utopia*, London, Routledge & Kegan Paul, 1936, p. 71.

81  Hegel, 1952, sect. 118. The. recent contribution by Lassman and
    Velody argues that the interventionist role of science in politics
    consisted in enabling the political actor to gain a heightened
    awareness of the tragedy of action, but says nothing about the point
    at which this awareness stifles action.
82  Ibid. sects 129–40.

# Bibliography

## WORKS BY WEBER

'Referat des Generalsekretars Pastor Paul Göhre und Professor Max Weber über die deutschen Landarbeiter', *Bericht über die Verhandlungen des 5. Evangelischen–Sozialen Kongresses*, Berlin, Rehtwisch & Seeler, 1894.

'Geschäftesbericht der Deutschen Gesellschaft für Soziologie' (1910), *Verhandlugen des ersten Deutschen Soziologentages*, Tübingen, J.C.B. Mohr (Paul Siebeck), 1911.

*Gesammelte Aufsätze zur Religionssoziologie*, Tübingen, J.C.B. Mohr (Paul Siebeck), 1920.

*General Economic History*, London, Allen & Unwin, 1927.

*Jugendbriefe*, Tübingen, J.C.B. Mohr (Paul Siebeck), 1936.

*From Max Weber*, London, Routledge & Kegan Paul, 1948.

*The Methodology of The Social Sciences*, New York, Free Press, 1949.

*The Religion of China*, New York, Free Press, 1951.

*Ancient Judaism*, New York, Free Press, 1952.

*The Religion of India*, New York, Free Press, 1958.

*Gesammelte Aufsätze zur Wissenschaftslehre* 3. Auflage, Tübingen, J.C.B. Mohr (Paul Siebeck), 1968.

*Max Weber: The Interpretation of Social Reality*, London, Nelson, 1971.

*Wirtschaft und Gesellschaft 5. Auflage*, Tübingen, J.C.B. Mohr (Paul Siebeck), 1972.

*Roscher and Knies*, New York, Free Press, 1975.

*The Protestant Ethic and the Spirit of Capitalism* 2nd edn, London, Allen & Unwin, 1976.

*Critique of Stammler*, New York, Free Press, 1977a.

*The Agrarian Sociology of Ancient Civilisations*, London, New Left Books, 1977b.

*Selections in Translation*, Cambridge, CUP, 1978a.

*Economy and Society*, Berkeley, University of California Press, 1978b.

*Gesammelte Politische Schriften 4. Auflage*, Tübingen, J.C.B. Mohr (Paul Siebeck), 1980a.

'The National State and Economic Policy', *Economy and Society* vol. 9, no. 4, 1980b.

'Some Categories of Interpretive Sociology', *The Sociological Quarterly* vol. 22, no. 2, 1981.
*Gesamtausgabe II: Briefe 1906–08*, Tübingen, J.C.B. Mohr (Paul Siebeck), 1990.

## COMMENTARIES

Aron, R., 'Max Weber and Power Politics', in O. Stammer, *Max Weber and Sociology Today*, Oxford, Blackwell, 1971.
Beetham, D., *Max Weber and the Theory of Modern Politics*, Cambridge, Polity, 1985.
Brubaker, R., *The Limits of Rationality*, London, Allen & Unwin, 1984.
Brugger, W., *Menschenrechtsethos und Verantwortungspolitik*, Freiburg, Alber, 1981.
Burger, T., *Max Weber's Theory of Concept Formation (expanded edn)*, Durham NC, Duke University Press, 1987.
Eden, R., 'Doing Without Liberalism', *Political Theory*, vol. 10, no. 3, 1982, pp. 379–408.
——, 'Bad Conscience for a Nietzschean Age: Weber's Calling for Science', *Review of Politics*, vol. 45, no. 3, 1983a.
——, *Political Leadership and Nihilism*, Tampa, University Press of Florida, 1983b.
Freund, D., 'Aktuelle Gedanken zur Demokratie bei Alexis de Tocqueville und Max Weber', *Schweizer Monatshefte für Politik, Wirtschaft und Kultur*, vol. 53.2, 1974, pp. 857–62.
Goldman, H., *Max Weber and Thomas Mann*, Berkeley, University of California Press, 1989.
Hennis, W., *Max Weber: Essays in Reconstruction*, London, Allen & Unwin, 1988.
Henrich, D., *Die Einheit der Wissenschaftslehre Max Webers*, Tübingen, J.C.B. Mohr (Paul Siebeck), 1952.
Honigsheim, P. (1950): 'Max Weber: His Religious and Ethical Background and Development', *Church History*, vol. 19, no. 4, 1950, pp. 219–39.
Huff, T., *Max Weber and the Methodology of the Social Sciences*, New Brunswick, Transaction Books, 1984.
Jaspers, K., *Leonardo, Descartes, Max Weber*, London, Routledge & Kegan Paul, 1965.
Kahler, E., 'The Vocation of Science', in Lassman, P. and Velody, I. (eds), *Max Weber's Science as a Vocation*, London, Allen & Unwin, 1988.
Kalberg, S., 'The Search for Thematic Orientations in a Fragmented Ouevre', *Sociology*, vol. 13, 1979, pp. 127–40.
——, 'Max Weber's Types of Rationality', *American Journal of Sociology*, vol. 65, no. 5, 1980, pp. 1145–79.
Lash, S. and Whimster, S., *Max Weber, Rationality and Modernity*, London, Allen & Unwin, 1987.
Lassman, P., 'Value-Relations and General Theory: Parsons' Critique of Weber', *Zeitschrift für Soziologie*, 1980.

Lassman, P. and Velody, I. (eds), *Max Weber's Science as a Vocation*, London, Allen & Unwin, 1988.
Löwith, K., *Max Weber and Karl Marx*, London, Allen & Unwin, 1982.
Marcuse, H., 'Industrialisation and Capitalism', *New Left Review*, vol. 30, 1965, pp. 3–17.
Merquior, J.G., *Rousseau and Weber*, London, Routledge & Kegan Paul, 1980.
Midgeley, E.B.F., *The Ideology of Max Weber*, Aldershot, Gower, 1983.
Mommsen, W.J., 'Max Weber's Political Sociology and his Philosophy of World History', *International Social Science Journal*, vol. 17, 1965, pp. 9–22.
——, *Max Weber and German Politics 1890–1920*, Chicago, University of Chicago Press, 1984a.
Nelson, B., 'Max Weber's "Author's Introduction" (1920): A Master Clue to His Main Aims', *Sociological Inquiry*, vol. 44, no. 4, pp. 267–78.
Oakes, G., 'Methodological Ambivalence: The Case of Max Weber', *Social Research*, vol. 49, 1982, pp. 589–615.
Prager, J., 'Moral Integration and Political Inclusion: Durkheim's and Weber's Theories of Democracy', *Social Forces* vol. 59, no. 4, pp. 918–50.
Roth, G. and Schluchter, W., *Max Weber's Vision of History*, Berkeley, University of California Press, 1979.
Scaff, L., 'Max Weber's Politics and Political Education', *American Political Science Review*, vol. 67, 1973, pp. 128–41.
——, 'Weber, Simmel and The Sociology of Culture', *Sociological Review*, vol. 36, no. 1, 1988, pp. 1–30.
——, *Fleeing the Iron Cage*, California, California University Press, 1989.
Scheler, M., 'Max Weber's Exclusion of Philosophy', in Lassman, P. and Velody, I. (eds), *Max Weber's Science as a Vocation*, London, Allen & Unwin, 1988.
Schluchter, W., 'The Paradox of Rationalisation', 1979a.
——, 'Value-Neutrality and the Ethic of Responsibility', both in Roth, G. and Schluchter, W., *Max Weber's Vision of History*, Berkeley, University of California Press, 1979b.
——, *The Rise of Western Rationalism*, Berkeley: University of California, 1981.
—— (ed.), *Max Webers Studie über Hinduismus und Buddhismus*, Frankfurt, Suhrkamp, 1984.
Schöllgen, G., *Handlungsfreiheit und Zweckrationalität*, Tübingen, J.C.B. Mohr (Paul Siebeck), 1984.
Stammer, O., *Max Weber and Sociology Today*, Oxford, Blackwell, 1971.
Stark, W., 'Max Weber and the Heteronomy of Purpose', *Social Research*, vol. 34, 1967, pp. 249–64.
Tenbruck, F., 'Science as a Vocation Revisited', in Forsthoff, E. and Horstel, R. (eds) *Standorte im Zeitstrom: Festschrift für Arnold Gehlen*, Frankfurt, Athensum, 1974.
——, 'The Problem of Thematic Unity in the Works of Max Weber', *British Journal of Sociology*, vol. 31, no. 3, 1980, pp. 316–51.

Torrance, J., 'Max Weber: Methods and the Man', *European Journal of Sociology*, vol. 15, no. 1, 1974, pp. 127–65.
Turner, B.S., *For Weber*, London, Routledge & Kegan Paul, 1981.
——, *Theories of Modernity and Postmodernity*, London, Sage, 1990.
Turner, C., 'Weber, Simmel and Culture', *Sociological Review*, vol. 37, no. 3, 1989, pp. 518–29.
——, 'Lyotard and Weber: Postmodern Rules and neo-Kantian Values', in Turner, B.S., *Theories of Modernity and Postmodernity*, London, Sage, 1990.
Turner, S.P. and Factor, R., *Max Weber and the Dispute Over Reason and Value*, London, Routledge & Kegan Paul, 1984.
Wagner, G., *Geltung und Normativer Zwang*, Freiburg, Alber, 1987.
Warren, M., 'Max Weber's Liberalism For a Nietzschean World', *American Political Science Review*, vol. 82, no. 1, 1988, pp. 31–50.
Weber, M., *Max Weber: A Biography*, New York, Wiley & Sons, 1975.
Wolin, S., 'Max Weber: Legitimation, Method, and the Politics of Theory', in Connolly, W.E., *Legitimacy and The State*, Oxford, Blackwell, 1984.

## OTHER WRITINGS REFERRED TO

Adorno, T.W. and Horkheimer, M., *Dialectic of Enlightenment*, London, Allen Lane, 1973.
Albert, H., *Treatise on Critical Reason*, Princeton, Princeton University Press, 1984.
Apel, K.-O., *Diskurs und Verantwortung*, Frankfurt, Suhrkamp, 1988.
Arendt, H., *The Human Condition*, Chicago, University of Chicago Press, 1958.
——, *On Revolution*, London, Penguin, 1963.
Arendt, H and Jaspers, K., *Briefwechsel*, München, Piper, 1985.
Aristotle, *Politics*, Oxford, OUP, 1948.
Arnason, J.P., *Praxis und Interpretation*, Frankfurt, Suhrkamp, 1988.
Barnard, F.M., *Herder on Social and Political Culture*, Cambridge, CUP, 1969.
Beiner, R., *Political Judgement*, London, Methuen, 1983.
Bendersky, J., *Carl Schmitt, Theorist for the Reich*, Princeton, Princeton University Press, 1983.
Berlin, I., *Four Essays on Liberty*, Oxford, OUP, 1969.
Berman, M., *All That is Solid Melts into Air*, London, Verso, 1983.
Black, A., *Guilds and Civil Society*, London, Methuen, 1985.
Bloom, A., *The Closing of the American Mind*, New York, Simon & Schuster, 1987.
Blumenberg, H., *The Legitimacy of the Modern Age*, Cambridge, MIT, 1985.
Bruch, R.V., Graf, F. and Hübinger, G., *Kultur und Kulturwissenschaften um 1900*, Stuttgart, Steiner, 1989.
Bruford, W.H., *The German Tradition of Self-cultivation*, Oxford, OUP, 1975.
Brunkhorst, H., 'Kultur und bürgerliche Gesellschaft', in Honneth, A. u.a. (Hsg), *Zwischenbetrachtung*, Frankfurt, Suhrkamp, 1990.

Bunyan, J., *The Pilgrim's Progress*, London, Dent, 1954.
Calinescu, M., *Faces of Modernity*, Bloomington, Indiana University Press, 1977.
Cassirer, E., *Zur Logik der Kulturwissenschaften*, Darmstadt, Wissenschaftliche Buchgemeinschaft, 1961.
Connolly, W. (ed.), *Legitimacy and the State*, Oxford, Blackwell, 1984.
Conze, W., Koselleck, R., Brunner, O. (Hsg), *Geschichtliche Grundbegriffe*, Stuttgart, Klett-Cotta, 1972–89.
Croce, B. and Vossler, K., *Briefwechsel*, Berlin, Suhrkamp, 1955.
Deleuze, G., *Nietzsche and Philosophy*, London, Athlone Press, 1983.
de Tocqueville, A., *Democracy in America*, New York, Vintage Books, 1945.
Dilthey, W., *Selected Writings*, Cambridge, CUP, 1976.
Dostoyevsky, F., *The Brothers Karamazov*, London, Penguin, 1953.
Dubiel, H., *Was ist Neokonservatismus?*, Frankfurt, Suhrkamp, 1985.
Durkheim, E., *Professional Ethics and Civic Morals*, London, Routledge & Kegan Paul, 1957.
——, *Suicide*, London, Routledge & Kegan Paul, 1981.
——, *The Division of Labour in Society*, London, Macmillan, 1984.
Elias, N., *The Civilising Process*, Oxford, Blackwell, 1978.
Elshtain, J.B., *Public Man, Private Woman*, Oxford, Martin Robinson, 1981.
Emerson, R., *State and Society in Modern Germany*, New Haven, Yale University Press, 1928.
Eucken, R., *Geistige Strömungen der Gegenwart* 4. Auflage, Leipzig, Veit, 1909.
Fichte, J.G., *Beitrag zur Berichtigung des Publikums über die Französische Revolution*, Hamburg, Meiner, 1973.
Foucault, M., *The Order of Things*, London, Tavistock, 1970.
——, *Language, Counter-memory, Practice*, Ithaca, Cornell University Press, 1977.
——, *The Foucault Reader*, New York, Pantheon, 1985.
Freud, S., 'Civilisation and Its Discontents', in *Pelican Freud Library*, vol. 12, London, Penguin, 1985.
Gadamer, H.-G., *Philosophical Hermeneutics*, Berkeley, University of California Press, 1976.
Gierke, O., *Das Wesen des menschlichen Verbandes*, Darmstadt, Wissenschaftliche Buchgemeinschaft, 1902.
——, *Natural Law and The Theory of Society*, Cambridge, CUP, 1957.
Goethe, J.W., *Wilhelm Meisters Lehrjahre*, Stuttgart, Reclam, 1982.
Graf, F.W., 'Kulturprotestantismus', *Archiv für Begriffsgeschichte*, vol. 28, 1984.
Green, M., *Mountain of Truth*, Hanover NH, University Press of New England, 1986.
Habermas, J., *Towards a Rational Society*, London, Heinemann, 1971.
——, *Theory and Practice*, London, Heinemann, 1974.
——, *Legitimation Crisis*, London, Heinemann, 1976.
——, *Knowledge and Human Interests*, 2nd edn, London, Heinemann, 1978.
——, 'Modernity: An Incomplete Project', in Foster, H. (ed.), *Postmodern Culture*, London, Pluto, 1983.

———, *The Theory of Communicative Action*, vol. 1, Cambridge, Polity, 1984a.

———, 'Uber Moralität und Sittlichkeit: Was macht eine Lebensform rational?', in Schnädelbach, H. (ed.) *Rationalität*, Frankfurt, Suhrkamp, 1984b.

———, *The Philosophical Discourse of Modernity*, Cambridge, Polity, 1987a.

———, *The Theory of Communicative Action*, vol. 2, Cambridge, Polity, 1987b.

Hausenstein, W., 'Die Politisierung der Unpolitischen', *Die Neue Merkur*, 2. Jg., 1915, pp. 174–88.

Hegel, G.W.F., *Philosophy of Right*, Oxford, OUP, 1952.

———, *Lectures on the Philosophy of History*, New York, Dover, 1956.

———, *Phenomenology of Spirit*, Oxford, OUP, 1977.

Heidegger, M., *The Question Concerning Technology and Other Essays*, New York, Harper & Row, 1977.

———, *Basic Writings*, London, Routledge & Kegan Paul, 1978.

Hennis, W., *Politik und Praktische Philosophie*, Frankfurt, Suhrkamp, 1963.

Herzog, R. and Koselleck, R., *Poetik und Hermeneutik XII: Epochenschwelle und Epochenbewusstsein*, München, Fink, 1987.

Hobbes, T., *Leviathan*, London, Penguin, 1968.

Honneth, A. u.a. (Hsg) *Zwischenbetrachtung*, Frankfurt, Suhrkamp, 1990.

Horkheimer, M., *The Eclipse of Reason*, New York, OUP, 1947.

Humboldt, W. von, 'Ideen zu einem Versuch, die Grenzen der Wirksamkeit des Staats zu bestimmen', in *Gesammelte Schriften* Bd. 1, Berlin, Behr, 1903.

———, *On Language*, Cambridge, CUP, 1988.

Jay, M., 'Review of Blumenberg's *The Legitimacy of the Modern Age*', *History and Theory*, vol. 24, no. 2, 1985, pp. 185–96.

Kant, I., *Groundwork of the Metaphysics of Morals*, New York, Harper & Row, 1964.

———, *Critique of Practical Reason*, New York, Bobbs Merrill, 1965.

———, *Political Writings*, Cambridge, CUP, 1970.

Kierkegaard, S., *Either/Or*, Princeton, Princeton University Press, 1987.

Kluckhohn, P., *Persönlichkeit und Gemeinschaft*, Halle, Niemeyer, 1925.

Koselleck, R., *Critique and Crisis*, Oxford, Berg, 1988.

Laclau, E. and Mouffe, C., *Hegemony and Socialist Strategy*, London, Verso, 1985.

Landman, M., *Pluralität und Antinomie*, München, Beck, 1963.

Lepenies, W., *Between Literature and Science: the Rise of Sociology*, Cambridge, CUP, 1988.

Liebersohn, H., *Religion and Industrial Society*, Philadelphia, American Philosophical Society, 1986.

Löwith, K., *Meaning in History*, Chicago, University of Chicago Press, 1949.

Löwith, K. and Strauss, L., 'Correspondence Concerning Modernity', *Independent Journal of Philosophy*, vol. 4, 1983, pp. 105–19.

Lukács, G., *Taktik und Ethik*, Darmstadt, Luchterhand, 1975.

———, *History and Class Consciousness*, London, Merlin Press, 1984.

Luxemburg, R., *The Russian Revolution*, Ann Arbor, University of Michigan Press, 1970.

Lyotard, J.-F., *The Postmodern Condition*, Manchester, Manchester University Press, 1984.

Lyotard, J.-F. and Thebaud, J.-L., *Just Gaming*, Manchester, Manchester University Press, 1985.

Machiavelli, N., *Discourses*, London, Penguin, 1970.

——, *The Prince*, London, Penguin, 1981.

MacIntyre, A., *After Virtue*, London, Duckworth, 1981.

Makreel, R.A., 'Dilthey and the neo-Kantians', *Journal of the History of Philosophy*, vol. 7, no. 4, 1969, pp. 423–40.

Mann, T., *Reflections of a Non-Political Man*, New York, Frederick Ungar, 1983.

Mannheim, K., *Ideology and Utopia*, London, Routledge & Kegan Paul, 1936.

Marcuse, H., 'Bemerkungen zu einer Neubestimmung der Kultur', in *Schriften* Bd. 8, Frankfurt, Suhrkamp, 1975.

Marquard, O., *Schwierigkeiten mit der Geschichtsphilosophie*, Frankfurt, Suhrkamp, 1973.

——, 'Temporale Positionalität', in Herzog, R., and Koselleck, R., *Poetik und Hermeneutik XII: Epochenschwelle und Epochenbewusstsein*, München, Fink, 1987.

Marx, K., *The Eighteenth Brumaire of Louis Bonaparte*, Moscow, Progress, 1954.

——, *Grundrisse*, London, Penguin, 1973.

——, *The Poverty of Philosophy*, Moscow, Progress, 1975a.

——, *Early Writings*, London, Penguin, 1975b.

Marx, K. and Engels, F., *The German Ideology*, London, Lawrence & Wishart, 1977.

Mayer-Tasch, P., *Korporativismus und Autoritärismus*, Frankfurt, Athensum, 1971.

Meinecke, F., *Weltbürgertum und Nationalstaat*, Oldenburg, 1907.

Mendelssohn, M., 'Über die Frage: Was heisst aufklären?', in Bahr, E. (Hsg), *Was ist Aufklärung?*, Stuttgart, Reclam, 1974.

Musil, R., *The Man Without Qualities*, London, Picador, 1979.

Nehamas, A., 'Immanent and Transcendent Perspectivism', *Nietzsche Studien*, vol. 12, 1983, pp. 473–90.

——, *Nietzsche: Life as Literature*, London, Harvard University Press, 1985.

Niedermann, J., *Kultur: Werden und Wandlungen des Begriffs und seiner Ersatzbegriffe von Cicero bis Herder*, Firenze, Libreria Editrice, 1941.

Nietzsche, F., *Beyond Good and Evil*, New York, Vintage Books, 1966.

——, *The Genealogy of Morals and Ecce Homo*, New York, Vintage Books, 1967a.

——, *The Will to Power*, New York, Vintage Books, 1967b.

——, *Twilight of the Idols and The Anti-Christ*, London, Penguin, 1968.

——, *The Gay Science*, New York, Vintage, 1974.

——, *Untimely Meditations*, Cambridge, CUP, 1983.

——, *Human, All Too Human*, Cambridge, CUP, 1986.

Oakeshott, M., *On Human Conduct*, Oxford, Clarendon, 1975.

Parsons, T., *The Structure of Social Action*, New York, Free Press, 1968.

——, *The System of Modern Societies*, New Jersey, Prentice Hall, 1971.

Perpeet, W., ' "Kulturphilosophie" '. *Archiv für Begriffsgeschichte*, Bd. 20, 1976, pp. 42–99.

Popper, K., *The Open Society and Its Enemies*, 5th edn, London, Routledge & Kegan Paul, 1966.

Radbruch, G., 'Über den Begriff der Kultur', *Logos*, Bd. 1, 1911, pp. 200–7.
Rauhut, F., 'Die Herkunft der Worte und Begriffe "Kultur", "Civilisation", und "Bildung" ', *Germanisch-Romanische Monatsschrift*, 1953, pp. 81–91.
Reiss, H.S., *The Political Thought of the German Romantics*, Oxford, OUP, 1955.
Rickert, H., 'Lebenswerte und Kulturwerte', *Logos*, Bd. 1, 1911, pp. 131–66.
——, *Science and History*, Princeton, D. Van Nostrand Company Inc., 1962.
——, *The Limits of Concept Formation in Natural Science*, Cambridge, CUP, 1986.
Ricouer, P., *Hermeneutics and the Human Sciences*, Cambridge, CUP, 1981.
Riedel, M. (Hsg), *Rehabilitation der praktischen Philosophie*, Frankfurt, Suhrkamp, 1975.
Rorty, R., *Philosophy and the Mirror of Nature*, Oxford, Blackwell, 1980.
——, 'Habermas and Lyotard on Postmodernity', *Praxis International*, vol. 4, no. 1, 1985, 161–75.
Rose, G., *Hegel Contra Sociology*, London, Athlone Press, 1981.
Rosen, S., *The Ancients and the Moderns*, New Haven, Yale University Press, 1989.
Scheler, M., 'Kultur und Religion: Eine Beschprechung zu Rudolf Euckens "Der Wahrheitsgehalt der Religion" ', in *Gesammelte Werke*, vol. 1, München, Francke, 1971.
Schiller, F., *Letters on The Aesthetic Education of Man*, Oxford, Clarendon, 1967.
Schmidt, A., *History and Structure*, Cambridge, MIT, 1983.
Schmitt, C., *Römischer Katholizismus und Politische Form*, Heilbronn, 1923.
——, *Politische Romantik* 2. Auflage, München, Duncker & Humblot, 1925.
——, *Der Leviathan in der Staatslehre des Thomas Hobbes*, Hamburg, Hanseatische Verlagsanstalt, 1938.
——, *The Concept of the Political*, New Brunswick, NJ, Rutgers University Press, 1976.
——, *Political Theology*, Cambridge, MIT, 1985a.
——, *The Crisis of Parliamentary Democracy*, Cambridge, MIT, 1985b.
Schnädelbach, H., *German Philosophy 1831–1933*, Cambridge, CUP, 1984a.
—— (ed.), *Rationalität*, Frankfurt, Suhrkamp, 1984b
——, 'What is neo-Aristotelianism?', *Praxis International*, vol. 7, no. 3/4, 1988.
Schopenhauer, A., *The World as Will and Representation*, New York, Dover, 1966.
Schutz, A., *The Phenomenology of the Social World*, London, Heinemann, 1977.
Schwab, F.-Z., 'Beruf und Jugend', *Die weissen Blätter*, 4. Jg., 1917, pp. 97–113.
Sennett, R., *The Fall of Public Man*, London, Faber & Faber, 1986.

Simmel, G., *Kant: Sechzehn Vorlesungen*, Leipzig, Duncker & Humblot, 1904.
——, *Brücke und Tür*, Stuttgart, Köhler, 1957.
——, *The Conflict of Modern Culture and other essays*, New York, Teachers College Press, 1968.
——, *On Individuality and Social Forms*, Chicago, University of Chicago Press, 1971.
——, *Problems of the Philosophy of History*, New York, Free Press, 1977.
——, *The Philosophy of Money*, London, Routledge & Kegan Paul, 1978.
——, *Essays on Interpretation in Social Science*, Manchester, Manchester University Press, 1980.
——, *Gesammelte Schriften zur Religionssoziologie*, Berlin, Duncker & Humblot, 1989.
Sombart, W., 'Kulturphilosophie'; 'Politik und Bildung'; 'Die Politik als Beruf', *Morgen, Wochenschrift für Deutsche Kultur*, vol. 1, 1907.
Spengler, O., *Der Untergang des Abendlandes*, München, Beck, 1920.
Spranger, E., *Lebensformen*, Halle, Niemeyer, 1930.
Strauss, L., *Natural Right and History*, Chicago, University of Chicago Press, 1953.
——, *Thoughts on Machiavelli*, Seattle, University of Washington Press, 1958.
——, 'The Three Waves of Modernity', in *Political Philosophy*, New York, Pegasus, 1975.
——, *Studies in Platonic Political Philosophy*, Chicago, Chicago University Press, 1983.
Tallis, R., *Not Saussure*, London, Macmillan, 1988.
Taylor, C., 'Interpretation and the Sciences of Man', *Review of Metaphysics*, vol. 25, 1971, pp. 3–51.
Tenbruck, F., 'Formal Sociology', in Coser, L. (ed.), *Georg Simmel*, Englewood Cliffs, Prentice–Hall, 1965.
Thurn, H.-P., 'Kultursoziologie – zur Begriffsgeschichte der Disziplin', *Kölner Zeitschrift für Soziologie und Sozialpsychologie*, vol. 31, 1971, pp. 422–9.
Troeltsch, E., *The Social Teachings of the Christian Churches*, London, Allen & Unwin, 1931.
Voegelin, E., *Wissenschaft, Politik und Gnosis*, München, Kosel, 1959.
——, *The New Science of Politics*, Chicago, Phoenix Books, 1966.
Willey, T.E., *Back To Kant*, Detroit, Wayne State University Press, 1978.
Windelband, W., *Introduction to Philosophy*, London, T. Fisher Unwin, 1921.
——, 'History and Natural Science', *History and Theory*, vol. 19, no. 2, 1980.

# Name index

# Subject index